CAMBRIDGE
UNIVERSITY PRESS

Economics

for Cambridge International AS & A Level

EXAM PREPARATION AND PRACTICE

Susan Grant & George Vlachonikolis

Contents

Digital questions for all chapters can be found online at Cambridge GO. For more information on how to access and use your digital resource, please see inside front cover.

> How to use this series

This suite of resources supports students and teachers following the Cambridge International AS & A Level Economics syllabus (9708). All of the components in the series are designed to work together and help students develop the necessary knowledge and skills for this subject. With clear language and style, they are designed for international students.

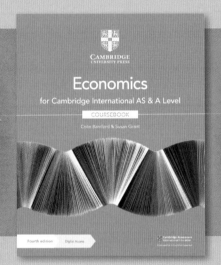

The coursebook is designed for students to use in class with guidance from the teacher. It offers complete coverage of the Cambridge International AS & A Level Economics syllabus (9708). Each chapter contains an in-depth explanation of Economics concepts with a variety of activities, case studies and images to engage students, help them make real-world connections and develop their analysis and evaluation skills.

The workbook provides further practice of all the skills presented in the coursebook and is ideal for use in class or as homework. It provides engaging exercises, worked examples and opportunities for students to evaluate sample answers so they can put into practice what they have learnt.

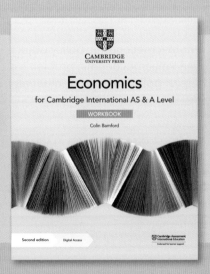

The teacher's resource is the foundation of this series because it offers inspiring ideas about how to teach this course. You'll find everything you need to deliver the course in here, including teaching guidance, lesson plans, suggestions for differentiation, assessment and language support, answers and extra materials, including downloadable worksheets and PPTs.

The Exam Preparation and Practice provides dedicated support for students in preparing for their final assessments. Hundreds of questions in the book and accompanying digital resource will help students to check that they understand, and can recall, syllabus concepts. To help students to show what they know in an exam context, a specially developed checklist of exam skills with corresponding questions, and past paper question practice, is also included. Self-assessment and reflection features support students to identify any areas that need further practice. This resource should be used alongside the coursebook, throughout the course of study, so students can most effectively increase their confidence and readiness for their exams.

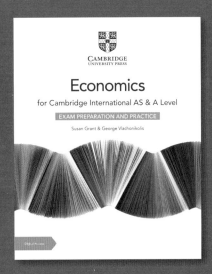

> How to use this book

This book will help you to check that you **know** the content of the syllabus and practise how to **show** this understanding in an exam. It will also help you be cognitively prepared and in the **flow**, ready for your exam. Research has shown that it is important that you do all three of these things, so we have designed the Know, Show, Flow approach to help you prepare effectively for exams.

| Know | You will need to consolidate and then recall a lot of syllabus content. |

| Show | You should demonstrate your knowledge in the context of a Cambridge exam. |

| Flow | You should be cognitively engaged and ready to learn. This means reducing test anxiety. |

Exam skills checklist

Category	Exam skill
Understanding the question	Recognise different question types
	Understand command words
	Mark scheme awareness
Providing an appropriate response	Understand connections between concepts
	Keep to time
	Know what a good answer looks like
Developing supportive behaviours	Reflect on progress
	Manage test anxiety

This **Exam skills checklist** helps you to develop the awareness, behaviours and habits that will support you when revising and preparing for your exams. For more exam skills advice, including understanding command words and managing your time effectively, please go to the **Exam skills chapter**.

Know

The full syllabus content of your *Cambridge International AS & A Level Economics* course is covered in your Cambridge coursebook. This book will provide you with different types of questions to support you as you prepare for your exams. You will answer **Knowledge recall questions** that are designed to make sure you understand a topic, and **Recall and connect questions** to help you recall past learning and connect different concepts.

KNOWLEDGE FOCUS

Knowledge Focus boxes summarise the topics that you will answer questions on in each chapter of this book. You can refer back to your Cambridge coursebook to remind yourself of the full detail of the syllabus content.

You will find **Knowledge recall questions** to make sure you understand a topic, and **Recall and connect questions** to help you recall past learning and connect different concepts. It is recommended that you answer the Knowledge recall questions just after you have covered the relevant topic in class, and then return to them at a later point to check you have properly understood the content.

Knowledge recall question

Testing yourself is a good way to check that your understanding is secure. These questions will help you to recall the core knowledge you have acquired during your course, and highlight any areas where you may need more practice. They are indicated with a blue bar with a gap, at the side of the page. We recommend that you answer the Knowledge recall questions just after you have covered the relevant topic in class, and then return to them at a later point to check you have properly understood the content.

« RECALL AND CONNECT «

To consolidate your learning, you need to test your memory frequently. These questions will test that you remember what you learned in previous chapters, in addition to what you are practising in the current chapter.

UNDERSTAND THESE TERMS

These list the important vocabulary that you should understand for each chapter. Definitions are provided in the glossary of your Cambridge coursebook.

Show

Exam questions test specific knowledge, skills and understanding. You need to be prepared so that you have the best opportunity to show what you know in the time you have during the exam. In addition to practising recall of the syllabus content, it is important to build your exam skills throughout the year.

EXAM SKILLS FOCUS

This feature outlines the exam skills you will practise in each chapter, alongside the Knowledge focus. They are drawn from the core set of eight exam skills, listed in the exam skills checklist. You will practise specific exam skills, such as understanding command words, within each chapter. More general exam skills, such as managing text anxiety, are covered in the Exam skills chapter.

Exam skills question

These questions will help you to develop your exam skills and demonstrate your understanding. To help you become familiar with exam-style questioning, many of these questions follow the style and use the language of real exam questions, and have allocated marks. They are indicated with a solid red bar at the side of the page.

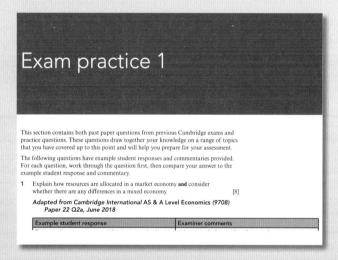

Exam practice 1

This section contains both past paper questions from previous Cambridge exams and practice questions. These questions draw together your knowledge on a range of topics that you have covered up to this point and will help you prepare for your assessment.

The following questions have example student responses and commentaries provided. For each question, work through the question first, then compare your answer to the example student response and commentary.

1   Explain how resources are allocated in a market economy **and** consider whether there are any differences in a mixed economy.   [8]

Adapted from Cambridge International AS & A Level Economics (9708) Paper 22 Q2a, June 2018

| Example student response | Examiner comments |

Looking at sample answers to past paper questions helps you to understand what to aim for.

The **Exam practice** sections in this resource contain example student responses and examiner-style commentary showing how the answer could be improved (both written by the authors).

Flow

Preparing for exams can be stressful. One of the approaches recommended by educational psychologists to help with this stress is to improve behaviours around exam preparation. This involves testing yourself in manageable chunks, accompanied by self-evaluation. You should avoid cramming and build in more preparation time. This book is structured to help you do this.

Increasing your ability to recognise the signs of exam-related stress and working through some techniques for how to cope with it will help to make your exam preparation manageable.

REFLECTION

This feature asks you to think about the approach that you take to your exam preparation, and how you might improve this in the future. Reflecting on how you plan, monitor and evaluate your revision and preparation will help you to do your best in your exams.

SELF-ASSESSMENT CHECKLIST

These checklists return to the Knowledge focus from your coursebook, as well as the Exam skills focus boxes from each chapter. Checking in on how confident you feel in each of these areas will help you to focus your exam preparation. The 'Show it' prompts will allow you to test your rating. You should revisit any areas that you rate 'Needs more work' or 'Almost there'.

Now I can	Show it	Needs more work	Almost there	Confident to move on

Increasing your ability to recognise the signs of exam-related stress and working through some techniques for how to cope with it will help to make your exam preparation manageable. The **Exam skills chapter** will support you with this.

Digital support

Extra self-assessment knowledge questions for all chapters can be found online at Cambridge GO. For more information on how to access and use your digital resource, please see inside the front cover.

You will find **Answers** for all of the questions in the book on the 'supporting resources' area of the Cambridge GO platform.

Multiple choice questions

These ask you to select the correct answer to a question from four options. These are auto-marked and feedback is provided.

Flip card questions

These present a question on one screen, and suggested answers on the reverse.

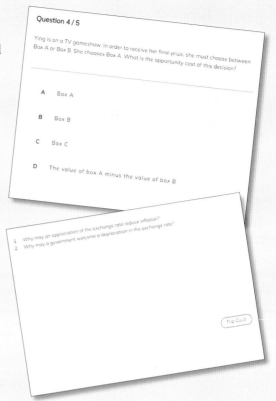

Question 4 / 5

Ying is on a TV gameshow. In order to receive her final prize, she must choose between Box A or Box B. She chooses Box A. What is the opportunity cost of this decision?

A   Box A

B   Box B

C   Box C

D   The value of box A minus the value of box B

1   Why may an appreciation of the exchange rate reduce inflation?
2   Why may a government welcome a depreciation in the exchange rate?

Flip Card

Syllabus assessment objectives for *Cambridge International AS & A Level Economics*

You should be familiar with the Assessment Objectives from the syllabus, as the examiner will be looking for evidence of these requirements in your responses and allocating marks accordingly.

The assessment objectives for this syllabus are:

Assessment objective	AS Level weighting	A Level weighting
AO1: Knowledge and Understanding	35%	35%
AO2: Application	40%	40%
AO3: Analysis	25%	25%

Exam skills

by Lucy Parsons

What's the point of this book?

Most students make one really basic mistake when they're preparing for exams. What is it? It's focusing far too much on learning 'stuff' – that's facts, figures, ideas, information – and not nearly enough time practising exam skills.

The students who work really, really hard but are disappointed with their results are nearly always students who focus on memorising stuff. They think to themselves, 'I'll do practice papers once I've revised everything.' The trouble is, they start doing practice papers too late to really develop and improve how they communicate what they know.

What could they do differently?

When your final exam script is assessed, it should contain specific language, information and thinking skills in your answers. If you read a question in an exam and you have no idea what you need to do to give a good answer, the likelihood is that your answer won't be as brilliant as it could be. That means your grade won't reflect the hard work you've put into revising for the exam.

There are different types of questions used in exams to assess different skills. You need to know how to recognise these question types and understand what you need to show in your answers.

So, how do you understand what to do in each question type?

That's what this book is all about. But first a little background.

Meet Benjamin Bloom

The psychologist Benjamin Bloom developed a way of classifying and valuing different skills we use when we learn, such as analysis and recalling information. We call these thinking skills. It's known as Bloom's Taxonomy and it's what most exam questions are based around.

If you understand Bloom's Taxonomy, you can understand what any type of question requires you to do. So, what does it look like?

Bloom's Taxonomy of thinking skills

Increasing difficulty →

- Evaluation — **Passing judgement** on something
- Synthesis — **Putting together knowledge,** understanding, application and analysis **to create something new**
- Analysis — **Taking apart** information or data in order to **discover relationships**, motives, causes, patterns and connections
- Application — **Using knowledge** and understanding in **new and different circumstances**
- Understanding — **Distinguishing between two similar ideas** or things by using knowledge to **recognise the difference**
- Knowledge — **Recalling, memorising and knowing**

The key things to take away from this diagram are:

- Knowledge and understanding are known as lower-level thinking skills. They are less difficult than the other thinking skills. Exam questions that just test you on what you know are usually worth the lowest number of marks.

- All the other thinking skills are worth higher numbers of marks in exam questions. These questions need you to have some foundational knowledge and understanding but are far more about how you think than what you know. They involve:

    - Taking what you know and using it in unfamiliar situations (application).
    - Going deeper into information to discover relationships, motives, causes, patterns and connections (analysis).
    - Using what you know and think to create something new – whether that's an essay, long-answer exam question a solution to a maths problem, or a piece of art (synthesis).
    - Assessing the value of something, e.g. the reliability of the results of a scientific experiment (evaluation).

In this introductory chapter, you'll be shown how to develop the skills that enable you to communicate what you know and how you think. This will help you achieve to the best of your abilities. In the rest of the book, you'll have a chance to practise these exam skills by understanding how questions work and understanding what you need to show in your answers.

Every time you pick up this book and do a few questions, you're getting closer to achieving your dream results. So, let's get started!

Exam preparation and revision skills

What is revision?

If you think about it, the word 'revision' has two parts to it:

- re – which means 'again'
- vision – which is about seeing.

So, revision is literally about 'seeing again'. This means you're looking at something that you've already learned.

Typically, a teacher will teach you something in class. You may then do some questions on it, write about it in some way, or even do a presentation. You might then have an end-of-topic test sometime later. To prepare for this test, you need to 'look again' or revise what you were originally taught.

Step 1: Making knowledge stick

Every time you come back to something you've learned or revised you're improving your understanding and memory of that particular piece of knowledge. This is called **spaced retrieval**. This is how human memory works. If you don't use a piece of knowledge by recalling it, you lose it.

Everything we learn has to be physically stored in our brains by creating neural connections – joining brain cells together. The more often we 'retrieve' or recall a particular piece of knowledge, the stronger the neural connection gets. It's like lifting weights – the more often you lift, the stronger you get.

However, if you don't use a piece of knowledge for a long time, your brain wants to recycle the brain cells and use them for another purpose. The neural connections get weaker until they finally break, and the memory has gone. This is why it's really important to return often to things that you've learned in the past.

Great ways of doing this in your revision include:

- Testing yourself using flip cards – use the ones available in the digital resources for this book.
- Testing yourself (or getting someone else to test you) using questions you've created about the topic.
- Checking your recall of previous topics by answering the Recall and connect questions in this book.
- Blurting – writing everything you can remember about a topic on a piece of paper in one colour. Then, checking what you missed out and filling it in with another colour. You can do this over and over again until you feel confident that you remember everything.
- Answering practice questions – use the ones in this book.
- Getting a good night's sleep to help consolidate your learning.

> **The importance of sleep and creating long-term memory**
>
> When you go to sleep at night, your brain goes through an important process of taking information from your short-term memory and storing it in your long-term memory.
>
> This means that getting a good night's sleep is a very important part of revision. If you don't get enough good quality sleep, you'll actually be making your revision much, much harder.

Step 2: Developing your exam skills

We've already talked about the importance of exam skills, and how many students neglect them because they're worried about covering all the knowledge.

What actually works best is developing your exam skills at the same time as learning the knowledge.

What does this look like in your studies?

- Learning something at school and your teacher setting you questions from this book or from past papers. This tests your recall as well as developing your exam skills.

- Choosing a topic to revise, learning the content and then choosing some questions from this book to test yourself at the same time as developing your exam skills.

The reason why practising your exam skills is so important is that it helps you to get good at communicating what you know and what you think. The more often you do that, the more fluent you'll become in showing what you know in your answers.

Step 3: Getting feedback

The final step is to get feedback on your work.

If you're testing yourself, the feedback is what you got wrong or what you forgot. This means you then need to go back to those things to remind yourself or improve your understanding. Then, you can test yourself again and get more feedback. You can also congratulate yourself for the things you got right – it's important to celebrate any success, big or small.

If you're doing past paper questions or the practice questions in this book, you will need to mark your work. Marking your work is one of the most important things you can do to improve. It's possible to make significant improvements in your marks in a very short space of time when you start marking your work.

Why is marking your own work so powerful? It's because it teaches you to identify the strengths and weaknesses of your own work. When you look at the mark scheme and see how it's structured, you will understand what is needed in your answers to get the results you want.

This doesn't just apply to the knowledge you demonstrate in your answers. It also applies to the language you use and whether it's appropriately subject-specific, the structure of your answer, how you present it on the page and many other factors. Understanding, practising and improving on these things are transformative for your results.

The most important thing about revision

The most important way to make your revision successful is to make it active.

Sometimes, students say they're revising when they sit staring at their textbook or notes for hours at a time. However, this is a really ineffective way to revise because it's passive. In order to make knowledge and skills stick, you need to be doing something like the suggestions in the following diagram. That's why testing yourself and pushing yourself to answer questions that test higher-level thinking skills are so effective. At times, you might actually be able to feel the physical changes happening in your brain as you develop this new knowledge and these new skills. That doesn't come about without effort.

The important thing to remember is that while active revision feels much more like hard work than passive revision, you don't actually need to do nearly as much of it. That's because you remember knowledge and skills when you use active revision. When you use passive revision, it is much, much harder for the knowledge and skills to stick in your memory.

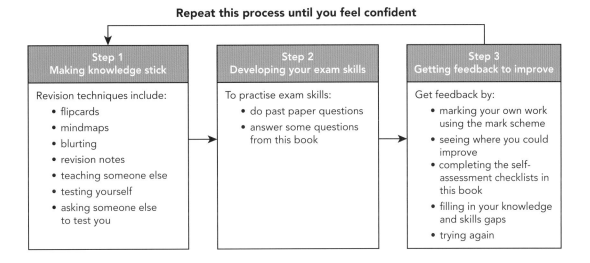

Repeat this process until you feel confident

Step 1 Making knowledge stick	Step 2 Developing your exam skills	Step 3 Getting feedback to improve
Revision techniques include: • flipcards • mindmaps • blurting • revision notes • teaching someone else • testing yourself • asking someone else to test you	To practise exam skills: • do past paper questions • answer some questions from this book	Get feedback by: • marking your own work using the mark scheme • seeing where you could improve • completing the self-assessment checklists in this book • filling in your knowledge and skills gaps • trying again

How to improve your exam skills

This book helps you to improve in eight different areas of exam skills, which are divided across three categories. These skills are highlighted in this book in the Exam skills focus at the start of each chapter and developed throughout the book using targeted questions, advice and reflections.

1 **Understand the questions: what are you being asked to do?**

   • Know your question types.

   • Understand command words.

   • Work with mark scheme awareness.

2 **How to answer questions brilliantly**

   • Understand connections between concepts.

   • Keep to time.

   • Know what a good answer looks like.

3 **Give yourself the best chance of success**

   • Reflection on progress.

   • How to manage test anxiety.

Understand the questions: what are you being asked to do?

Know your question types

In any exam, there will be a range of different question types. These different question types will test different types of thinking skills from Bloom's Taxonomy.

It is very important that you learn to recognise different question types. If you do lots of past papers, over time you will begin to recognise the structure of the paper for each of your subjects. You will know which types of questions may come first and which ones are more likely to come at the end of the paper. You can also complete past paper questions in the Exam practice sections in this book for additional practice.

You will also recognise the differences between questions worth a lower number of marks and questions worth more marks. The key differences are:

- how much you will need to write in your answer

- how sophisticated your answer needs to be in terms of the detail you give and the depth of thinking you show.

Types of questions

1   Multiple-choice questions

Multiple-choice questions are generally worth smaller numbers of marks. You will be given several possible answers to the question, and you will have to work out which one is correct using your knowledge and skills.

There is a chance of you getting the right answer with multiple-choice questions even if you don't know the answer. This is why you must **always give an answer for multiple-choice questions** as it means there is a chance you will earn the mark.

Multiple-choice questions are often harder than they appear. The possible answers can be very similar to each other. This means you must be confident in how you work out answers or have a high level of understanding to tell the difference between the possible answers.

Being confident in your subject knowledge and doing lots of practice multiple-choice questions will set you up for success. Use the resources in this book and the accompanying online resources to build your confidence.

This example of a multiple-choice question is worth one mark. You can see that all the answers have one part in common with at least one other answer. For example, palisade cells is included in three of the possible answers. That's why you have to really know the detail of your content knowledge to do well with multiple-choice questions.

Which two types of cells are found in plant leaves?

- **A**   Palisade mesophyll and stomata
- **B**   Palisade mesophyll and root hair
- **C**   Stomata and chloroplast
- **D**   Chloroplast and palisade mesophyll

2 Questions requiring longer-form answers

Questions requiring longer-form answers need you to write out your answer yourself.

With these questions, take careful note of how many marks are available and how much space you've been given for your answer. These two things will give you a good idea about how much you should say and how much time you should spend on the question.

A rough rule to follow is to write one sentence, or make one point, for each mark that is available. You will get better and better at these longer form questions the more you practise them.

In this example of a history question, you can see it is worth four marks. It is not asking for an explanation, just for you to list Lloyd George's aims. Therefore, you need to make four correct points in order to get full marks.

What were Lloyd George's aims during negotiations leading to the Treaty of Versailles? [4]

3 Essay questions

Essay questions are the longest questions you will be asked to answer in an exam. They examine the higher-order thinking skills from Bloom's Taxonomy such as analysis, synthesis and evaluation.

To do well in essay questions, you need to talk about what you know, giving your opinion, comparing one concept or example to another, and evaluating your own ideas or the ones you're discussing in your answer.

You also need to have a strong structure and logical argument that guides the reader through your thought process. This usually means having an introduction, some main body paragraphs that discuss one point at a time, and a conclusion.

Essay questions are usually level-marked. This means that you don't get one mark per point you make. Instead, you're given marks for the quality of the ideas you're sharing as well as how well you present those ideas through the subject-specific language you use and the structure of your essay.

Practising essays and becoming familiar with the mark scheme is the only way to get really good at them.

Understand command words

What are command words?

Command words are the most important words in every exam question. This is because command words tell you what you need to do in your answer. Do you remember Bloom's Taxonomy? Command words tell you which thinking skill you need to demonstrate in the answer to each question.

Two very common command words are **describe** and **explain**.

When you see the command word describe in a question, you're being asked to show lower-order thinking skills like knowledge and understanding. The question will either be worth fewer marks, or you will need to make more points if it is worth more marks.

The command word explain is asking you to show higher-order thinking skills. When you see the command word explain, you need to be able to say how or why something happens.

You need to understand all of the relevant command words for the subjects you are taking. Ask your teacher where to find them if you are not sure. It's best not to try to memorise the list of command words, but to become familiar with what command words are asking for by doing lots of practice questions and marking your own work.

How to work with command words

When you first see an exam question, read it through once. Then, read it through again and identify the command word(s). Underline the command word(s) to make it clear to yourself which they are every time you refer back to the question.

You may also want to identify the **content** words in the question and underline them with a different colour. Content words tell you which area of knowledge you need to draw on to answer the question.

In this example, command words are shown in red and content words in blue:

1   a   Explain **four** reasons why governments might support business start-ups.   [8]

Adapted from Cambridge IGCSE Business Studies (0450) Q1a Paper 21 June 2022

Marking your own work using the mark scheme will help you get even better at understanding command words and knowing how to give good answers for each.

Work with mark scheme awareness

The most transformative thing that any student can do to improve their marks is to work with mark schemes. This means using mark schemes to mark your own work at every opportunity.

Many students are very nervous about marking their own work as they do not feel experienced or qualified enough. However, being brave enough to try to mark your own work and taking the time to get good at it will improve your marks hugely.

Why marking your own work makes such a big difference

Marking your own work can help you to improve your answers in the following ways:

1   **Answering the question**

Having a deep and detailed understanding of what is required by the question enables you to answer the question more clearly and more accurately.

It can also help you to give the required information using fewer words and in less time, as you can avoid including unrelated points or topics in your answer.

2   **Using subject-specific vocabulary**

Every subject has subject-specific vocabulary. This includes technical terms for objects or concepts in a subject, such as mitosis and meiosis in biology. It also includes how you talk about the subject, using appropriate vocabulary that may differ from everyday language. For example, in any science subject you might be asked to describe the trend on a graph.

Your answer could say it 'goes up fast' or your answer could say it 'increases rapidly'. You would not get marks for saying 'it goes up fast', but you would for saying it 'increases rapidly'. This is the difference between everyday language and formal, scientific language.

When you answer lots of practice questions, you become fluent in the language specific to your subject.

3   Knowing how much to write

It's very common for students to either write too much or too little to answer questions. Becoming familiar with the mark schemes for many different questions will help you to gain a better understanding of how much you need to write in order to get a good mark.

4   Structuring your answer

There are often clues in questions about how to structure your answer. However, mark schemes give you an even stronger idea of the structure you should use in your answers.

For example, if a question says:

'Describe and explain two reasons why…'

You can give a clear answer by:

- Describing reason 1
- Explaining reason 1
- Describing reason 2
- Explaining reason 2

Having a very clear structure will also make it easier to identify where you have earned marks. This means that you're more likely to be awarded the number of marks you deserve.

5   Keeping to time

Answering the question, using subject-specific vocabulary, knowing how much to write and giving a clear structure to your answer will all help you to keep to time in an exam. You will not waste time by writing too much for any answer. Therefore, you will have sufficient time to give a good answer to every question.

How to answer exam questions brilliantly

Understand connections between concepts

One of the higher-level thinking skills in Bloom's Taxonomy is **synthesis**. Synthesis means making connections between different areas of knowledge. You may have heard about synoptic links. Making synoptic links is the same as showing the thinking skill of synthesis.

Exam questions that ask you to show your synthesis skills are usually worth the highest number of marks on an exam paper. To write good answers to these questions, you need to spend time thinking about the links between the topics you've studied **before** you arrive in your exam. A great way of doing this is using mind maps.

How to create a mind map

To create a mind map:

1   Use a large piece of paper and several different coloured pens.

2   Write the name of your subject in the middle. Then, write the key topic areas evenly spaced around the edge, each with a different colour.

3   Then, around each topic area, start to write the detail of what you can remember. If you find something that is connected with something you studied in another topic, you can draw a line linking the two things together.

This is a good way of practising your retrieval of information as well as linking topics together.

Answering synoptic exam questions

You will recognise questions that require you to make links between concepts because they have a higher number of marks. You will have practised them using this book and the accompanying resources.

To answer a synoptic exam question:

1   **Identify the command and content words.** You are more likely to find command words like **discuss** and **explain** in these questions. They might also have phrases like 'the connection between'.

2   **Make a plan for your answer.** It is worth taking a short amount of time to think about what you're going to write in your answer. Think carefully about what information you're going to put in, the links between the different pieces of information and how you're going to structure your answer to make your ideas clear.

3   **Use linking words and phrases in your answer.** For example, 'therefore', 'because', 'due to', 'since' or 'this means that'.

Here is an example of an English Literature exam question that requires you to make synoptic links in your answer.

1   Discuss Carol Ann Duffy's exploration of childhood in her poetry. Refer to two poems in your answer.   [25]

Content words are shown in blue; command words are shown in red.

This question is asking you to explore the theme of childhood in Duffy's poetry. You need to choose two of her poems to refer to in your answer. This means you need a good knowledge of her poetry, and to be familiar with her exploration of childhood, so that you can easily select two poems that will give you plenty to say in your answer.

Keep to time

Managing your time in exams is really important. Some students do not achieve to the best of their abilities because they run out of time to answer all the questions. However, if you manage your time well, you will be able to attempt every question on the exam paper.

Why is it important to attempt all the questions on an exam paper?

If you attempt every question on a paper, you have the best chance of achieving the highest mark you are capable of.

Students who manage their time poorly in exams will often spend far too long on some questions and not even attempt others. Most students are unlikely to get full marks on many questions, but you will get zero marks for the questions you don't answer. You can maximise your marks by giving an answer to every question.

Minutes per mark

The most important way to keep to time is knowing how many minutes you can spend on each mark.

For example, if your exam paper has 90 marks available and you have 90 minutes, you know there is 1 mark per minute.

Therefore, if you have a 5 mark question, you should spend five minutes on it.

Sometimes, you can give a good answer in less time than you have budgeted using the minutes per mark technique. If this happens, you will have more time to spend on questions that use higher-order thinking skills, or more time on checking your work.

How to get faster at answering exam questions

The best way to get faster at answering exam questions is to do lots of practice. You should practise each question type that will be in your exam, marking your own work, so that you know precisely how that question works and what is required by the question. Use the questions in this book to get better and better at answering each question type.

Use the 'Slow, Slow, Quick' technique to get faster.

Take your time answering questions when you first start practising them. You may answer them with the support of the textbook, your notes or the mark scheme. These things will support you with your content knowledge, the language you use in your answer and the structure of your answer.

Every time you practise this question type, you will get more confident and faster. You will become experienced with this question type, so that it is easy for you to recall the subject knowledge and write it down using the correct language and a good structure.

Calculating marks per minute

Use this calculation to work out how long you have for each mark:

Total time in the exam / Number of marks available = Minutes per mark

Calculate how long you have for a question worth more than one mark like this:

Minutes per mark × Marks available for this question = Number of minutes for this question

What about time to check your work?

It is a very good idea to check your work at the end of an exam. You need to work out if this is feasible with the minutes per mark available to you. If you're always rushing to finish the questions, you shouldn't budget checking time. However, if you usually have time to spare, then you can budget checking time.

To include checking time in your minutes per mark calculation:

(Total time in the exam – Checking time) / Number of marks available = Minutes per mark

Know what a good answer looks like

It is much easier to give a good answer if you know what a good answer looks like.

Use these methods to know what a good answer looks like.

1 **Sample answers** – you can find sample answers in these places:

   - from your teacher

   - written by your friends or other members of your class

   - in this book.

2 **Look at mark schemes** – mark schemes are full of information about what you should include in your answers. Get familiar with mark schemes to gain a better understanding of the type of things a good answer would contain.

3 **Feedback from your teacher** – if you are finding it difficult to improve your exam skills for a particular type of question, ask your teacher for detailed feedback. You should also look at their comments on your work in detail.

Give yourself the best chance of success

Reflection on progress

As you prepare for your exam, it's important to reflect on your progress. Taking time to think about what you're doing well and what could be improved brings more focus to your revision. Reflecting on progress also helps you to continuously improve your knowledge and exam skills.

How do you reflect on progress?

Use the 'reflection' feature in this book to help you reflect on your progress during your exam preparation. Then, at the end of each revision session, take a few minutes to think about the following:

	What went well? What would you do the same next time?	What didn't go well? What would you do differently next time?
Your subject knowledge		
How you revised your subject knowledge – did you use active retrieval techniques?		
Your use of subject-specific and academic language		
Understanding the question by identifying command words and content words		
Giving a clear structure to your answer		
Keeping to time		
Marking your own work		

Remember to check for silly mistakes – things like missing the units out after you carefully calculated your answer.

Use the mark scheme to mark your own work. Every time you mark your own work, you will be recognising the good and bad aspects of your work, so that you can progressively give better answers over time.

When do you need to come back to this topic or skill?

Earlier in this section of the book, we talked about revision skills and the importance of spaced retrieval. When you reflect on your progress, you need to think about how soon you need to return to the topic or skill you've just been focusing on.

For example, if you were really disappointed with your subject knowledge, it would be a good idea to do some more active retrieval and practice questions on this topic tomorrow. However, if you did really well you can feel confident you know this topic and come back to it again in three weeks' or a month's time.

The same goes for exam skills. If you were disappointed with how you answered the question, you should look at some sample answers and try this type of question again soon. However, if you did well, you can move on to other types of exam questions.

Improving your memory of subject knowledge

Sometimes students slip back into using passive revision techniques, such as only reading the coursebook or their notes, rather than also using active revision techniques, like testing themselves using flip cards or blurting.

You can avoid this mistake by observing how well your learning is working as you revise. You should be thinking to yourself, 'Am I remembering this? Am I understanding this? Is this revision working?'

If the answer to any of those questions is 'no', then you need to change what you're doing to revise this particular topic. For example, if you don't understand, you could look up your topic in a different textbook in the school library to see if a different explanation helps. Or you could see if you can find a video online that brings the idea to life.

You are in control

When you're studying for exams it's easy to think that your teachers are in charge. However, you have to remember that you are studying for your exams and the results you get will be yours and no one else's.

That means you have to take responsibility for all your exam preparation. You have the power to change how you're preparing if what you're doing isn't working. You also have control over what you revise and when: you can make sure you focus on your weaker topics and skills to improve your achievement in the subject.

This isn't always easy to do. Sometimes you have to find an inner ability that you have not used before. But, if you are determined enough to do well, you can find what it takes to focus, improve and keep going.

What is test anxiety?

Do you get worried or anxious about exams? Does your worry or anxiety impact how well you do in tests and exams?

Test anxiety is part of your natural stress response.

The stress response evolved in animals and humans many thousands of years ago to help keep them alive. Let's look at an example.

The stress response in the wild

Imagine an impala grazing in the grasslands of east Africa. It's happily and calmly eating grass in its herd in what we would call the parasympathetic state of rest and repair.

Then the impala sees a lion. The impala suddenly panics because its life is in danger. This state of panic is also known as the stressed or sympathetic state. The sympathetic state presents itself in three forms: flight, fight and freeze.

The impala starts to run away from the lion. Running away is known as the flight stress response.

The impala might not be fast enough to run away from the lion. The lion catches it but has a loose grip. The impala struggles to try to get away. This struggle is the fight stress response.

However, the lion gets an even stronger grip on the impala. Now the only chance of the impala surviving is playing dead. The impala goes limp, its heart rate and breathing slows. This is called the freeze stress response. The lion believes that it has killed the impala so it drops the impala to the ground. Now the impala can switch back into the flight response and run away.

The impala is now safe – the different stages of the stress response have saved its life.

What has the impala got to do with your exams?

When you feel test anxiety, you have the same physiological stress responses as an impala being hunted by a lion. Unfortunately, the human nervous system cannot tell the difference between a life-threatening situation, such as being chased by a lion, and the stress of taking an exam.

If you understand how the stress response works in the human nervous system, you will be able to learn techniques to reduce test anxiety.

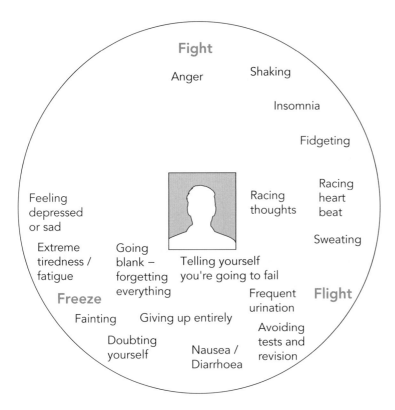

The role of the vagus nerve in test anxiety

The vagus nerve is the part of your nervous system that determines your stress response. Vagus means 'wandering' in Latin, so the vagus nerve is also known as the 'wandering nerve'. The vagus nerve wanders from your brain, down each side of your body, to nearly all your organs, including your lungs, heart, kidneys, liver, digestive system and bladder.

If you are in a stressful situation, like an exam, your vagus nerve sends a message to all these different organs to activate their stress response. Here are some common examples:

- **Heart** beats faster.
- **Kidneys** produce more adrenaline so that you can run, making you fidgety and distracted.
- **Digestive system** and **bladder** want to eliminate all waste products so that energy can be used for fight or flight.

If you want to feel calmer about your revision and exams, you need to do two things to help you move into the parasympathetic, or rest and repair, state:

1   Work with your vagus nerve to send messages of safety through your body.

2   Change your perception of the test so that you see it as safe and not dangerous.

How to cope with test anxiety

1   Be well prepared

Good preparation is the most important part of managing test anxiety. The better your preparation, the more confident you will be. If you are confident, you will not perceive the test or exam as dangerous, so the sympathetic nervous system responses of fight, flight and freeze are less likely to happen.

This book is all about helping you to be well prepared and building your confidence in your knowledge and ability to answer exam questions well. Working through the knowledge recall questions will help you to become more confident in your knowledge of the subject. The practice questions and exam skills questions will help you to become more confident in communicating your knowledge in an exam.

To be well prepared, look at the advice in the rest of this chapter and use it as you work through the questions in this book.

2   Work with your vagus nerve

The easiest way to work with your vagus nerve to tell it that you're in a safe situation is through your breathing. This means breathing deeply into the bottom of your lungs, so that your stomach expands, and then breathing out for longer than you breathed in. You can do this with counting.

Breathe in deeply, expanding your abdomen, for the count of four; breathe out drawing your navel back towards your spine for the count of five, six or seven. Repeat this at least three times. However, you can do it for as long as it takes for you to feel calm.

The important thing is that you breathe out for longer than you breathe in. This is because when you breathe in, your heart rate increases slightly, and when you breathe out, your heart rate decreases slightly. If you're spending more time breathing out overall, you will be decreasing your heart rate over time.

3   Feel it

Anxiety is an uncomfortable, difficult thing to feel. That means that many people try to run away from anxious feelings. However, this means the stress just gets stored in your body for you to feel later.

When you feel anxious, follow these four steps:

1   Pause.

2   Place one hand on your heart and one hand on your stomach.

3   Notice what you're feeling.

4   Stay with your feelings.

What you will find is that if you are willing to experience what you feel for a minute or two, the feeling of anxiety will usually pass very quickly.

4   Write or talk it out

If your thoughts are moving very quickly, it is often better to get them out of your mind and on to paper.

You could take a few minutes to write down everything that comes through your mind, then rip up your paper and throw it away. If you don't like writing, you can speak aloud alone or to someone you trust.

Other ways to break the stress cycle

Exercise and movement	Being friendly	Laughter
• Run or walk. • Dance. • Lift weights. • Yoga. Anything that involves moving your body is helpful.	• Chat to someone in your study break. • Talk to the cashier when you buy your lunch.	• Watch or listen to a funny show on TV or online. • Talk with someone who makes you laugh. • Look at photos of fun times.
Have a hug	Releasing emotions	Creativity
• Hug a friend or relative. • Cuddle a pet e.g. a cat. Hug for 20 seconds or until you feel calm and relaxed.	It is healthy to release negative or sad emotions. Crying is often a quick way to get rid of these difficult feelings so if you feel like you need to cry, allow it.	• Paint, draw or sketch. • Sew, knit or crochet. • Cook, build something.

If you have long-term symptoms of anxiety, it is important to tell someone you trust and ask for help.

Your perfect revision session

1	Intention	**What do you want to achieve in this revision session?** • Choose an area of knowledge or an exam skill that you want to focus on. • Choose some questions from this book that focus on this knowledge area or skill. • Gather any other resources you will need e.g. pen, paper, flashcards, coursebook.
2	Focus	**Set your focus for the session** • Remove distractions from your study area e.g. leave your phone in another room. • Write down on a piece of paper or sticky note the knowledge area or skill you're intending to focus on. • Close your eyes and take three deep breaths, with the exhale longer than the inhale.
3	Revision	**Revise your knowledge and understanding** • To improve your knowledge and understanding of the topic, use your coursebook, notes or flashcards, including active learning techniques. • To improve your exam skills, look at previous answers, teacher feedback, mark schemes, sample answers or examiners' reports.
4	Practice	**Answer practice questions** • Use the questions in this book, or in the additional online resources, to practise your exam skills. • If the exam is soon, do this in timed conditions without the support of the coursebook or your notes. • If the exam is a long time away, you can use your notes and resources to help you.
5	Feedback	**Mark your answers** • Use mark schemes to mark your work. • Reflect on what you've done well and what you could do to improve next time.
6	Next steps	**What have you learned about your progress from this revision session? What do you need to do next?** • What did you do well? Feel good about these things, and know it's safe to set these things aside for a while. • What do you need to work on? How are you going to improve? Make a plan to get better at the things you didn't do well or didn't know.
7	Rest	**Take a break** • Do something completely different to rest: get up, move or do something creative or practical. • Remember that rest is an important part of studying, as it gives your brain a chance to integrate your learning.

1 Scarcity, choice and opportunity cost

KNOWLEDGE FOCUS

You will answer questions on:

1.1 The fundamental economic problem

1.2 Unlimited wants

1.3 Choice and opportunity cost

1.4 What to produce, how to produce and for whom to produce?

EXAM SKILLS FOCUS

In this chapter you will:

- demonstrate that you understand the command word 'state' and answer a state question

- show that you understand the purpose of a short-answer question.

The command word 'state' means to express in clear terms. 'State' questions are checking the assessment objective of AO1 Knowledge and understanding only. You should write a concise answer that effectively demonstrates your knowledge of syllabus content, recall of facts or formulae. Sometimes, the command word 'state' may simply require a definition.

You will be faced with many different question types during your exam. A short-answer question will likely carry fewer marks than an extended response question and may contain an indication in the question as to how many points should be made.

1.1 The fundamental economic problem

For questions that have the command word 'state', you should give an uncomplicated yet valid factual statement. The question will usually only carry one or two marks.

It is important that you use specific economic terminology as much as possible in every question. For 'state' questions, however, you only need to use the terminology correctly; you do not need to provide an explanation of each of the terms you use within your answer.

1 State 'the fundamental problem' in economics. [2]

> **UNDERSTAND THESE TERMS**
> - fundamental economic problem
> - resources
> - scarcity

1.2 Unlimited wants

1 To support your understanding of the key terms 'wants' and 'needs', try this matching activity.

Look at the following list of goods. Copy the following table and identify whether households would normally consider these goods to be a want or a need.

> luxury car   baby clothes   bread   dartboard
> staple foods   premium brand of TV

Want	Need

Table 1.1: Wants and needs

> **UNDERSTAND THESE TERMS**
> - wants
> - needs

1.3 Choice and opportunity cost

1 State what is meant by the term 'opportunity cost'. [1]

This is a short-answer question. It carries a relatively small number of marks and it does not require a lot of explanation. That said, all exam answers can usually be improved with the use of an example. Sometimes, you will be able to use an example from the case study. On other occasions, you can use your own example.

For example, consider how you could use examples in your answers to these two short-answer questions:

- Using an example from the data, state what is meant by the term 'opportunity cost'. [2]

- Using your own example, state what is meant by the term 'opportunity cost'. [2]

Both questions still require you to state what is meant by the term 'opportunity cost'. But, the first question also requires you to select some economic information from the case study as well. This checks whether you can apply the concept of opportunity cost to a new context. The second question requires you to create your own example. This checks whether you understand the syllabus content.

You should now try to answer these two questions. You can use the following short extract as a stimulus:

2

> ### Hamna's choice
>
> Hamna receives $500 from her family on her 18th birthday. Her friend, Zoya, says she should spend the money on clothes but she decides to save all of the money in a bank.

Using an example from the data, state what is meant by the term 'opportunity cost'.   [2]

3   Using your own example, state what is meant by the term 'opportunity cost'.   [2]

4

> ### Cy's choice
>
> A board game costs $30. Two economics paperback books cost $15 each. Cy cannot buy both the board game and the books. Cy must choose between the alternatives. He decides to buy the board game.

Using an example from the data, state what is meant by the term 'opportunity cost'.   [2]

REFLECTION

How should you prepare for these sorts of questions? There is no real substitute for extra reading. The more you read, the more you will become familiar with economic vocabulary and improve your capacity to identify key information that could be useful for a question like this.

- How much reading do you do outside of class?
- Are you challenging yourself to identify key economic concepts when you read?
- Do you read with a highlighter pen to hand?

It is always important to read exam case studies with a highlighter pen. This is so that you can highlight passages in the text and can use them in your answers later on.

1.4 What to produce, how to produce and for whom to produce?

1 What to produce? How to produce? For whom to produce? These are generally referred to as the questions related to the allocation of resources. Can you describe what these three questions mean?

SELF-ASSESSMENT CHECKLIST

Let's revisit the Knowledge focus and Exam skills focus for this chapter.
Decide how confident you are with each statement.

Now I can	Show it	Needs more work	Almost there	Confident to move on
explain the fundamental economic problem of scarcity	Define the concept of scarcity.			
explain the need for individuals, firms and governments to make choices	Explain why choices have to be made.			
define the meaning of opportunity cost	Define the concept of opportunity cost.			
explain how opportunity cost results from the need to make choices	Identify examples of opportunity cost in your life.			
explain the basic questions of resource allocation	Sit down with another student. Both write out a one-sentence explanation of each of the basic questions. Compare with each other.			
demonstrate that I understand the command word 'state' and answer a 'state' question	Describe what the command word 'state' means.			
show that I understand the purpose of a short-answer question.	Explain the difference between a short-answer question and a multiple-choice question.			

2 Economic methodology

5 >

KNOWLEDGE FOCUS

You will answer questions on:

2.1 What is economics?

2.2 Economics as a social science

2.3 Positive and normative statements

2.4 Meaning of the term 'ceteris paribus'

2.5 The importance of time periods

EXAM SKILLS FOCUS

In this chapter you will:

- show that you understand the command word 'identify' and answer an 'identify' question

- show that you understand what the assessment objective of AO1 Knowledge and understanding means.

The command word 'identify' means name/select/recognise. You should be precise about what you have identified. You do not need to add any explanation to your answer unless the question uses an additional command word.

Assessment objectives are a set of statements that are used to indicate what skill or skills you need to demonstrate in your response to the question. They are clearly labelled in mark schemes to show you where marks can be awarded. The assessment objective AO1 Knowledge and understanding is present in all question types. However, it is normally associated with short-answer questions. For example, the command words 'state' and 'identify' are checking your AO1 Knowledge and understanding skills.

2.1 What is economics?

≪ RECALL AND CONNECT 1 ≪

a State the fundamental economic problem.

b State what is meant by the term 'opportunity cost'.

c Using examples of your choosing, state what is meant by the term 'resource'.

2.2 Economics as a social science

1 Identify **one** reason why economics is considered a social science. [2]

2 Identify **one** reason why economists choose to use models. [2]

2.3 Positive and normative statements

UNDERSTAND THESE TERMS

- positive statement
- normative statement

1 This activity will help you identify positive and normative statements when reading data.

Here are a selection of newspaper headlines. Copy the table below and sort the headlines into two columns: positive statements and normative statements.

> Inflation hits 9% – a 50 year-high.
> People are spending too much money buying cryptocurrencies.
> Young people are not saving enough money.
> Interest rates have doubled in the last 2 months.
> The government should spend more on healthcare services.
> Government spending on healthcare fell in real terms last year.

Positive	Normative

Table 2.1: Positive and normative statements

2   You should now create your own examples.

   a   **Three** examples of normative statements.

   b   **Three** examples of positive statements.

3
> **House prices in Cambridge**
>
> It is often stated that house prices are too high across the city of Cambridge, UK. In economics, affordability studies are often conducted to calculate the average house price in terms of the average wage. In 2022, the average wage in Cambridge was reported to be £35000. According to a leading property website, the average house price in the city was £544000. These data tell us the average house price is an incredible 15.5 times the average wage.

Using the data, identify **one** normative statement and **one** positive statement.   [2]

REFLECTION

Strong learning is built on feedback. Having tried these questions, how do you think you performed?

If you found any of the questions difficult so far, then it is important to identify the reasons why. For example, you might be finding it difficult to remember some of the key terms. Or you might be finding it difficult to understand the case studies. Make a note of any reflections you have about the questions so far.

2.4 Meaning of the term 'ceteris paribus'

1   State what is meant by the term 'ceteris paribus'.

2   Can you use the term 'ceteris paribus' in a sentence?

2.5 The importance of time periods

At such an early stage of your course, you should mainly be concerned with AO1 Knowledge and understanding. Knowledge is progressively acquired throughout your course and will often be assessed by recalling the definitions of key terms. Understanding is something you develop from your knowledge.

It is important not to over-write your answer. AO1 requires an accurate understanding, and so the more you write, the more you might signal that there is some doubt in your mind. Thus, keep your answer short and to the point of the question.

Some of the command words that assess only AO1 Knowledge and understanding are 'calculate', 'define', 'describe', 'identify', 'outline' and 'state'. You looked at 'state' questions in the previous chapter.

1   State what is meant by the term 'short run'.   [1]

2   State what is meant by the term 'long run'.   [1]

3   State what is meant by the term 'very long run'.   [1]

Let's look at Question 1 again and consider the following two possible answers. Read them both. Do you understand why Answer A is better than Answer B?

Answer A:

time period when a firm can change at least one but not all factor inputs

Answer B:

Time period when a firm can change at least one but not all factor inputs. Time periods do not have an exact timetable such as three months or one year. But the concept of the short run suggests that, in this hypothetical time period, a firm might be able to change at least one factor of production (e.g., labour) but not others (e.g., capital). It is different to the long run, which is a time period in which a firm can change all its factors of production.

Both answers would have gained full marks, but Answer A is better. It is concise and to the point. Answer B is correct, but it uses 86 words (compared to Answer A's 15 words). This means there is more possibility for Answer B to go wrong. It also means that that student has less time to spend on other questions in the exam.

SELF-ASSESSMENT CHECKLIST

Let's revisit the Knowledge focus and Exam skills focus for this chapter. Decide how confident you are with each statement.

Now I can	Show it	Needs more work	Almost there	Confident to move on
explain why economics is a social science	State at least two reasons why economics is a social science.			
differentiate between facts and opinions (positive and normative statements)	Identify positive and normative statements from a selection of statements.			
explain why economists use the term 'ceteris paribus'	Use 'ceteris paribus' in a sentence correctly.			
explain when to refer to a time period such as 'short run', 'long run' and 'very long run'	Define each term succinctly.			
show that I understand the command word 'identify' and answer an 'identify' question	Answer an 'identify' question from a past paper.			
show that I understand what the assessment objective of AO1 Knowledge and understanding means.	Explain verbally to a fellow student what AO1 Knowledge and understanding means.			

3 Factors of production

The command word 'explain' means set out purposes or reasons, make the relationships between things evident or provide why and/or how links and support with relevant evidence. The command word 'explain' can cover a lot of different types of questions, such as short-answer questions and extended response questions. You will consider its use here in short-answer questions only.

Short-answer questions are often referred to as low-mark questions since they do not carry many marks. Because of this, you do not need to spend a lot of time on them. Your time is often better spent on the higher-mark questions later in the exam. To get a sense of how long you should spend on a question, divide the length of time for the paper by the number of marks. This will give you a (maximum) time to spend per mark.

3.1 The factors of production

1 Match the following terms with the correct definition.

Terms		Definitions	
a	land	i	human resources available in an economy.
b	labour	ii	a physical resource made by humans that aids the production of goods and services.
c	capital	iii	organising production and taking risks.
d	enterprise	iv	natural resources in an economy.

2 Match the following terms with the correct reward.

Terms		Rewards	
a	land	i	profit
b	labour	ii	rent
c	capital	iii	interest
d	enterprise	iv	wages

3 Match the following terms with the correct examples.

Terms		Examples	
a	land	i	businessperson, angel investor
b	labour	ii	factory, machinery, IT equipment (computers)
c	capital	iii	the population
d	enterprise	iv	oil reserves, soil, sunlight

Before completing Questions 4 to 6, consider how much time you should spend per mark. Paper 2: AS Level Data Response and Essays is two hours and 60 marks, and so you should aim to spend a maximum of two minutes per mark. However, this timing includes other activities such as reading the case study, planning your answer and then reviewing your answer.

4 Define the term 'enterprise'. [1]

5 State the reward for labour. [1]

6 With the help of an example, state what economists mean by the term 'land'. [2]

3.2 The difference between human capital and physical capital

1   Here are some examples of different types of capital (human and physical). Copy the table and sort them into the relevant columns.

> factory   knowledge   machinery   skills
> experience   IT equipment (computers)

Physical capital	Human capital

Table 3.1: Physical and human capital

It is always good practice, where possible, to use data from the case study to support your answers. This can be in the form of quotes or facts and figures. With that in mind, a good tip is to read the questions before you read the case study. You can then highlight important elements in the case study that you can use later in your answer.

2

Tesla and the gigafactory

Tesla is the world's largest producer of electric vehicles. In 2019, Tesla built its first factory in Europe (called the gigafactory) in Berlin, Germany. The firm spent over $15 billion investing in new machinery. By 2022, the gigafactory was producing 1 000 vehicles per week and employing roughly 4 500 people – many of them are skilled experts in their area of work.

Using the data, identify **one** example of physical capital and **one** example of human capital.   [2]

3.3 Specialisation and the division of labour

In general, for an 'explain' question you should aim to write an answer that contains clearly identifiable reasons for something happening. You may have to draw upon data or other information to make your explanation clear. It will often be a lengthier answer than a 'state' question, and so it will carry more marks accordingly.

1   State what is meant by the term 'specialisation'. [1]

2   Explain why division of labour should lead to an increase in productivity. [2]

In many exam papers, you will be asked to 'contextualise' your answer. For example, the previous question could have been written differently so that you apply your economic knowledge and understanding (your AO1 Knowledge and understanding skills) to a unique context, such as car manufacturing. In this case, you should look to explain how the concept of division of labour might be applied in a car factory. For example, you could mention that some workers might become specialised in engine building whilst others are quicker at fitting wheels and tyres.

3   Explain why the division of the labour in a car factory should lead to an increase in productivity. [3]

3.4 The role of the entrepreneur

1   'Fill in the gaps' can be a useful retrieval practice strategy. Copy the following text and complete the gaps using terminology from Chapter 3.

> | fail | production | risks | factors of production |

Entrepreneurs are individuals who organise _____ by putting together the various _____ to form a business opportunity.

Entrepreneurs are prepared to take _____. They use their own money or borrow from banks or other people to try to achieve their ambitions. If their plans _____, they will lose their own money and that of others.

2   Can you list **four** characteristics of a successful entrepreneur?

3   Can you list **four** examples of famous entrepreneurs?

SELF-ASSESSMENT CHECKLIST

Let's revisit the Knowledge focus and Exam skills focus for this chapter.
Decide how confident you are with each statement.

Now I can	Show it	Needs more work	Almost there	Confident to move on
define the meaning of the factors of production: land, labour, capital and enterprise	Define the meaning of the factors of production: land, labour, capital and enterprise.			
explain the importance of the factors of production	Use the term 'factors of production' in an explanation of the basic economic problem.			
describe the rewards to the factors of production	List the different rewards to each one of the factors of production.			
explain the difference between human capital and physical capital	Give **two** examples each of human capital and physical capital.			
explain the division of labour and specialisation	Explain the division of labour and specialisation.			
explain the role of the entrepreneur in the organisation of the factors of production in 21st-century economies and as a risk taker	List the characteristics of a successful entrepreneur and provide some examples of 21st-century entrepreneurs.			
understand the command word 'explain' and answer an 'explain' question	Answer an 'explain' question confidently, such as: explain the difference between the terms 'productivity' and 'production'.			
show that I can spend a proportionate amount of time on short-answer questions.	Write the answer to a 3-mark question in 6 minutes or less, such as Question 3 in Section 3.3.			

4 Resource allocation in different economic systems

EXAM SKILLS FOCUS

In this chapter you will:

- show that you understand the command word 'describe' and can answer a 'describe' question.

The command word 'describe' means to state the points of a topic or give characteristics and main features. For example, you might be asked to describe a process, the main characteristics of a concept, the main trends in a set of data or the key features of a particular situation. 'Describe' questions are more like explain questions than state, define or identify questions. Your answer should show that you can write at least a couple of sentences of prose rather just than one or two words.

4.1 What are economic systems?

≪ RECALL AND CONNECT 1 ≪

Read the following excerpt:

> The fundamental problem of scarcity requires choices to be made. The choices that are made are determined by a country's economic system. The economic system identifies the means by which decisions can be made relating to the three resource allocation questions.

Let's look at some of the key terms from that excerpt.

a   State what is meant by the term scarcity.

b   Explain how an opportunity cost arises when choices are made.

c   Identify the **three** resource allocation questions.

UNDERSTAND THESE TERMS

- market economy
- planned economy
- mixed economy
- market mechanism

4.2 The market economy

1   Use the following activity to put the different stages of the market mechanism in order.

a   There is a decrease in demand.

i	fall in price
ii	decrease in quantity supplied
iii	excess supply from firms
iv	less profit incentive to produce

b   There is an increase in demand.

i	increase in quantity supplied
ii	more profit incentive to produce
iii	excess demand from consumers
iv	rise in price

Like most of the command words you have seen so far, 'describe' is likely to feature as a command word for short-answer questions that are checking your level of AO1 Knowledge and understanding only. Therefore, you need to demonstrate strong knowledge of a particular topic or issue. Try the following questions, which ask you to 'describe' a process.

2   Describe how the market mechanism works when there is a fall in demand for a given product.   [2]

3   Describe how the market mechanism allocates resources following an increase in demand.   [2]

4.3 The planned economy

1   The word box contains six desirable economic issues. According to standard economic theory, three of them are associated with planned economies. That is, they are more likely to result from a planned economy than from a market economy. Three of them are associated with a market economy. Copy the following table and categorise them correctly.

| low levels of income inequality   high level of innovation |
| strong incentives to work   high levels of social welfare |
| higher levels of efficiency   low levels of unemployment |

Planned economy	Market economy

Table 4.1: Planned economy and market economy advantages

In this set of 'describe' questions, you are being asked to describe the advantages or disadvantages for a particular economic concept. It is good practice to show that you understand the concept (or the key term) by offering a short definition at the start of your answer. Then, you must outline at least two advantages or disadvantages. There is no need to offer any counter-arguments in a short-answer question.

2   Describe **one** advantage of a planned economy over a market economy.   [2]

3   Many economists argue that market economies are more advantageous than planned economies. Describe **one** disadvantage of a planned economy.   [2]

4.4 The mixed economy

UNDERSTAND THESE TERMS

- private sector
- public sector
- privatisation

This question is asking you describe the main features of an economic concept. A before, you should start your answer with a short definition of the concept (or key term). Then, you should outline at least two important characteristics but without excessive detail.

1   Describe the main features of a mixed economy.   [3]

REFLECTION

At this stage, you have mostly been looking at short-answer questions that assess AO1 Knowledge and understanding. Check now that you can remember the purpose of short-answer questions and what AO1 Knowledge and understanding means.

What strategies could you use to improve your confidence regarding question types and mark scheme language?

SELF-ASSESSMENT CHECKLIST

Let's revisit the Knowledge focus and Exam skills focus for this chapter. Decide how confident you are with each statement.

Now I can	Show it	Needs more work	Almost there	Confident to move on
explain decision-making in market, planned and mixed economic systems	Write a short paragraph that outlines the difference between the two concepts.			
analyse the advantages and disadvantages of resource allocation in market, planned and mixed economic systems	List the key advantages associated with all **three** systems.			
show that I understand the command word 'describe' and can answer a 'describe' question.	Complete a past paper question with the command word 'describe'.			

5 Production possibility curves

The command word 'calculate' means to work out from given facts, figures or information. Depending on the complexity of the calculation, you may be expected to rearrange a formula and this will likely carry more marks. You should always show your working because the mark scheme may reward a partially correct answer.

Economics is a subject of diagrams. This is because economists regularly use diagrams to create a simplified way of analysing complex situations. You will learn many diagrams during your time studying economics, and it is important that you include them in your answers. Mark schemes often state that a diagram is necessary within an answer to achieve higher marks. This is because diagrammatic forms are a key part of AO1 Knowledge and understanding in many parts of the syllabus.

5.1 The production possibility curve

UNDERSTAND THIS TERM
• production possibility curve (PPC)

1 To check your understanding of the PPC model, copy the following text and fill in the blanks.

To understand how the production possibility curve works, imagine that the economy produces just two goods: cars (manufacturing) and rice (agriculture).

maximum produced resources utilised

These two industries use all of the economy's current _____ between them in their production of cars and rice. The production technology available is being fully _____. The PPC shows the _____ level of output of each of the two goods that can be _____.

5.2 The production possibility curve and opportunity cost

≪ RECALL AND CONNECT 1 ≪
a Define the term 'opportunity cost'.
b Zikri is deciding whether to go to the opera or a football game. He chooses to go to the opera. What is the opportunity cost of this decision?

Quantitative skills are an important aspect of studying economics. Sometimes, exam questions ask you to calculate figures. Other times, you will be expected to conduct calculations in order to justify part of your analytical writing. Here are some tips for conducting calculations:

• Show your working.

• Make sure it is clear which part of your response is your final answer.

• Check if the question requires you to round up/down your answer to a certain number of significant figures.

• State the units of your answer.

These elements are often overlooked by students, and yet they are easy things to get right and score marks.

Read this short extract which relates to the following Exam skills question:

1

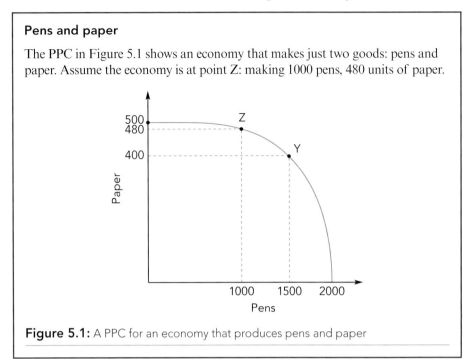

Pens and paper

The PPC in Figure 5.1 shows an economy that makes just two goods: pens and paper. Assume the economy is at point Z: making 1000 pens, 480 units of paper.

Figure 5.1: A PPC for an economy that produces pens and paper

The economy moves from point Z to point Y. Calculate how many units of paper it gives up. [1]

Read this short extract which relates to the two following Exam skills questions:

2

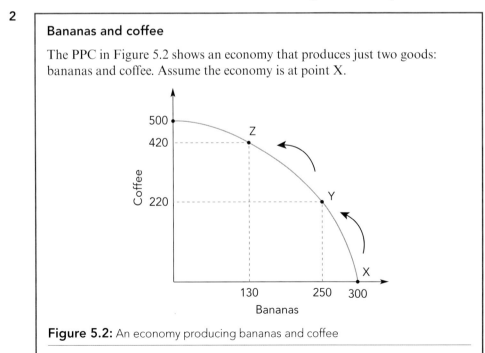

Bananas and coffee

The PPC in Figure 5.2 shows an economy that produces just two goods: bananas and coffee. Assume the economy is at point X.

Figure 5.2: An economy producing bananas and coffee

Calculate the opportunity cost of moving from point X to point Y. [1]

3   Calculate the opportunity cost of moving from point Y to point Z.   [1]

> **REFLECTION**
>
> Mathematical skills are crucial to your success in economics. It is important that you look at all the mathematical demands of the syllabus and make sure that you are confident with everything required.
>
> How could you improve your mathematical skills during your revision?

When answering economics questions, always consider whether a diagram is required or would be useful in your answer. In Chapter 3, you looked at the command word 'explain'; it stated that you must support your points or reasons with relevant evidence. In many cases, a good diagram will satisfy that requirement for 'evidence'. Sometimes this will be explicit in the question, but other times it will not.

Read the following question. Your task is to note down the mark scheme's expectations. You do not need to write an answer. You just need to write down the criteria needed for a question like this.

4   Explain, with the aid of a PPC diagram, why there will be an opportunity cost of every choice that a firm makes.   [3]

5.3 The shape of the PPC

'Explain' questions come up frequently in exams. Two more examples follow. In each case, identify the mark scheme's expectation first. Then, plan how you would go about answering these two different questions to make sure you have met every expectation of the mark scheme. For example, do you need to draw a diagram, or do you need to perform a calculation?

Write out your answer to each question.

1   Explain why a PPC is often drawn concave to the origin.   [2]

2   With the help of a diagram, explain why a PPC is often drawn concave to the origin.   [3]

REFLECTION

By now you should be becoming more familiar with the style of 'explain' questions, and you should be developing your mark scheme awareness such that you can identify the mark scheme's expectations. What strategies could you use to improve your confidence with 'explain' questions? What strategies could you use to improve your confidence with identifying mark scheme expectations?

Some strategies might include:

- Find several explain question from past papers.

- Read through the relevant mark schemes.

- Highlight the aspects of the mark scheme that continue to come up. You should find that the criteria stay relatively constant, even though the indicative content might change.

The PPC in Figure 5.3 shows an economy that makes just two goods: pens and paper. Assume the economy is making 100 pens and 0 units of paper.

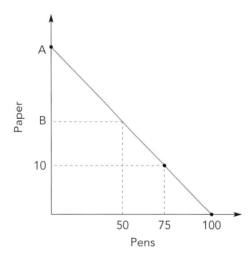

Figure 5.3: An economy producing pens and paper

3   Calculate how many pens the economy gives up when it chooses to make 10 units of paper.   [1]

4   Calculate how many units of paper are produced at point A.   [1]

5   Calculate how many units of paper are produced at point B.   [1]

5.4 Shifts in the PPC

1   An economy splits its resources between making manufactured goods and agricultural goods. Copy the following table and, from the following list, identify whether each item would lead to an outward shift or an inward shift of the PPC.

> birth rate decline   technology innovation
> an increase in immigration numbers   earthquake
> increase in income tax rates   government infrastructure investment

Outward shift	Inward shift

Table 5.1: Outwards and inwards shifts of a PPC

2   With this information in mind, read the following news story:

> **The Pakistani economy**
>
> Pakistan's economy is highly concentrated in two key industries: textiles and agriculture. In 2022, Pakistan suffered deadly flooding that affected a significant portion of the country. Economic activity was dealt a severe blow due to infrastructure damage and tragic loss of life.

You should now draw a diagram that illustrates this news story.

SELF-ASSESSMENT CHECKLIST

Let's revisit the Knowledge focus and Exam skills focus for this chapter.
Decide how confident you are with each statement.

Now I can	Show it	Needs more work	Almost there	Confident to move on
explain the meaning and purpose of a production possibility curve	Define a PPC.			
explain the shape of the production possibility curve, including the difference between constant opportunity costs and increasing opportunity costs	Explain why PPCs can be drawn concave to the origin or as a straight line.			
analyse the causes and consequences of shifts in a production possibility curve	Explain, with a diagram, why a PPC might shift outwards or inwards.			
discuss the significance of a position within a production possibility curve	Explain what the various positions on a PPC diagram mean.			
show that I understand the command word 'calculate' and can answer a 'calculate' question	Draw a PPC graph with numbers (like Figure 5.3). Ask another student to do the same. Swap graphs with each other and answer each other's question. Share your answers.			
show that I understand the importance of drawing diagrams when answering economics questions.	Answer the following question: explain why a straight-line PPC has constant opportunity cost. Use a diagram as part of your answer.			

6 Classification of goods and services

The command word 'assess' means to make an informed judgement. In an 'assess' question, you should give a balanced account of both sides, for and against an issue or argument.

The command word 'define' means to give precise meaning. You should provide a clear and concise explanation whilst avoiding unnecessary details or tangents that could distract from your main point. Depending on the term or concept you are defining, it may be helpful to provide examples to illustrate your definition. These can be real-world examples or hypothetical scenarios.

Every student needs to understand what good answers look like. It is important that you compare your answers against example student responses. Sometimes, this will cause you to re-edit your own work, but this is a very useful strategy to improve the quality of your future answers.

6.1 Excludability and rivalry

<< RECALL AND CONNECT 1 <<

Outline what a factor of production is and explain how they are used to satisfy wants and needs.

UNDERSTAND THESE TERMS

- excludability
- rivalry

1   To support your understanding of the key terms in this chapter, try this labelling activity. Copy the following table and sort these different goods and services into the relevant quadrant of the table (**a**, **b**, **c** or **d**).

| cup of coffee | fishing | flood defences | cinema |

	Excludable	Non-excludable
Rival	a	b
Non-rival	c	d

Table 6.1

As a way of thinking about your answer to an assess question, you should always look for the hypothesis. That is, you should look out for a proposed explanation in the stem of the question.

A few ways you can do this are:

- Replacing the command word 'assess' with 'explain'. This will give you the first line of analysis.

- Thinking about what the standard economic theory would say.

Once you have offered one side of the argument, then you need to offer an opposing view. This might be a complete counter-argument, or it might be a evaluative point such as 'it depends on certain assumptions' or 'only under circumstances like ...'.

You must also write a conclusion. The final paragraph will answer the question with a well-reasoned judgement that is based on your previous lines of analysis.

2   Assess whether roads are always a good example of a public good.   [12]

REFLECTION

Make sure you are completely happy with the key terms from Section 6.1.

Some of the terms look very similar but have quite different meanings (e.g., 'private goods' and 'public goods'). The answer to an exam question about 'private goods' would be different to the answer to a question about 'public goods'.

How will you ensure that you do not misread an important key term in the question?

6.2 Private goods

1   With the use of an example, define the term 'private good'.   [2]

2   Explain what is meant by the terms 'excludability' and 'rivalry' and assess whether a cup of coffee and cinema tickets conform to both.   [8]

It is important that you understand what a good answer looks like. Once you have answered the two preceding questions, take a look at the following example student responses. These are weaker answers and would not score full marks. How can you improve the answers?

Example student response
1   One type of private good is a cup of coffee.
2   Buying a ticket to see a cinema movie is excludable. Buying a cup of coffee is rival.

If you need some help, here is some support:

*   The 'define' question needs you to offer a short sentence that confirms understanding and to state an example.

*   In the 'explain' question, it is important not only to outline the key terms in more detail but to also talk through the example(s) to show how it illustrates those key concepts.

*   You must also include some sort of evaluative statement in order to help support an informed judgement.

Now read the following stronger example student responses to see what a good answers looks like:

Example student response
1   Private goods are goods that are rival and excludable. An example would be a cup of coffee.
2   Excludability means it is possible to exclude some people from using a particular product. This is normally done through charging a price. Rivalry means that the consumption of a particular product by one person reduces the availability for others. Goods that are both excludable and rival are called private goods. A cup of coffee is a good example of a private good. Consumers must pay for a cup of coffee; they cannot drink coffee for free. Thus, it is excludable. If one consumer drinks a cup of coffee, that means no one else can drink that same cup of coffee. Thus, it is rival. By contrast, a cinema ticket is excludable but non-rival. People must pay for a ticket to watch the movie, but several people can watch the movie at the same time without affecting the utility for each other.

> **REFLECTION**
>
> Look at your two original answers again. Think about whether they need to be improved. If so, how can you improve them?

6.3 Public goods

Before you answer these questions, think about what you learned from the previous Reflection. These questions all carry a different number of marks and so they require a different length of answer.

1   With the use of an example, define the term 'public good'. [2]

2   With the use of an example, explain what is meant by the terms 'non-excludability' and 'non-rivalry'. [6]

3   Assess whether a beach should be considered a public good. [12]

6.4 Merit goods, demerit goods and information failure

> **UNDERSTAND THESE TERMS**
>
> • merit good
>
> • demerit good
>
> • information failure

1   Using your own knowledge, copy and complete the following table.

Merit goods	Under _____	Example 1
		Example 2
Demerit goods	Over _____	Example 1
		Example 2

Table 6.2: Merit and demerit goods

2   Assess the view that the only goods a government should produce are public goods. [12]

SELF-ASSESSMENT CHECKLIST

Let's revisit the Knowledge focus and Exam skills focus for this chapter.
Decide how confident you are with each statement.

Now I can	Show it	Needs more work	Almost there	Confident to move on
explain the meaning and importance of free goods and private goods (economic goods)	Explain the difference between a free good and a public good.			
explain the meaning and importance of public goods	List **three** examples of a public good.			
explain the meaning and importance of merit goods and demerit goods	Use the terms 'merit' and 'demerit good' in a sentence.			
analyse how underconsumption of merit goods results from imperfect information in the market	Explain how underconsumption of merit goods results from imperfect information in the market.			
analyse how overconsumption of demerit goods results from imperfect information in the market	Explain how overconsumption of demerit goods results from imperfect information in the market.			
show that I understand the command word 'assess' and answer an 'assess' question.	Identify an 'assess' question from a past paper and write an answer.			
show that I understand the command word 'define' and answer a 'define' question	Create some flashcards of your own with the key term on one side and the definition of that term on the other side.			
show that I understand what a good answer looks like.	Look at some of your previous work that you did not score full marks on. Re-edit it to try and improve your original score.			

Exam practice 1

This section contains both past paper questions from previous Cambridge exams and practice questions. These questions draw together your knowledge on a range of topics that you have covered up to this point and will help you prepare for your assessment.

The following questions have example student responses and commentaries provided. For each question, work through the question first, then compare your answer to the example student response and commentary.

1   Explain how resources are allocated in a market economy **and** consider whether there are any differences in a mixed economy.   [8]

Adapted from Cambridge International AS & A Level Economics (9708) Paper 22 Q2a, June 2018

Example student response	Examiner comments
There are four main resources of an economy: land, labour, capital and enterprise. The fundamental economic problem is that resources are scarce and people's wants and needs are unlimited. This means a choice always has to be made between competing uses for resources. It leads to three basic questions: how to allocate those resources, what to make and for whom.	**AO1 Knowledge and understanding** The student shows a good knowledge of syllabus content. There is a decent explanation of the fundamental problems and the three important questions. The student defines a market economy well, using technical terminology. *3/3*
In a market economy, resources are allocated through the price mechanism. This essentially means that the market forces of supply and demand dictate how resources are allocated. For example, there may be a large demand for avocados because of a particular food trend on social media. In the short-term, avocados will be relatively scarce but as more entrepreneurs see that there is profit to made from producing avocados, they will reallocate their resources away from other products and towards making avocados. This is known as the profit motive (the reason why entrepreneurs reallocate their resources) and consumer sovereignty (because consumers are making their own decisions about the things they want to buy).	**AO2 Analysis** There is a good example of how resources are allocated in a market economy. Having shown a strong understanding of syllabus content, the student is now examining the issue of resource allocation using relevant economic theory. Again, there is excellent technical terminology, and the chain of analysis is correct. *3/3*
In a mixed economy, resources are allocated through the price mechanism and the government. If resources are purely allocated by the government then this would be called a planned economy. A mixed economy is the most common form of economy in the real world. Norway, Singapore and Vietnam, for example, all have mixed economies. Mixed economies are often more advantageous than market economies because they can solve market failures like public goods.	**AO3 Evaluation** The final paragraph is not as good. The student defines the mixed economy accurately (AO1) but fails to elaborate any further with regards to the question about differences in a mixed economy. The points about planned economies and the examples of mixed economies are irrelevant to the question being asked. The student needed to elaborate further in terms of the provision of public goods and merit goods. Just saying mixed

Example student response	Examiner comments
	economies can help to provide public goods is not enough. The student should have defined what public goods are, why the market economy cannot provide them and how a mixed economy does provide them. *0/2* *Total: 6/8 marks*

2   Explain, with the aid of a production possibility curve (PPC) diagram, why scarcity makes choice inevitable for firms **and** consider whether each choice has an opportunity cost. [8]

Adapted from Cambridge International AS & A Level Economics (9708) Paper 21 Q2a, June 2020

Example student response	Examiner comments
A PPC is a simple representation of the different combinations of goods that an economy can make given its current resources and state of technology. Regardless of the economic system (free market or planned), the economy cannot make a limitless number of goods and services; it must make choices about what goods to make. In the diagram below, the PPC shows that an economy can produce different combinations of manufactured goods (M) and agricultural goods (A). Opportunity cost is defined as the benefits foregone of the next best alternative. If, for example, an economy chooses to produce more agricultural goods then it will produce less manufactured goods. The number of manufactured goods given up are the opportunity cost. This is the cost of the choice that has been made.	**AO1 Knowledge and understanding** A definition of a keyword is often a good way to begin an answer to a question with the command word 'explain'. The PPC definition shows a good understanding of the term, and later on, there is a good definition of opportunity cost. In the second paragraph, the student states that choices must be made in an economy but, critically, does not say why. The student never explains why scarcity makes choice inevitable (which is the question). The answer only states that choices must be made and only ever explains why choices lead to opportunity cost. *2/3* **AO2 Analysis** The question asks for diagrams. The student has used their initiative to designate the axes labels (manufactured goods and agricultural goods). This is fine, but make sure you look to see if there are certain axes that you should be using from any data that you may have been given. The diagram is well drawn. The student applies their knowledge to the diagram by successfully illustrating a movement along the curve. The explanation is correct, but it is difficult to read. The student would benefit from simplifying their writing if possible. Nevertheless, the student is using relevant economic concepts, such as a PPC diagram, to examine the question with regards to opportunity cost and choice. This is strong AO2 Analysis. *3/3*

Example student response	Examiner comments
If a PPC is drawn as a straight line, this implies that the opportunity cost of production is constant. The economy can be at any point on (or below) the PPC and the economic system will dictate that choice. For example, as the economy goes from point X to point Y, it gains 100 agricultural goods and gives up 20 manufactured goods. From point Y to point Z, the economy again gains 100 agricultural goods and gives up 20 agricultural goods. The ratio of agricultural goods to manufactured goods is constant. The choice of being at X, Y or Z has led to an opportunity cost. If the PPC is drawn as a curved line, like in the diagram below, this indicates that the opportunity cost of production is increasing. For example, when the economy moves from point X to point Y now, the economy gains 280 agricultural goods and gives up 20 manufactured goods. The ratio is 14:1. When the economy moves from point Y to point Z, the economy gains just 50 more agricultural goods, yet still gives up 20 manufactured goods. The ratio is now 2.5:1. The opportunity cost of producing agricultural goods has increased. 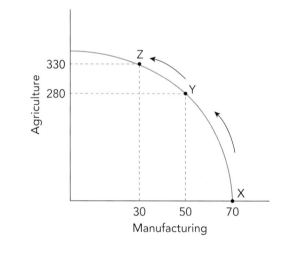	**AO3 Evaluation** The student has not quite gotten the evaluation correct though. The paragraph about the straight line PPC had already analysed the key issues of opportunity cost and choice. A curved PPC does not add very much to the analysis about opportunity cost. It effectively explains why the opportunity cost is increasing along a curved PPC, but the question instead asks whether there is always opportunity cost – not whether it is always constant/increasing. Instead, the student should be thinking about movements within the PPC. *0/2* Note: the student may now have spent too long on this question writing irrelevant content. They may run out of time on later questions. *Total: 5/8 marks*

3   Explain how capital goods contribute to production in a modern economy
     and consider how capital is rewarded.   [8]

*Adapted from Cambridge International AS & A Level Economics (9708)
    Paper 21 Q2a, November 2018*

Example student response	Examiner comments
There are four factors of production. Land, such as natural resources like sunlight and water. Labour, such as people. Capital, such as manufactured resources like machines and equipment. Enterprise such as entrepreneurship. The factors of production are limited. Because of this, the economy cannot satisfy everyone's wants and needs and so choices have to be made. A market economy will allocate the factors of production via the 'invisible hand', which means the forces of demand and supply. Capital goods are probably the main factor of production. They can be used in combination with the other factors like land and labour to make the things that people want and need like yachts. This output (yachts) can be sold for money. However, firms need to buy the capital goods like machines first, so the reward for making capital goods is money.	**AO1 Knowledge and understanding** Ultimately, the student correctly identifies that capital is a factor of production and that it includes all human-made aids to production such equipment and machinery. They also identify that capital is a factor of production that can be used in combination with the other factors of production to produce goods and services which can be sold. This is all correct, and despite the lack of structure, the student demonstrates good knowledge of syllabus content. *3/3* **AO2 Analysis** There is a lot of irrelevant material at the beginning of the answer, which suggests the students does not completely understand the demands of the question. This may indicate that the student's content knowledge is slightly confused. By extension, there is very little analysis that can be credited. The student does not link to PPC growth (outward shift) or potential growth of the economy. *0/3* **AO3 Evaluation** There is very little evaluation to credit. The reward for capital is interest payments, not money. The student should offer an example of how capital is rewarded via interest payments but does not. *0/2* Note: This answer has very little structure (it is just one long paragraph). The answer would have benefitted from being structured into logical paragraphs, which would help to demonstrate a student's understanding of the topic. *Total: 3/8 marks*

Here are two practice questions which you should attempt. Use the guidance in the
commentaries in this section to help you as you answer the questions.

4   Using examples, explain the concept of division of labour **and** consider
     the likely effects of division of labour on a PPC diagram.   [8]

5   Explain why it is difficult for economists to conduct experiments **and**
     consider the importance of the term *ceteris paribus* in economic analysis.   [8]

7 Demand and supply curves

EXAM SKILLS FOCUS

In this chapter you will:

- show that you understand what 'data response' questions are

- show that you understand how to integrate diagrams into your answer as part of meeting the AO2 Analysis assessment objective.

'Data response' questions require you read to a case study closely and then answer questions that are based on that context. All 'data response' questions require you to refer to the case study and use examples in order to justify your economic analysis.

AO2 Analysis means using relevant economic concepts to examine economic issues and relationships. This means that you will frequently use diagrams in your answer. Many students, however, make the mistake of just drawing a diagram and never referring to it in their answer. You not only need to select the correct diagram, but you need to integrate that diagram into your answer. That means you must refer to it and use it as part of your analysis.

7.1 The price mechanism and markets

- price mechanism
- consumers
- market

Question 1 is a short-answer question. Before you attempt it, you should highlight the key words (including the command word) so that you answer the entirety of the question. Ensure you use technical terms where possible.

1   Describe how the price mechanism can solve the basic questions of resource allocation when there is a shortage in the market.   [3]

7.2 Demand

- national demand
- effective demand
- demand curve (D)
- market demand
- demand schedule

You have been studying economics for a while now. How easy is it to learn definitions?

By now, you should have realised that learning definitions is an important exam skill. This is not because there are lots of 'define' questions in exams. Generally, there are not. But learning definitions is important because it will, first, help you to understand what a question is asking and, second, help you focus your answer to the question being asked. By contrast, misreading questions and not answering the questions are common errors that students make in exams.

How can you improve your learning of definitions?

7.3 The demand curve

1   Name some of the main features of the demand curve.

2   Draw a demand curve for a product.

Quite often, you will need to draw a demand curve, or similar diagram, in support of your AO2 Analysis skills. When drawing a diagram, ensure that you have included all its important elements. Here is a list of things you must remember when drawing a demand curve:

•   Axes must be labelled (price and quantity).

•   The demand curve should be drawn as a downward sloping line, preferably drawn straight.

•   The demand curve must be labelled D.

Sometimes you might also be asked to draw, or plot, a demand curve from data onto a set of grid squares. In this case, make sure you use the correct scale on the grid squares you are given.

> **REFLECTION**
>
> How comfortable are you with plotting co-ordinates on grid squares?

7.4 The factors that affect demand

1   Consider the factors in the box below. Each factor will either lead to an increase in demand or a decrease in demand for hot coffee. Copy the table and put each factor into the relevant column. Assume that hot coffee is a normal good.

> **UNDERSTAND THESE TERMS**
> •   substitute
> •   complement
> •   joint demand

> national income rises   the price of a substitute rises
> the price of a substitute falls   fashion trends move away from coffee
> the season changes to summer   the price of a complement falls

Demand increase	Demand decrease

Table 7.1: Factors that shift the demand curve

7.5 Supply

≪ RECALL AND CONNECT 1 ≪

State what the term 'ceteris paribus' means.

7.6 The supply curve

1   Name some of the main features of the supply curve.

2   Draw a supply curve for a product.

7.7 The factors affecting supply

1   Consider the factors in the following box. Each factor will either lead to an increase in demand or a decrease in demand for tomatoes. Copy the table and put each factor into the relevant column.

> there is a good harvest   the price of farming labour rises
> the level of agricultural productivity rises with the use of fertiliser
> severe weather causes a drought
> the government offers a subsidy for farmers
> the government chooses to increase tax on tomatoes

Supply increase	Supply decrease

Table 7.2: Factors that shift the supply curve

7.8 Causes of a shift in the demand curve

In this chapter, you should develop two key skills:

- applying examples from the case study to your answers (for data response questions)

- integrating economic diagrams to support your analysis.

The questions in Sections 7.4 and 7.7 checked that you can identify whether demand or supply increases or decreases. In this section, you need to make sure you can apply these concepts to a real-life scenario and ensure that you can draw an appropriate demand curve. Note that it will be important to use the data in your analysis as well.

1

Coffee consumption

A report in May 2022 stated that global coffee consumption was increasing. The COVID-19 pandemic had severely affected demand for the two prior years, but as countries opened back up from their respective lockdowns, people were returning to former habits such as meeting friends in coffee shops, gathering around the coffee machine at work and buying a coffee on the morning commute to work.

Using a diagram, explain why global coffee consumption is rising.   [3]

REFLECTION

Review your answer to Question 1 and go through the following checklists.

Data response checklist:

●   Is your answer in context?

●   Did you reference the case study at least once?

Diagram checklist:

●   Are the axes labelled?

●   Are both curves labelled?

●   Do you have an arrow to show the direction of movement between the two curves?

●   Have you plotted (with dotted lines) the price and quantity?

●   Have you accurately labelled any changes to price and quantity?

●   Have you referred to your diagram in your analysis?

Consider how you could improve your use of case study examples and economic diagrams in answering questions.

7.9 Causes of a shift in the supply curve

1

Olive production in Europe

In 2022, the historic drought and incredible heatwaves across southern Europe caused many olives trees to drop their olives as they tried to conserve water. Producers recorded the weakest harvest on record, and as a result, the price of olive oil is expected to nearly double over the coming months.

Using a diagram, explain the impact of the weather conditions in southern Europe in 2022 on the supply of olives.   [3]

7.10 How to distinguish between a shift in the demand or supply curve and a movement along the curves

1 Consider the difference between a movement along a demand curve and the shift of a demand curve. [4]

2 Consider the difference between a movement along a supply curve and the shift of a supply curve. [4]

SELF-ASSESSMENT CHECKLIST

Let's revisit the Knowledge focus and Exam skills focus for this chapter. Decide how confident you are with each statement.

Now I can	Show it	Needs more work	Almost there	Confident to move on
define the term effective demand	Distinguish between the terms 'demand' and 'effective demand'.			
explain the importance of individual and market demand and supply	Explain how market curves are derived from individual ones.			
explain the factors that affect demand	List **five** factors that affect the demand curve.			
explain the factors that affect supply	List **five** factors that affect the supply curve.			
analyse the causes of a shift in the demand curve (D)	Explain why the demand curve shifts.			
analyse the causes of a shift in the supply curve (S)	Explain why the supply curve shifts.			
distinguish between the shift in the demand or supply curve and the movement along these curves	Research the global price changes of a commodity and identify whether it has been caused by a shift in demand or supply.			

CONTINUED

show that I understand what data response questions are	Explain to another student why examples are so important to data response questions.			
show that I understand how to integrate diagrams into my answer as part of meeting the AO2 Analysis assessment objective.	Create a case study question that requires a diagram to answer it. Ask another student to do the same. Answer each other's questions using well-integrated diagrams in your answers.			

8 Price elasticity, income elasticity and cross elasticity of demand

Planning your answer means giving some forethought to your answer before you actually write it. You might even write a small plan before you write your full answer. Planning is not for everyone, though. Some students might prefer just going straight into an answer without planning. The benefit with that approach is time. But planning helps you keep your focus on the exam question. For some students it can also help reduce the stress of not knowing what the next step of your answer is whilst writing it.

Time management in exams is critical. For example, you need to spend (much) less time on questions that carry a low number of marks in order to give yourself the best possible chance with the questions that carry more marks.

8.1 What do economists mean by elasticity?

UNDERSTAND THESE TERMS

- elasticity
- elastic
- inelastic

8.2 Price elasticity of demand

≪ RECALL AND CONNECT 1 ≪

a What is effective demand?

b Draw a demand curve.

UNDERSTAND THESE TERMS

- price elasticity of demand (PED)
- price elastic
- price inelastic
- perfectly elastic
- perfectly inelastic
- unit elasticity

1 State the formula for PED. [1]

   Note that it is important in a question to show your working and to state your answer with units. In terms of PED, there are no units. Students often give elasticity coefficients as percentages, but they are not.

2 In the following two scenarios, calculate the PED coefficient and state whether it is price elastic demand or price inelastic demand.

   a The price of a bag of potato crisps rises from $0.40 to $0.44. As a result, sales fall but only by 2.5%. [2]

   b A car company tries to increase sales by reducing the price of its cars. The average price reduction is 15%. As a result, they record their highest-ever level of sales. Sales increase by 45%. [2]

3 Copy the following table and then consider the following list of characteristics. Do you think they apply more to a price-elastic good or a price-inelastic good?

> lots of substitutes   addictive   low price   a luxury good
> strong brand loyalty   considered over the long term

Price elastic	Price inelastic

Table 8.1: Characteristics of a good that is price elastic in demand and a good that is price inelastic in demand

The price elasticity of demand can be denoted by name, number or diagram.

For example, price-elastic demand can be denoted as any negative coefficient below −1 (e.g., −2, −2.5 or −10) and can be illustrated as a shallow downward-sloping line.

4 Draw **two** diagrams:

    a a perfectly elastic demand curve

    b a perfectly inelastic demand curve.

8.3 Income elasticity of demand

1 In the following two scenarios, calculate the YED coefficient and state whether the product is a normal or an inferior good.

    a An economy suffers a downturn. Average income falls by 2%. As a result, the quantity demanded falls by 5%. [2]

    b Freya sees her income rise from $30 000 per year to $31 500 per year. As a result, her consumption of beans falls from 40 cans per year to 32 cans. [2]

> **UNDERSTAND THESE TERMS**
>
> - income elasticity of demand (YED)
> - necessity good
> - superior good

8.4 Cross elasticity of demand

> **《 RECALL AND CONNECT 2 《**
>
> **a** Define the terms 'substitutes' and 'complements'.
>
> **b** How do substitutes and complements influence demand?

A good tip for questions that carry a high number of marks is to plan your answer. Your teacher may have given you the feedback before: 'not answering the question'. Planning your answer is meant to ensure that you will answer all elements of a question and that you will remain focused on the question throughout your answer.

Be aware that planning takes time. Therefore, your planning should be quick; it should be in note or bullet point form. Ultimately, you are still going to have to write the essay in full, so do not take up too much time with the plan.

Take a look at the following question. Spend one to two minutes planning an answer. Highlight the key words and write a set of bullet points that sets out the structure of your answer. Then write out your answer in full.

1   Explain how economists use the concept of cross elasticity to distinguish between substitute goods and complementary goods **and** consider how firms might use this information.   [8]

> REFLECTION
>
> How successful was your planning? How long did the planning process take? How do you think taking the time to plan benefitted you once you were writing the answer?

8.5 How price, income and cross elasticities of demand can affect decision-making

1   Firms will always be keen to know the elasticities of their own products. In particular, they might use the information to inform new decisions.

Copy and complete the following table. What business decision might a firm make in each of the situations listed in order to increase their revenue? The first one is done for you.

The firm produces a ...	It should ...
price inelastic good	raise its price in order to raise revenue.
price elastic good	
normal good	
inferior good	
good that has a close substitute	
good that has a close complement	

Table 8.2: Business decision-making

Look at the following questions and plan your answer for no more than one or two minutes. Then try writing a full answer.

2   With reference to the concept of income elasticity, assess whether a firm selling cheap plastic shoes is likely to have more success in a high-income country like Canada.   [12]

3   Assess how an electronic goods firm might attempt to change the price elasticity of demand for their products **and** consider which approach is most likely to be successful.   [12]

REFLECTION

In this chapter, you have answered some short-answer questions and some more extended answer questions. Consider the length of time you have taken for each of your answers. To what extent are you spending an appropriate amount of time on different questions?

You should make sure that the length of time you spend on writing your answers reflects the mark allocation in an exam. For example, 'calculate' questions are relatively short, and there is no time for planning. By contrast, 'assess' questions tend to have more marks allocated to them, so there is more time for planning and writing.

What strategies could you use to speed up your witing?

SELF-ASSESSMENT CHECKLIST

Let's revisit the Knowledge focus and Exam skills focus for this chapter. Decide how confident you are with each statement.

Now I can	Show it	Needs more work	Almost there	Confident to move on
define the meaning of price elasticity, income elasticity and cross elasticity of demand (PED, YED, XED, respectively)	Define each term.			
use formulae to calculate price elasticity, income elasticity and cross elasticity of demand	Complete **three** elasticity calculations, one for each of the elasticities.			
explain the importance of relative percentage changes, the size and sign of the coefficient in relation to price elasticity, income elasticity and cross elasticity of demand	Explain the difference between a negative and positive coefficient value for YED and XED.			

CONTINUED

describe elasticity values: perfectly elastic, (highly) elastic, unitary elasticity, (highly) inelastic, perfectly inelastic	Write out a short explanation for each of these terms.			
explain the variation in price elasticity of demand along the length of a straight-line demand curve	Identify the price inelastic and the price elastic points along a demand curve.			
analyse the factors that affect price, income and cross elasticity of demand	List three factors that affect PED, YED and XED.			
analyse the relationship between price elasticity of demand and total expenditure on a product	Explain why firms that sell inelastic products want to increase prices.			
discuss how price, income and cross elasticity of demand can affect decision-making	Discuss with another student the different decisions that a firm can make, depending on the type of product it makes.			
understand why planning my answer is necessary	Plan the answer to your next assess question. Consider whether it improves the speed and/or quality of your writing.			
show that I can manage the distribution of my time across the whole paper.	Complete a full past paper in timed conditions.			

9 Price elasticity of supply

The command word 'outline' means to set out the main points. It can be used for relatively short-answer questions and for more extended answer questions. It is associated with AO1 Knowledge and understanding and AO2 Analysis. Therefore, you will need to look at the number of marks for the question in order to plan the length of your answer, but you will not be required to write any evaluative comments.

The concept of price elasticity of supply (PES) is closely connected to the concept of price elasticity of demand (PED). Therefore, you should look to revise the Chapter 9 content in conjunction with the Chapter 8 content. They are similar in many ways (such as the formulae) but different in many ways too (such as the factors affecting the elasticity coefficient). Therefore, it is easy to get muddled between the two.

9.1 Price elasticity of supply

≪ RECALL AND CONNECT 1 ≪

a   What is meant by price elasticity of demand?

b   What is the form for price elasticity of demand?

c   Draw the diagrams for price inelastic demand and price elastic demand.

UNDERSTAND THESE TERMS

- price elasticity of supply (PES)
- price elastic supply
- price inelastic supply

1   State the formula for PES.   [1]

2   In the following two scenarios, calculate the PES coefficient and state whether it is price elastic supply or price inelastic supply.

    a   The price of a product rises from \$80 to \$100. As a result, supply rises by 50%.   [2]

    b   The price of a product rises from \$25 to \$35. As a result, supply rises from 6000 units to 6600 units.   [2]

The PES can be denoted by name, number or diagram. For example, price elastic supply can be denoted as any positive coefficient above +1 and can be illustrated as a steep upward-sloping line.

3   Draw the different supply curves for price elastic supply and price inelastic supply.

4   Now make sure you can also draw the extreme scenarios of perfectly elastic supply and perfectly inelastic supply.

9.2 Factors influencing price elasticity of supply

≪ RECALL AND CONNECT 2 ≪

List **three** factors that affect the price elasticity of demand.

1   Before completing the next Exam skills question, try this matching activity. Copy the table and categorise the factors under the headings of price elastic or price inelastic.

> short time taken   not very complicated   handmade
> can be stored   perishable   scarce resources used in production

Price elastic supply	Price inelastic supply

Table 9.1: Characteristics of a good that is price elastic in supply and a good that is price inelastic in supply

'Outline' questions often work like 'explain' questions. For example, the question may refer to a case study in the exam. Therefore, you need to select the relevant information from the extract to support your answer. This is all part of AO2 Analysis, and every case study will have facts, figures and quotes embedded within them that you can use in your answer.

2
> **COVID-19 vaccine production**
>
> COVID-19 vaccines were produced at great speed. They were, however, the result of unprecedented international cooperation and focus. Generally, vaccines tend to take a long time to make: anything up to ten years. Vaccines must go through many stages such as:
>
> * research phase
> * preclinical stage (which often includes animal testing)
> * clinical development (which often includes human testing)
> * government approval
> * manufacture and distribution.

Using the data, outline **two** factors that are likely to influence the price elasticity of supply for medical vaccines. [5]

9.3 Implications of PES for the ways in which businesses react to changing market conditions

1   Copy the text and fill in the blanks.

> can   cannot   inelastic   elastic   long   short   unstable
> stored   perishable   automated   productive capacity

Agricultural goods tend to be price _____ in supply. This is because they can take a _____ time to grow and they are _____. Therefore, farmers _____ respond to price changes quickly. This will mean that agricultural prices are more _____ compared to manufactured goods.

Manufactured goods tend to price _____ in supply. This is because they can take a _____ time to produce, production is often _____ and products can be _____ in a warehouse. Therefore, firms _____ respond to price changes quickly. If demand is high for a long time, firms may choose to increase their _____.

2

Pumpkin production

Pumpkins are a popular vegetable. China is the world's largest grower of pumpkins, followed by Mexico and Iran. Pumpkins can take three to four months to grow. From harvest, they are then packaged and sent around the world. The typical journey time from China to the USA is a further three to four weeks. Even if the consumers are prepared to pay high prices at times of high demand (like Thanksgiving), the process cannot be sped up. By contrast, an electronic watch from China can usually be ordered, made, and delivered within 10–12 working days at any time of the year.

Explain the concept of price elasticity of supply (PES) **and** consider the likely difference in PES for pumpkins and electronic watches. [8]

3   Assess which factors are most important in determining whether the PES for an agricultural good is likely to be relatively elastic or relatively inelastic. [12]

4   Consider whether pumpkins should be considered both price inelastic in supply and demand. [5]

REFLECTION

The purpose of Question 4 was to check your understanding of two concepts: PES and PED. It is important that you take time to revise each elasticity individually and do not assume that your understanding of one is sufficient for all. For example, a strong understanding of PES will not necessarily extend to a strong understanding of XED.

Students tend to understand PES less well than the other elasticities they have learnt (PED, YED and XED). How confident are you about the different elasticities? If you struggled with PES, how could you consolidate your understanding?

In addition, students often make the mistake of writing about PED when they should be writing about PES. How will you ensure that you avoid making this mistake?

SELF-ASSESSMENT CHECKLIST

Let's revisit the Knowledge focus and Exam skills focus for this chapter.
Decide how confident you are with each statement.

Now I can	Show it	Needs more work	Almost there	Confident to move on
define the meaning of price elasticity of supply (PES)	Explain the term 'price elasticity of supply'.			
calculate price elasticity of supply using the formula	State the PES formula.			
explain the significance of the relative percentage changes and the size and sign of the coefficient of price elasticity of supply	Create a number line that has the PES coefficients running from 0 to +10 and insert the labels of inelastic and elastic onto it.			
analyse the factors affecting price elasticity of supply	List **three** factors that would cause an agricultural product, like rice, to have price inelastic supply.			
discuss how price elasticity of supply is related to the speed and ease with which businesses react to changed market conditions	Explain why agricultural goods are considered to be price inelastic in supply but manufactured goods are not.			
show that I understand the command word 'outline' and answer an 'outline' question	Explain to another student what the command word 'outline' means.			
understand some of the connections between concepts from previous chapters.	Make a mind map of some of the connection between other chapters in this book (not just Chapters 8 and 9).			

10 The interaction of demand and supply

KNOWLEDGE FOCUS

You will answer questions on:

10.1 Market equilibrium and disequilibrium

10.2 The effects of shifts in demand and supply curves on equilibrium price and quantity

10.3 Relationships between markets

10.4 The functions of price in resource allocation

EXAM SKILLS FOCUS

In this chapter you will:

- understand the importance of selecting, interpreting and organising economic information in numerical form

- show that you understand what command word 'compare' means and answer a 'compare' question

- be able to identify a high-quality response.

Part of the skills of AO2 Analysis is to select, interpret and organise economic information in numerical form. Therefore, you should be prepared for questions that refer to a table of numerical data. These data might be transferred from a real-life set, or it might refer to a hypothetical situation. Nevertheless, you need to demonstrate your understanding of economics by using the data to justify your written analysis. For example, this might mean including a calculation as part of your analysis or it might mean identifying a pattern or trend to support your argument.

The command word 'compare' means to identify and comment on similarities and/ or differences. You should make sure that your answer really does compare two things in terms of their similarities and differences and not just state what the two things are.

Every student should see some concrete examples of high-quality answers as part of their learning. This will enable you to identify what a high-quality answer looks like and, by extension, understand how to improve your own answers.

10.1 Market equilibrium and disequilibrium

1

Market price	Quantity demanded	Quantity supplied
$10	4000	1600
$11	3800	2200
$12	3600	2800
$13	3400	3400
$14	3200	4000

Table 10.1: Demand and supply schedule for a premium brand of chocolate

Table 10.1 shows a demand and supply schedule for a premium brand of chocolate. Using the table, identify a market price where:

a   The market is in equilibrium.

b   The market is in disequilibrium, and there is an over-supply.

c   The market is in disequilibrium, and there is a shortage.

REFLECTION

Data can be presented both in tabular form and diagrammatic form.
Plot the data from Table 10.1. Now, make sure you can identify the same points (equilibrium and disequilibrium) on a diagram. Did you find it easier to answer the question using a table or a diagram?

2   State what is meant by the following terms.

a   over-supply

b   shortage

c   market adjustment

10.2 The effects of shifts in demand and supply curves on equilibrium price and quantity

1

Market price	Original demand schedule: Quantity demanded (D$_1$)	New demand schedule: Quantity demanded *after change* (D$_2$)
$10	4000	
$11	3800	
$12	3600	
$13	3400	
$14	3200	

Table 10.2: Original and new demand schedule for a premium brand of chocolate

Table 10.2 shows the demand schedule for the same premium brand of chocolate as Table 10.1. However, the price of a substitute brand rises. Therefore, the quantity demanded for this premium brand of chocolate rises by 800 units at any given price.

a Copy Table 10.2 and complete the column on the right-hand side of the table.

b Using your results from the new demand schedule, identify the new equilibrium price and quantity for the chocolate. You will need to look at Table 10.1 again.

The purpose of the previous questions was to check your ability to select and interpret economic information in numerical form. The following question will check your ability to integrate that data into your explanation. Where numerical data are present, mark schemes will almost certainly have marks reserved for whether you used that data in your answer.

2 Table 10.1 shows a demand and supply schedule for a premium brand of chocolate. The rising cost of electricity and gas means that the firm now reduces the quantity supplied at any given price by 800 units. With the help of a diagram and Table 10.1, explain how the market has led to a new equilibrium. [3]

REFLECTION

Self-assess your answer by considering all the points on this checklist:

• Did you use technical terms?

• When using a diagram to support your explanation, did you refer to the changes in your diagram?

• Did you use the numbers in the question?

How can you improve your answer to a similar question in the future?

3

> ### Cocoa supply
>
> It has been reported that the world demand for chocolate is decreasing at a time when recent weather conditions have been near-perfect to produce cocoa beans. Cocoa beans are the key raw ingredient in the production of chocolate and a 'glut' in world supply of cocoa beans is expected.

Using a diagram, assess the likely effects of these changes on the equilibrium price and quantity of chocolate products. [8]

The command word 'compare' implies that there are two things going on in the question. Therefore, you should acknowledge both things and explain what is going on in each case. You should also provide some commentary on any similarities or differences between the two.

4

> ### Coffee prices
>
> Brazil is the largest producer of coffee in the world. As a result, the decisions that Brazilian coffee producers make will have a very large impact on global coffee prices.
>
> Between 2014 and 2019, the global coffee price fell as Brazilian government deregulation policies led to more firms entering the market. At the same time, a large subsidy programme led to an increase in capital investment in the industry. In 2020–2022, however, coffee prices rose exponentially as the COVID-19 pandemic led to many factories closing, staff absences and supply chain problems.

Compare, using supply and demand diagrams, how the decisions of Brazilian firms affected the price mechanism for the world price of coffee in 2014–2019 and 2020–2022. [6]

10.3 Relationships between markets

《 RECALL AND CONNECT 1 《

a State what is meant by the terms 'alternative demand' and 'joint demand'.

b The concept of XED is closely related to the concepts of alternative demand and joint demand. List the definitions for 'cross elasticity of demand', 'substitute' and 'complement'.

UNDERSTAND THESE TERMS

- derived demand
- joint supply

1 Try this matching activity to consolidate your understanding of the previous concepts. This helps to practise the exam skill of application.
Copy the key terms and match each one to its example.

Key term	
a	alternative demand
b	joint demand
c	derived demand
d	joint supply

Example	
i	mobile phones and lithium batteries
ii	Starbucks coffee and Costa coffee
iii	lamb and wool
iv	Nintendo Switch and games

10.4 The functions of price in resource allocation

《 RECALL AND CONNECT 2 《

a State the fundamental allocation questions.

b State the different functions of the price mechanism.

It is important that you can recognise high quality responses.

In Question 1, you will not need to write an answer. Instead, you should try to comment on the good (and bad) things about the sample student answer. The question is assessing elements from all parts of the chapter but, specifically, the content from Sections 10.3 and 10.4.

Read the following question and example student response. Make your own notes in an exercise book and give the sample answer a score out of six.

1

Palm oil production

Palm oil is used in the production of many varied goods such as cooking oil, chocolate, instant coffee and soaps and shampoos. Palm oil is produced from the flesh of the palm fruit, which is grown through South-East Asia. When farmers harvest the fruit, they collect the palm oil that is released. Any waste is then turned into palm kernel cake that is then sold for animal feed.

Assess, with the aid of diagrams, the impact of an increase in demand for palm oil on the markets for palm oil and palm kernel cake.   [6]

Example student response	Your comments
An increase in demand for palm oil means that the demand curve for palm oil should shift to the right (D to D_1). As a result, the price will rise from P to P_1. The price mechanism sends a signal to producers that they should produce more. This is shown by the movement from Q to Q_1 on the diagram. Firms have an incentive to do produce more because they can now make more profit. 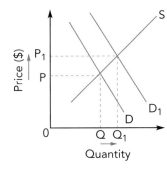 Palm kernel cake is in joint supply as a by-product of palm oil. This is shown in the data by the words: 'any waste is then turned into palm kernel cake'. Therefore, if production for palm oil rises (to meet the extra demand), then the supply of kernel cake will rise. This is shown by an increase in the supply curve (S to S_1) for kernel cake. As a result, the price of kernel cake falls (P to P_1) and the quantity rises (Q to Q_1). 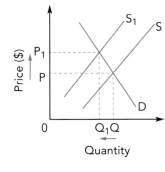	

SELF-ASSESSMENT CHECKLIST

Let's revisit the Knowledge focus and Exam skills focus for this chapter.
Decide how confident you are with each statement.

Now I can	Show it	Needs more work	Almost there	Confident to move on
define the meaning of equilibrium and disequilibrium in a market	Explain the difference between the terms 'equilibrium' and 'disequilibrium' regarding the market.			
explain the effects of shifts in demand and supply curves on equilibrium price and quantity	Draw **four** market equilibrium diagrams, each showing a different shift of the demand or supply curve. Write a short paragraph for each example, which explain the impact of those shifts.			
explain the relationships between different markets, including joint demand (complements), alternative demand (substitutes), derived demand and joint supply	Define each of these terms.			
analyse the functions of price in resource allocation, signalling (transmission of preferences) and the provision of incentives	List the **three** functions of the price mechanism.			
understand the importance of selecting, interpreting and organising economic information in numerical form	Read a news article about the economy. Try to summarise the article in just 100 words by selecting the key information.			
show that I understand the command word 'compare' and answer a compare question	Select a compare question from a past paper and answer it.			
identify a high-quality response.	Ask your teacher for a high-quality answer to a previous homework (or classroom task). Mark it yourself and try to understand why it gained full marks.			

11 Consumer and producer surplus

The command word 'assess' means to make an informed judgement. Assess questions will always include AO3 Evaluation marks. Therefore, in your answer you must seek to assess the strengths and weaknesses of an argument or to identify the limitations of a particular model.

As has been established, it is likely that you will need to integrate diagrams into your economic analysis. It is important that you know how to illustrate changes to those diagrams effectively so that you can demonstrate a high level of understanding.

11.1 The significance of consumer surplus

In the first half of the question, you must define consumer surplus and identify the correct area on a diagram. The second half of the question assesses your understanding of how consumer surplus changes when the price changes. Adapting the consumer surplus area implies that the price has moved.

1   Using a diagram, describe how the consumer surplus changes when there is an increase in price from $4 to $6.

« RECALL AND CONNECT 1 «

Outline the difference between a movement along the demand curve and a shift of the demand curve.

An 'assess' question means that you should review and respond to given information but also that you should include a brief point that contains some evaluation. Even if there are not a high number of marks allocated to an assess question, you do need to include evaluation. This evaluation does not need to be substantial, though.

2   Using diagrams, assess whether a fall in price will always lead to large rise in consumer surplus. [6]

REFLECTION

It is possible to denote the areas of a diagram with letters rather than shading. In fact, this may even be preferable as too much shading can become messy. Try both methods.

However, you should never use different colours. Although it may stand out better on your script, remember that exam papers are often photocopied and/or scanned before they are marked. Therefore, colour may not show up on the photocopy.

Have a look at how the same diagrams are illustrated online. Do you have a preference?

UNDERSTAND THIS TERM
• consumer surplus

11.2 The significance of producer surplus

1   Draw a supply curve for a restaurant meal and shade in the producer surplus if the price is $40.

2   Outline **two** reasons why the price of a restaurant meal might fall and, therefore, the producer surplus will fall.

UNDERSTAND THIS TERM
• producer surplus

Question 3 follows up on the previous question. In the first half of the question, you must define producer surplus and identify the correct area on a diagram. The second half of the question assesses your understanding of how producer surplus changes when the price changes.

3   Using diagrams, describe how the producer surplus changes when there is an increase in price from \$4 to \$6. [3]

≪ RECALL AND CONNECT 2 ≪

The concept of producer surplus can relate to the concept of PES.

a   State the formula for PES.

b   Draw a price elastic and a price inelastic supply curve.

4   Using diagrams, assess whether a rise in price will lead to large rise in producer surplus. [6]

SELF-ASSESSMENT CHECKLIST

Let's revisit the Knowledge focus and Exam skills focus for this chapter.
Decide how confident you are with each statement.

Now I can	Show it	Needs more work	Almost there	Confident to move on
explain the meaning and significance of consumer surplus	Define 'consumer surplus' and identify it on a diagram.			
explain the meaning and significance of producer surplus	Define 'producer surplus' and identify it on a diagram.			
explain the causes of changes in consumer and producer surplus	State **two** reasons why the consumer surplus might increase in the market for cosmetics.			
analyse the significance of price elasticity of demand and supply in determining the extent of changes in consumer and producer surplus	Draw the change to both consumer and producer surplus on diagram when PED and PES are elastic/inelastic.			
show that I understand the command word 'assess' and answer an 'assess' question	Identify an assess question from a past paper and write out a full answer.			
Show how changes to diagrams can be illustrated.	Shade the changes to consumer and producer surplus on a supply and demand after one of the curves has shifted.			

Exam practice 2

This section contains both past paper questions from previous Cambridge exams and practice questions. These questions draw together your knowledge on a range of topics that you have covered up to this point and will help you prepare for your assessment.

The following questions have example student responses and commentaries provided. For each question, work through the question first, then compare your answer to the example student response and commentary.

1   Using diagrams, explain what is meant by consumer surplus **and** consider the impact on consumer surplus when an indirect tax is imposed on a good with price-elastic demand compared with the impact when the demand is price-inelastic.   [8]

Adapted from Cambridge International AS & A Level Economics (9708) Paper 22 Q3a, November 2021

Example student response	Examiner comments
Consumer surplus is the area between the demand curve and the supply curve. It is measure of social utility in the economy. 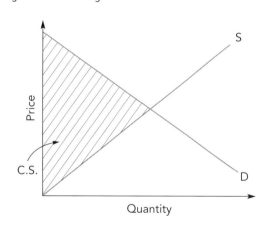 Price elasticity of demand is the responsiveness of the quantity demanded to a change in price. Price elastic is when the quantity demanded changes more than proportionately to the price. Price inelastic is when the quantity demanded changes less than proportionately to the price.	**AO1 Knowledge and understanding** The student makes a number of errors at the beginning. In the first sentence, the student fails to demonstrate a satisfactory understanding of consumer surplus. In the second sentence, the definition is incorrect. Finally, the shaded area on the diagram is incorrect. However, in the first couple of sentences in the second paragraph, the student demonstrates good knowledge of price elasticity of demand (PED). *1/3* **AO2 Analysis** There is very little analysis that can be credited. The question specifically asks the student to apply the concept of PED to an indirect tax diagram. There is no indirect tax diagram. Some of the analysis is correct, but there is limited reference back to the core concept of PED. *1/3*

Example student response	Examiner comments
When an indirect tax is imposed on producers, the supply curve shifts left. This is because the costs of production to the firm rise. This leads to the price rising and the consumer surplus falls. When the demand curve is inelastic, then the quantity demanded does not fall by a significant amount and so the change in consumer surplus will be relatively small.	**AO3 Evaluation** There is no real evaluation. Again, the question specifically asks for a diagram and requires a strong technical understanding of the scenario. No evidence of evaluation is presented. *0/2* *Total: 2/8 marks*

2 a Explain how economists use the concept of elasticity to distinguish between inferior goods and necessary goods **and** consider the effect on both types of goods of a change in consumer incomes. [8]

Adapted from Cambridge International AS & A Level Economics (9708) Paper 22 Q2a, June 2019

Example student response	Examiner comments
Income elasticity of demand (YED) is the responsiveness of the quantity demanded to a change in income. The formula for YED is: % change in quantity demanded ———————————— % change in income An economist would observe an inferior good if the YED coefficient had a negative value. That is, if income rises then the quantity demanded falls. Good examples of inferior goods might include supermarket own brand sugary drinks or cheap takeaway food. As incomes rise, people will generally substitute these inferior goods for superior goods (such as branded sugary drinks or restaurant meals). A necessary good, however, will have a positive value that is between 0 and +1. The positive value means that it is a normal good. Good examples of necessities might include table salt or petrol.	**AO1 Knowledge and understanding** There is a strong start to the answer. The student immediately demonstrates a strong understanding of the concept of YED by presenting a definition and formula. The student understands that inferior goods have a negative YED. The correct use of the term 'coefficient' also signals strong understanding. *3/3* **AO2 Analysis** The student correctly identifies that necessary goods have a positive YED between 0 and +1, and good examples are offered. The question doesn't explicitly ask for examples but, in this case, they really help to explain the impact of a change in income. There is a good analysis of the effect of income changes on inferior goods. *3/3* **AO3 Evaluation** There is not enough evaluation. The question asks about 'when consumer incomes change' for both goods, and yet there is no explanation of the effect on necessary goods. The student ought to have explained the effect that an increase in income will have on the quantity demanded of a necessary good. *0/2* *Total: 6/8 marks*

b Assess the ways in which a business might attempt to change the price elasticity of demand of its products and the likelihood of success. [12]

Adapted from Cambridge International AS & A Level Economics (9708) Paper 22 Q2b, June 2019

Example student response	Examiner comments
PED is the responsiveness of demand to a change in price. Most firms seek to have an inelastic product. This means that even significant price rises for the good will have a relatively small effect on the sales for the good. The firm can make more revenue by increasing its price.	**AO1 Knowledge and understanding** This answer has a good opening. The student immediately demonstrates a strong understanding with a definition and sets the scene by focusing on making goods more price inelastic.
Different businesses might try to change the PED to make them more inelastic in different ways. For example, a clothes retailer is likely to have lots of substitutes in the market. One way in which they can try to make their goods more price inelastic is through branding. A good example of this strategy is seen with 'designer labels' such as Gucci or Armani. Each brand has a distinctive logo and perhaps there are distinctive designs as well. Consumers will begin to perceive differences between the brands and, as a result, the substitution relationships are not as strong. If businesses successfully use influencers to endorse their clothes even this may lead to further brand loyalty. Even if the price increases, people will continue to buy the clothes.	**AO2 Analysis** In the second paragraph, there is an excellent explanation. What makes it so good is that it is rooted in real world application and is not generic. All that is missing is a diagram (inelastic demand curve) and an explanation of the diagram. Diagrams are not absolutely essential, but they really do provide evidence of understanding.
However, not all consumers will perceive the differences. Some consumers are less easily persuaded by marketing campaigns and they do not value a logo on their clothes. For these consumers, PED for clothes will remain elastic.	In the fourth paragraph, the student successfully identifies another factor. This one is less developed than the first and the example is less realistic. The student never elaborates on why the monopoly would cause the PED to be become more inelastic. Presumably it is because there are fewer substitutes as the two main rival firms in the market are now one. This answer does not score full marks for AO2 Analysis because the explanation is not developed enough.
Some firms may seek to merge in order to reduce their PED coefficient. Mergers can be effective because they reduce the number of substitutes in the market. For example, if Coca-Cola merges with Pepsi then all that is left is one very large seller in the market (a monopoly).	Later on, the student proposes a third line or argument. There is normally no requirement for a third analytical point but, in this case, the student does well to include a third one because their second point could have been stronger. *AO1 and AO2: 6/8*
However, mergers are often fraught with difficulty. The businesses may not adapt well to working together after having an intense rivalry. The merged business may eventually break up and the two rivals are competing again. Even if it successful, merging is an expensive process and it could lead to opportunities for promising new brands to enter the market.	**AO3 Evaluation** The third paragraph offers a decent evaluation. It is not a complete counterargument; rather it recognises the limitations of the preceding analysis. Recognising the limitations of economic models in this way is part of AO3 Evaluation.

Example student response	Examiner comments
One way that an electronics firm can seek to change their PED is through creating a unique product. In particular, they might design a product that has a particular function that no other product on the market can do. In this case, consumers have no other option but to buy that product. There are no substitutes. This would create a very inelastic good. In conclusion, branding is probably a cheaper and reliable way to create an inelastic product. Developing an entirely new product (whilst effective) and merging with a rival firm come with no guarantees of success.	The second evaluative section is present but saying that mergers are expensive and may not work does not really help to answer this question. The question asks whether the strategies will be effective at changing PED. Whether or not mergers are expensive is not particularly relevant. This answer does not score full marks for AO3 Evaluation because it is does not assess the strength of the argument in relation to the question well enough. There is a neat conclusion which proposes a clear answer and justifies it. 3/4
	Total: 9/12 marks

Here are two practice questions which you should attempt. Use the guidance in the commentaries in this section to help you as you answer the questions.

3   Explain why demand curves are generally downward-sloping **and** consider the reasons that cause a movement along the demand curve compared to a shift of the demand curve.   [8]

4   Assess the reasons why agricultural goods are considered to be price inelastic in supply and whether that means food is always scarce.   [12]

12 Reasons for government intervention in markets

KNOWLEDGE FOCUS

You will answer questions on:

12.1 What is market failure?

12.2 How governments intervene in markets

12.3 Controlling prices in markets

EXAM SKILLS FOCUS

In this chapter you will:

- understand how to read a mark scheme so that you can improve the quality of your own answers

- understand the term 'interleaving' so that you can improve your own learning.

Students often report that they do not understand why marks are awarded or not awarded for their answers. Therefore, knowing what a mark scheme looks like, and the language it uses, is an important step in becoming more familiar with understanding how to write successful answers. It also helps with self-assessment and preparing effectively.

Learning is often described as a change in long-term memory. Metacognition means that students try to understand more about the learning and the most effective ways to improve their long-term memory. An important strand of metacognition is the idea of interleaving. This a process where you revisit a particular concept in your learning, often approaching it from a different perspective, in order to improve your understanding.

12.1 What is market failure?

1 Copy this text and fill in the blanks.

> inefficient   scarce   mechanism

Market failure is an _____ allocation of goods and services in the market. In this case, the free market _____ does not make the best use of _____ resources.

≪ RECALL AND CONNECT 1 ≪

This is a great opportunity to revise certain concepts from previous chapters that might lead to market failure.

a   What is the fundamental economic problem?

b   Can you define public goods and also give an example?

c   Can you define a merit good and also give an example?

d   Can you define a demerit good and also give an example?

e   Can you define information failure and also give an example?

REFLECTION

How easy was it to remember the definitions from previous chapters?

Revisiting concepts from previous chapters is a process called interleaving (or spaced-retrieval practice). Research into education explains that learning new information, waiting for a period of time to elapse and then trying to retrieve that information again helps to reinforce your long-term memory.

How could you embed interleaving into your revision routine?

12.2 How governments intervene in markets

1 Copy Table 12.1 and match the market failure with a possible solution. You should also illustrate how that solution solves the market failure on a demand and supply diagram.

The first one is done for you.

Possible solutions:

> Government may ban the consumption of certain goods or tax their consumption.
> Government provision of the good or a subsidy to incentivise more private production.
> Government provision of the good.
> ~~Government imposes legislation such that producers have to label products with details about their ingredients.~~

Illustration on demand and supply diagram:

> supply curve shifts left   supply curve shifts right   ~~demand curve shifts left~~

Market failure	Possible solution	Illustration on demand and supply diagram
Addressing information failure	Government imposes legislation such that producers have to label products with details about their ingredients.	demand curve shifts left
Addressing the overconsumption of demerit goods		
Addressing the underconsumption of merit goods		
Addressing the non-provision of public goods		not applicable

Table 12.1: Solutions to market failures

2 Using examples, assess how a government might behave differently to address the market failure of merit goods and demerit goods.   [8]

12.3 Controlling prices in markets

Before you write your answer to Question 1, read the following suggested mark scheme. Then, write a list of what you need to include to get full marks.

Mark scheme

- Up to four marks will be awarded for analysing the advantages and disadvantages of indirect taxes.

- If the analysis only considers either the advantages or the disadvantages, a maximum of three marks will be given.

- Similarly, up to four marks will be awarded for analysing the advantages and disadvantages of indirect taxes. If the analysis only focuses on either the advantages or the disadvantages, a maximum of three marks will be given.

- The analysis must incorporate the use of data.

- Up to three marks will be awarded for evaluative comments that compare the relative strengths and weaknesses of each approach.

- An additional one mark will be given for a reasoned conclusion.

1

> **Hungary's 'chip tax'**
>
> Hungary has an obesity prevalence rate of 29%. This compares favourably with countries like the USA (36%), but it is still well above the global average of 20%. Hungary was one of the first countries in the world to introduce a tax on unhealthy foods, which was widely known as the 'chip tax' at the time. In 2022, however, the Hungarian government added some new details to the tax. Products with high levels of sugars and sweeteners (like cereals, candies, fruit and sugary drinks) now incurred the tax. The government has also run a series of campaigns to provide more information to people about the health risks of over-consuming sugary drinks. Some international commentators argued that the government's aim would have been better served by using a minimum price strategy.

Assess whether minimum price legislation or indirect taxes are more likely to reduce obesity levels in Hungary.   [12]

> **REFLECTION**
>
> It is important that you understand what mark schemes look like.
>
> How successful were you in meeting all of the requirements of the mark scheme?
>
> How can you improve your understanding of the mark scheme?

SELF-ASSESSMENT CHECKLIST

Let's revisit the Knowledge focus and Exam skills focus for this chapter.
Decide how confident you are with each statement.

Now I can	Show it	Needs more work	Almost there	Confident to move on
explain why there is the non-provision of public goods	Explain what the market failure associated with public goods is.			
explain why there is overconsumption of demerit goods and the underconsumption of merit goods	Explain why there is overconsumption of demerit goods and the underconsumption of merit goods.			
explain why governments control prices in markets.	Explain why governments control prices in markets.			
understand how to read a mark scheme so that I can improve the quality of my own answers	Download a mark scheme from Cambridge Assessment International Education's website that relates to a past paper question that you will complete. Highlight all the key words in the mark scheme that will enable you to write a high quality answer.			
understand the term 'interleaving' so that I can improve my own learning.	Create a revision schedule that ensures you revisit the same material at least three times during your study period.			

13 Methods and effects of government intervention in markets

AO2 Analysis means that you must be able to explain the impacts and consequences of changes in economic variables. A common mistake that students make is that they miss out important stages in their analysis. When explaining impacts or consequences of policies, you should provide a logical chain of analysis that considers all the different stages of economic theory. This will help you demonstrate a strong understanding of economic theory, which means you can access more marks.

AO3 Evaluation is the final assessment objective. Evaluation really means to qualify the chain of analysis that has just been made. For example, you might acknowledge the assumptions and limitations of economic models that were used as part of the analysis section. The mistake that many students make is to think that evaluation always needs to be a complete counter argument. It does not.

Example student responses are often used by teachers to show examples of work (usually completed by former students) that gained high marks. Every student should see examples of excellent answers during their study so that they can identify any areas for improvement in their own work.

13.1 The impact and incidence of specific indirect taxes

1   Explain the difference between a specific tax and an *ad valorem* tax.

2   Identify whether the taxes in the word box are an example of a specific tax or an *ad valorem* tax. Copy and complete the table into your own notebook.

UK Value Added Tax (20%)   India tobacco tax (28%)
Turkey fuel duty ($0.07 per litre)
France sugary drink tax (7.55 eurocents per litre)

Specific tax	Ad valorem tax

Table 13.1: Examples of indirect taxes

3   Draw a specific tax diagram and an *ad valorem* tax diagram.

4   Draw **two** specific indirect tax diagrams. Read the following instructions:

  • One should have a price inelastic demand curve and one should have a price elastic demand curve.

  • You should shade in the producer incidence of the tax in both diagrams.

5   With the aid of diagrams, assess whether the government should impose an indirect tax to reduce the level of consumption of a demerit good like petrol.   [12]

Before you write your answer, remember that an 'assess' question means you must provide a chain of analysis and an evaluation.

With regards to a chain of analysis, you can use a writing scaffold like this:

Analysis start: The government imposes an indirect tax.
Analysis end: Therefore, the quantity demanded for petrol falls.

Copy the writing scaffold and fill in the missing links.

> **UNDERSTAND THESE TERMS**
>
> • consumer incidence
> • producer incidence

After the analysis, you need an evaluative point. Evaluation means that you are looking to qualify your previous chain of analysis. Here are some general approaches that you could take: the quantity demanded for petrol falls but:

- How much is it falling by (large/small)?
- When is it falling (short run/long run)?
- Is this good for everyone (consumers/producers)?
- Does it depend on elasticity (elastic/inelastic)?
- Are there any major side effects?

Now put it all together and write a full answer.

13.2 The impact and incidence of subsidies

1   Define the term 'subsidy'.

2   Identify the producer incidence and the consumer incidence of the subsidy in Figure 13.1.

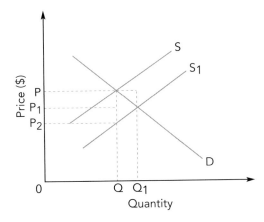

Figure 13.1: The incidence of a subsidy

Students often make a common mistake by mixing up the tax incidence diagram with the subsidy diagram. They frequently mislabel the subsidy diagram by forgetting that the producer/consumer incidences are the opposite way round compared to the tax diagram.

Can you come up with a mnemonic or an easy short-hand way of remembering the correct order?

3   With the aid of diagrams, assess whether the government should use a subsidy to increase the level of consumption of a merit good like electric vehicles.   [6]

13.3 The direct provision of goods and services

≪ RECALL AND CONNECT 1 ≪

a   Define the term 'market failure'.

b   Explain why public goods are likely to lead to market failure.

1   State **two** criticisms of the direct provision of goods and services.   [2]

2   Assess whether a government that wants to increase the consumption of healthcare should use a policy of subsidies or a policy of direct provision.   [12]

13.4 Maximum and minimum prices

Economics is full of new vocabulary. Sometimes economists use synonyms (interchangeable words) to convey the same meaning.

1   Copy and complete the table, identifying the synonyms for the terms.

UNDERSTAND THESE TERMS
• maximum price
• minimum price

shortage	glut	price ceiling	price floor

Key term	Synonym
maximum price	
minimum price	
excess demand	
excess supply	

Table 13.2: Synonyms for key terms

2   List **three** markets in which a government might use a minimum price.

3   List **three** markets in which a government might use a maximum price.

4 Draw the minimum price diagram and the maximum price diagram.

5 With the aid of a diagram, explain how minimum prices work to keep the price above the market equilibrium **and** consider the effects of a minimum price policy on consumers and producers. [8]

Rather than write your own answer to this question, read the following example student response.

In your notebook, you should make notes on the following areas:

- answer structure
- chains of analysis
- use of technical terminology
- how diagrams are integrated into the analysis
- how the letter notation is used to identify areas on the diagram.

Example student response	Your comments
A minimum price is price floor that is set above the equilibrium price. Minimum prices are often used by the government to reduce demand for demerit goods like petrol. The diagram shows that consumers now face a higher price. P_1 has risen to P_{min}. As a result, consumers will buy less of the product (Q_1 to Q_D). As a result, consumer surplus has fallen from ACP_1 to ABP_{min}. Therefore, minimum prices are undesirable for consumers. The diagram shows that producers will also see a fall in sales. Q_1 falls to Q_D. However, this might advantageous to producers in terms of revenue and producer surplus if their product is price inelastic in demand. If we assume this is a demerit good like petrol, which has a low inelastic PED, then producers are better off. Revenue rises ($P_1CQ_{10} < PminBQ_DO$) because consumers will continue to buy the product even if prices rise. As a result, the producer surplus rises as well ($P_1C0 < PminBDO$).	

REFLECTION

You may wish to compare the notes that you made with another student afterwards. How can example student responses help improve your own answers? Where can you find more example student responses?

Write a full answer to the following question.

6   Assess whether a government that wants to lower the price of natural gas should use a policy of subsidies or a maximum price.   [12]

13.5 Buffer stock schemes

1   Copy the following text and fill in the blanks.

stored	minimum	maximum	raise	fallen	supplies
	buy up	growers	consumers	decrease	

In general terms, buffer stick schemes combine the principles of minimum and maximum price controls. A buffer stock scheme starts by setting a _____ price for a particular product, say, potatoes. If the market price looks like it is going below this price, the buffer stock scheme will _____ stocks of potatoes from _____. These will be _____ in warehouses. This action should _____ the price of potatoes since supply in the market has _____. The scheme can also set a _____ price. The effect will be to increase _____ from producers which in time will see a _____ in the price of the product. _____ are happier.

13.6 Provision of information

« RECALL AND CONNECT 2 «

a   List **two** non-price determinants of demand.

b   Illustrate the impact of a non-price determinant on the demand curve.

1   With the help of a diagram, consider whether the provision of information on food packaging may reduce consumption of junk food.   [4]

2   State **two** limitations of the government using information provision to reduce the consumption of junk food.   [2]

SELF-ASSESSMENT CHECKLIST

Let's revisit the Knowledge focus and Exam skills focus for this chapter.
Decide how confident you are with each statement.

Now I can	Show it	Needs more work	Almost there	Confident to move on
analyse the impact and incidence of specific indirect taxes	Draw a specific tax diagram.			
analyse the impact and incidence of subsidies	Draw a subsidy diagram.			
explain direct provision of goods and services	List **three** goods/services that are provided for by the government in your country.			
analyse maximum and minimum prices	Draw the diagrams for maximum and minimum prices.			
analyse buffer stock schemes	Describe how a buffer stock works to another student.			
explain provision of information	Identify a government information campaign in your country.			
consider how a writing scaffold can help me to build a strong chain of analysis in my answers	Use a writing scaffold in your next written assignment.			
understand the meaning of AO3 Evaluation	List **three** general ways to approach evaluation.			
understand how I can learn from example student responses.	Start a study group with other students where you can share example student responses with each other.			

14 Addressing income and wealth inequality

EXAM SKILLS FOCUS

In this chapter you will:

- consider a particular approach to data response questions that can help reduce test anxiety

- have an opportunity to write a series of questions under time limits.

Test anxiety can adversely affect exam performance. One of the ways to reduce test anxiety is to create a set routine for answering certain types of questions. In this chapter, how you can approach data response questions so that you can support your analysis and evaluation points is considered.

Exams are time-limited, so students need to demonstrate their understanding in a fixed time frame. At some point, every student needs to practise writing their answers under time limits. In the first few attempts, you should monitor the time you take and, if necessary, look for ways you can write more efficiently in the future.

14.1 Income and wealth

《 RECALL AND CONNECT 1 《

a   List the **four** factors of production and the reward that is generated from the use of each one.

b   Define the term income.

1   Copy and complete the following table. Classify the terms in the word box as a type of income or a type of wealth.

> wages earned on over-time   rent earned from a second home
>
> value of a second home   interest paid on savings
>
> total savings   pension fund

Income	Wealth

Table 14.1: Types of income and wealth

2   With the help of examples, consider the difference between income inequality and wealth inequality.   [4]

14.2 Measuring income and wealth inequality

1   Copy the text below and fill in the blanks

The Gini coefficient is a numerical measure of the extent of _____ in an economy. If the income _____ in an economy is equal, the Gini coefficient will have a value of _____. At the other extreme, if _____ income accrues to just one person, then the Gini coefficient will be _____.

zero	distribution	one	income inequality	all

REFLECTION

A common error that students make is to misinterpret the Gini coefficient. It is important that you remember 1 = unequal and 0 = equal.

Think of an easy way to help yourself remember this.

14.3 Economic reasons for inequality of income and wealth

Data response questions can sometimes seem quite daunting. This is because they are focused on case studies that you know very little about. Therefore, when responding to data questions, it is a good idea to read the question before you read the data. The reason for this is that you can begin thinking about the general structure of your answer quickly. You can then read the data and highlight key words and phrases that you can use in your answer to support your analysis and evaluation. This strategy should help reduce any test anxiety that you have. Try this technique with Question 1.

1
> **South Africa's GINI coefficient**
>
> Nigeria is Africa's largest economy. Its Gini coefficient of 0.35 is on par with developed countries such as the UK and France. By contrast, South Africa is the continent's third-largest economy. It has a Gini coefficient of 0.65, which is one of the highest in the world. Of South Africa's workforce, 18% is made up primarily of informal workers, many of whom work in agriculture and retail. Informal workers generally work without contracts, workplace regulation or trade union rights. According to the UN, South Africa's population has 10.1 mean years of schooling, but there are large disparities between income levels.

With reference to the data, assess the most likely cause of South Africa's high Gini coefficient.   [6]

14.4 Policies to redistribute income and wealth

UNDERSTAND THESE TERMS

- minimum wage
- transfer payment
- progressive tax
- regressive tax

1   State **three** examples of transfer payments.

2   State **three** examples of progressive taxes.

3   State **three** examples of regressive taxes.

Questions 4–7 offer a great opportunity to practise writing to time. Each question has a different command word and carries a different number of marks. All the assessment objectives are being assessed.

You should aim to spend no more than 42 minutes on this set of four questions. Try to allocate your time correctly so that you write enough for each question and finish on time. Set an alarm to go off after 42 minutes. If you do not finish on time, then swap pen colours but keep writing. This is so you can see how close you are to writing to the time limit.

4   State **two** criticisms of increasing progressive taxes. [2]

5   Define, with an example, what is meant by the term 'transfer payment'. [3]

6   Outline **two** criticisms of increasing a minimum wage in a country like Nigeria. [4]

7   Assess whether a government should increase the minimum wage or increase progressive taxes to reduce income inequality [12]

REFLECTION

If you did not write to the 42-minute time limit, then you should consider strategies that might enable you to achieve this. How can you write more efficiently?

SELF-ASSESSMENT CHECKLIST

Let's revisit the Knowledge focus and Exam skills focus for this chapter.
Decide how confident you are with each statement.

Now I can	Show it	Needs more work	Almost there	Confident to move on
explain the difference between income as a flow concept and wealth as a stock concept	Define the **two** concepts.			
measure inequality in income and wealth with a Gini coefficient	Explain what a Gini coefficient values of 0 and 1 mean.			
explain the economic reasons for inequality of income and wealth	Explain at least **three** causes of income and/or wealth inequality.			
discuss policies that redistribute income and wealth, including the minimum wage, transfer payments, progressive income taxes, inheritance and capital taxes and state provision of essential goods and services	State the advantages and disadvantages of each policy.			
consider a particular approach to data response questions that can help reduce text anxiety	Explain to another student how you will approach data response questions.			
have an opportunity to write a series of questions under time limits.	Complete a full past paper question in the specified time. Reflect on ways to write more efficiently if necessary.			

Exam practice 3

This section contains both past paper questions from previous Cambridge exams and practice questions. These questions draw together your knowledge on a range of topics that you have covered up to this point and will help you prepare for your assessment.

The following questions have example student responses and commentaries provided. For each question, work through the question first, then compare your answer to the example student response and commentary.

1   Explain the difference between regressive and progressive taxes **and** consider whether you would use an income tax or a specific indirect tax to make post-tax incomes more equal.   [8]

Adapted from Cambridge International AS & A Level Economics (9708)
    Paper 22 Q3a, June 2019

Example student response	Examiner comments
A progressive tax is one where the tax rate rises more than proportionately to the rise in income.	**AO1 Knowledge and understanding**
A good example of a progressive tax is income tax. As income rises, workers pay a greater percentage of their income on the tax. For example, Malaysia has several levels to its income tax rates. Tax rates start at 0%, and then progress through 1%, 3%, 8%, 14%, 21%, 24%, 25%, 26%, 28% to 30% for the highest income earners.	The student demonstrates a strong understanding of both progressive and regressive taxes. The addition of real-life examples is always welcome. It is not essential to use your own examples, but it is a way of demonstrating your knowledge to someone marking your answer.
If a government chooses to raise progressive taxes, like income tax, then it follows that high-income earners will pay more and low-income earners will pay less. This should help to reduce income inequality. Increasing progressive taxes helps to make post-tax income more equal.	*3/3*
	AO2 Analysis
A regressive tax is one where the percentage of income spent on the tax decreases as income increases. A good example of a regressive tax is sales tax or an indirect specific tax. For example, in Malaysia there is a 'sales and service tax (SST)' of 5% or 10% depending on the product being taxed.	The structure of the answer is good and, in the third paragraph, the student analyses the impact of increasing income tax on post-tax income. The final sentence is a good example of a mini-conclusion about the impact on post-tax income, which clearly answers the question. Overall, the student shows an excellent understanding of progressive tax and offers an excellent explanation of the impact of increasing progressive taxes on income inequality.
	3/3

Example student response	Examiner comments
If a government chooses to raise regressive taxes, like sales tax, then it follows that low-income earners will pay more tax and high-income earners will pay less tax. This would worsen income inequality.	**AO3 Evaluation** The final paragraph is not quite right. It states: 'that low-income earners will pay more tax'. But, whilst low-income earners will pay a higher percentage of their income on tax, they would not pay more in nominal terms. Even though the final sentence is correct, the explanation is incorrect, and therefore economic theory has not been used effectively. *1/2* *Total: 7/8 marks*

2   A government is considering whether to adopt a policy of maximum price legislation in the market for food or to provide food subsidies to alleviate hunger in a period of food shortages.

Assess whether maximum price legislation or food subsidies are more likely to alleviate hunger under these circumstances. [12]

Adapted from Cambridge International AS & A Level Economics (9708) Paper 22 Q3b, November 2021

Example student response	Examiner comments
Food is often considered a necessity. As a result, governments are often are keen to ensure that all households are able to buy food at an affordable price. This is a question of equity. One policy they can use is to impose a maximum price. The diagram below shows a maximum price in action. The maximum price will lower the price from P_1 to P_{max}. This satisfies the main aim of the policy: to make food more affordable. 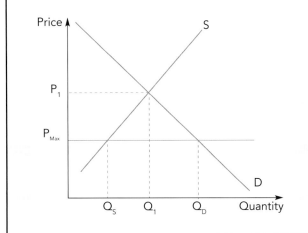	**AO1 Knowledge and understanding and AO2 Analysis** This is a skilful introduction. Introductions are not necessary in economics, but the student frames their answer nicely here. The answer uses a diagram to support a technical analysis of how maximum prices can help to reduce food prices. The policy is well explained. Economic theory is used to examine an economic issue, part of AO2 Analysis. The format is then repeated but for subsidies. Again, the answer uses diagrams to support a technical analysis of how subsidies can help to reduce food prices. *8/8* **AO3 Evaluation** There is an early evaluative point of maximum prices (that they may lead to excess demand) that recognises the limitations of this diagram. The use of a paragraph break and a phrase like 'on the other hand' gives a good indication that the student is now starting the second half of the question.

Example student response	Examiner comments
On the other hand, producers have less incentive to produce food if the price is lower. This is because they will find it harder to make profit. As a result, the producers will reduce supply to Q_s. This causes excess demand (Q_d to Q_s), or a shortage, in the market. Less food is now available to purchase. Therefore, it is not clear that hunger is alleviated for all. Instead, the government could use a subsidy policy. A subsidy is a grant given to producers in order to lower the costs of production. The diagram below shows this policy in action. The supply shifts right (S_1 to S_2) because costs are lower. Therefore, the price of food decreases (P_1 to P_2). This also satisfies the main aim of the policy: to make food more affordable. It also leads to an increase in the supply of food. This is a clear advantage of subsidies over maximum prices, which actually reduced supply. Hunger should be alleviated. 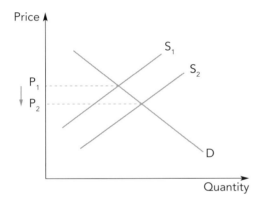 The main downside to subsidies is that it is a very expensive policy for the Government to run. There is an opportunity cost to this spending; the money could have been better spent possible on healthcare or education. Also, it is not clear that just making food cheaper to produce would solve a food shortage that had resulted from a drought or a supply chain crisis.	The subsidy policy is also well evaluated. In this instance, the student identifies that subsidies will actually increase the supply of food (and alleviate hunger for most). The evaluation points about drought and/or a supply chain crisis are pertinent in a question about 'food shortage'. The student uses terms from the question (notably, 'alleviating hunger') in their answer. Unfortunately, this answer is not able to score full marks. This is because the student has failed to offer a conclusion. Conclusions must be well-reasoned and based on the arguments that have already been put forward in the essay. *3/4* Note: Overall, this is a very strong answer apart from one critical element: it has no conclusion. *Total: 11/12 marks*

3   Fuel duties are higher in Europe than in any other part of the world.

Assess whether an indirect tax on fuel or a national awareness campaign that promotes the use of more environmentally friendly fuel is more likely to improve air pollution.   [12]

Example student response	Examiner comments
Fuel (petrol) is often described as a demerit good. It is often overconsumed because consumers have a lack of information about its external costs. When consumers over-consume petrol this causes air pollution. Therefore, governments will aim to decrease the consumption of fuel. One policy that a government could choose is to impose an indirect tax, shifting the demand curve to the left. The quantity of fuel demanded falls. 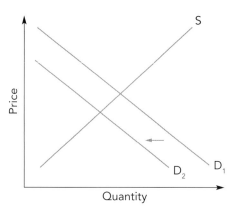 However, the increase in price is regressive. This means that it disproportionately affects low-income households. In addition, petrol fuel could be considered PED inelastic due to habitual consumption. As a result, when the price rises, the quantity demanded only falls by a relatively small amount. The policy has had limited success. By contrast, a government can choose to run a national awareness campaign. This will likely inform people of the negative costs associated with using petrol. As a result, it is expected that the demand curve will shift left. Consumption of petrol fuel falls and it is hoped that the demand for greener fuels (a substitute good) will rise.	**AO1 Knowledge and understanding and AO2 Analysis** The answer has a good introduction. It demonstrates knowledge of the syllabus, part of AO1. It also frames the answer by explaining why this is an economic issue. Unfortunately, the economic analysis in the second paragraph is incorrect. The use of an indirect tax does not shift demand to the left. Instead, the student should have explained that raising the costs of production will have the effect of shifting the supply curve to the left, putting upwards pressure on price and causing a contraction along the demand curve. However, the second analytical paragraph is correct. The diagram could be improved by drawing Q_1 and Q_2. This would show a fall in the quantity demanded. 4/8

Example student response	Examiner comments
Quantity However, this all depends on the effectiveness of the campaign. If people ignore the campaign or simply do not see it, or if people are irrational in their purchasing choices, then consumption may not fall. In addition, campaigns are expensive to run. Overall, a combination of both policies is probably the best way forward. That is, a tax will generate enough money (tax revenue) to run the information campaign. In addition, either policy may have limited effects (for the reasons shown) but running both policies together will maximise the impact.	**AO3 Evaluation** The first evaluation paragraph is good, in particular the analysis with regards to price elasticity. The student recognises the limitation of the economic theory under a specific circumstance, part of AO3 Evaluation. The second evaluation paragraph could be improved with a bit more detail. The student should identify the type of irrational behaviour, for example consumer inertia or herd behaviour. The conclusion works well enough in that it answers the question, however, most of the time it is better to state which policy is better rather than just saying a combination/mixture of both. This is because the AO3 Evaluation objective includes being about to come to a reasoned judgement. *3/4* *Total: 7/12 marks*

Here are two practice questions which you should attempt. Use the guidance in the commentaries in this section to help you as you answer the questions.

4   Explain how imposing a maximum price on oil can benefit consumers **and** consider its impact on other economic agents.   [8]

5   Assess whether the best way to redistribute income is by increasing transfer payments to those in poverty.   [12]

15 National income statistics

EXAM SKILLS FOCUS

In this chapter you will:

- show that you understand how to approach multiple-choice questions

- show that you can interpret and comment on bar charts and line graphs

- show you understand the 'consider' command word.

Paper 1: AS Level Multiple Choice consists of 30 multiple-choice questions. The time given for Paper 1 is one hour. This works out at two minutes per question, although you will be able to answer some questions more quickly than others. You should read the question carefully and consider each of the options. You might think that you can identify the correct option quickly, but always read each of the other options so that you can be sure that they can be rejected. Why not, after studying a topic, try writing some of your own multiple-choice questions and try these out on other students.

A variety of diagrams may be used in Paper 1: AS Level Multiple Choice and in the data response question of Paper 2: AS Level Data Response and Essays. Two of the most common of these are bar charts and line graphs. The more you practise and interpret diagrams, the more confident and the more skilled you will become in answering questions which include diagrams.

The command 'consider' contains an evaluative element. It may require you, for example, to decide why something is likely to happen but also why it may not.

15.1 National income statistics

UNDERSTAND THESE TERMS

- national income
- national income statistics

1 Why is total output equal to total income and total expenditure?

2 In 2023 Economy A had a national income of $500 billion while Economy B had a national income of $80 billion. If Economy A's national income rises to $520 billion and Economy B's national income rises to $88 billion after a year, which country had the highest:

a total increase in national income

b growth rate of national income?

As you know, the command word 'identify' only requires you to name, select or recognise. So, in Question 3(a) you would not gain any more marks for describing the international organisation you have selected, and in Question 3(b) the two marks available should indicate that you only need to identify two aims.

3 Identify:

a an international organisation that makes use of national income statistics to compare the economic performance of countries [1]

b the aims a government is likely to have for its country's national income. [2]

《 RECALL AND CONNECT 1 《

What is the difference between microeconomics and macroeconomics?

15.2 Gross domestic product and gross national income

UNDERSTAND THESE TERMS

- gross domestic product (GDP)
- gross national income (GNI)
- compensation of employees
- gross national disposable income
- multinational companies (MNCs)

1   Why would you expect China's GDP to be greater than Singapore's GDP?

2   Why may a country's GDP decrease but its GNI increase?

Line graphs are widely used in economics. They show how one or more variables change, usually over time. The vertical axis, also known as the y-axis, shows the variable or variables. The horizontal axis, also called the x-axis, usually shows time. Lines connect the individual data points.

When examining a line graph, first check what is shown on the axes and then look for trends. If you are comparing two sets of variables, as in Question 3, look at whether they are following similar trends and how they differ. Consider possible reasons for any differences.

3
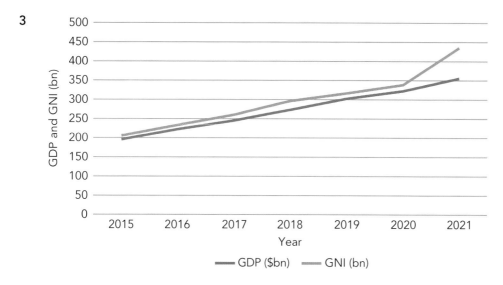

Figure 15.1: Bangladesh's GDP and GNI 2015–2021

Compare Bangladesh's GDP and GNI over the period shown.   [4]

≪ RECALL AND CONNECT 2 ≪

What effect is a fall in the cost of production likely to have on firms' output?

15.3 Methods of measuring GDP

UNDERSTAND THESE TERMS

- circular flow of income
- output method
- value added
- income method
- expenditure method

1 Why are exports added and imports deducted in the expenditure method?

2 Why are transfer payments not included in measures of GDP?

When more than one mark is given for a calculation, make sure you include your workings in your answer.

3 a In Pakistan in 2021, consumer expenditure was $221 billion, investment was $29 billion and government spending was $19 billion. The country's GDP was $251 billion. Calculate the value of Pakistan's net exports. [2]

   b In 2021, the UK had a GDP of $3180 billion. The country's income from profit, rent and interest was $1450 billion. Calculate the proportion of the country's income from wages. [2]

≪ RECALL AND CONNECT 3 ≪

a Give **three** examples of transfer payments.

b Why do governments make transfer payments?

15.4 Market prices and basic prices

1 Decide in each case whether the prices are based on basic prices or market prices:

   a prices paid by buyers of products

   b prices that would be paid to producers in the absence of government intervention.

UNDERSTAND THESE TERMS

- market prices
- basic prices

A bar chart shows the number of units of a variable. These are represented by bars, also called blocks. Each bar has the same width. It is the height of the bars that shows the difference in the numerical values.

Again, first check what the axes are measuring. Then look for differences in the relative heights and consider reasons for their differences.

2

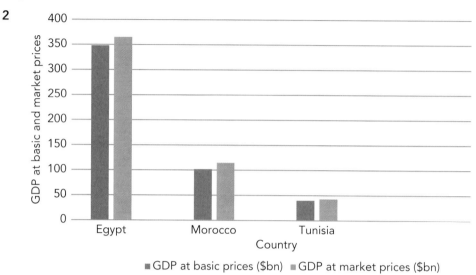

■ GDP at basic prices ($bn) ■ GDP at market prices ($bn)

Figure 15.2: GDP at basic and market prices in Egypt, Morocco and Tunisia 2020

a Explain what the word 'domestic' in gross domestic product means. [1]

b Explain whether indirect taxes are higher or lower than subsidies in the three countries shown in Figure 15.2. [3]

REFLECTION

How confident did you feel in interpreting this bar chart? Look back at your answer to Question 2(b) and think about any ways in which you could have improved your answer.

《 RECALL AND CONNECT 4 《

What are the **four** factors of production whose income is used to measure GDP?

15.5 Gross values and net values

1 Why may net investment be negative?

2 What effect are advances in technology likely to have on depreciation and gross investment?

3

> **Measuring GDP and GNI**
>
> In recent years, US government statisticians have found discrepancies between different measures of GDP. In 2021, for example, it was thought that profits had been overestimated while spending had been underestimated. In other years, total spending recorded has been higher than total incomes deducted. Some people had not declared all the incomes they had earned. In 2021, both US GDP and GNI increased. The United States's GNI was influenced by the performance of the country's MNCs.

UNDERSTAND THESE TERMS

- gross investment
- net domestic product (NDP)
- net investment
- depreciation (of capital goods)

a   Identify which method of measuring GDP:

    i   includes profits [1]

    ii   adds up total spending. [1]

b   Explain how US multinational companies could influence US GNI. [3]

When answering multiple-choice questions, first read the question carefully. Then try to work out the answer before you look at the options. In Question 4, first calculate NDP at basic prices. Then look at the options. If your figure does not match one of these options, you must have made a mistake. Note, however, that just because an option equals your answer, it does not necessarily mean it is right. The wrong options (known as distractors) will be based on the mistakes students may make.

4   A country has a GNI at market prices of $850 billion, depreciation is $20 billion, subsidies are $30 billion, indirect taxes are $55 billion and net income from abroad is $8 billion. What is NDP at basic prices?

    A $797 billion

    B $813 billion

    C $822 billion

    D $863 billion

In Question 5(a), considering why the two measures are likely to be equal can be relatively brief, but remember the two methods are not the same thing. To provide a strong answer to Question 5(b), the nature of each measure should be examined. Once this is done, it becomes easier to judge and explain why GDP at market prices may be higher than NNI at basic prices.

5   **a**   Explain **two** methods of measuring GDP **and** consider whether the two methods will give the same figure for GDP. [8]

    b   Assess whether a country's GDP at market prices is likely to be higher than its NNI at basic prices. [12]

SELF-ASSESSMENT CHECKLIST

Let's revisit the Knowledge focus and Exam skills focus for this chapter.
Decide how confident you are with each statement.

Now I can	Show it	Needs more work	Almost there	Confident to move on
define the meaning of national income	Explain to another student what is meant by national income.			
explain the purpose of national income statistics	Identify **two** reasons why governments measure national income statistics.			
explain the difference between gross domestic product (GDP), gross national income (GNI) and net national income (NNI)	Produce a flow chart showing what adjustments need to be made to move from GDP to GNI and then NNI.			
analyse the three methods of measuring GDP	Name the **three** methods of measuring GDP.			
explain how measures of national income are adjusted from market prices to basic prices	Produce a revision card which shows how national income figures are adjusted from market prices to basic prices.			
explain how measures of national income are adjusted from gross values to net values	Write a calculation question for another student which is based on the difference between GNI and NNI.			
show that I understand how to approach multiple-choice questions	Explain what a distractor is within a multiple-choice question.			
show that I can interpret and comment on bar charts and line graphs	Plot a line graph showing the GDP of your country over the last 10 years. One source of information is the World Bank's website.			
show that I understand the 'consider' command word.	Consider whether an increase in its GDP is more beneficial than an increase in its GNI.			

16 Introduction to the circular flow of income

You can check how you have performed on the Exam skills questions throughout the book by comparing your answers to those in the Answers section. If you feel confident with your answers, that is great. If you do not, do not worry. If you devote more time to working on these skills, you should soon feel more confident.

A wide variety of information can be provided in tables. These may appear in multiple-choice questions and in Question 1 on Paper 2: AS Level Data Response and Essays. A table has columns going down the page and rows going across the page. Columns and rows have headings. It is always important to check carefully what headings are showing.

16.1 The circular flow of income

1 How is the circular flow of income linked to methods of measuring gross domestic product (GDP)?

《 RECALL AND CONNECT 1 《

What is the difference between income and wealth?

16.2 The difference between an open and a closed economy

1 In the real world, are there any closed economies?

2 a Name **two** real flows between households and firms.

 b Name **two** money flows between households and firms.

Table 16.1 is a relatively short table. First read Question 3, then check the headings of the columns and rows to see what information they contain. Note, for example, that the figures are percentages and not absolute amounts.

3

Country	Exports as a % of GDP 2021	Imports as a % of GDP 2021
Kenya	11	20
Mauritius	31	56
Nigeria	14	20
Sudan	2	2
UAE	93	69

Table 16.1: Exports and imports as a percentage of GDP in selected countries

 a Calculate the contribution net exports made to the economy of Mauritius in 2021. [1]

 b Explain which country had the most open economy in 2021. [2]

16.3 The impact of injections and leakages on the circular flow

1 Give **two** reasons why households may not spend all of the income they earn.

2 Will an open economy have more injections and more leakages than a closed economy?

UNDERSTAND THESE TERMS

- open economy
- closed economy

UNDERSTAND THESE TERMS

- injections
- leakages

Analysis involves building up links. The more you practise analysing, the more you will start to think like an economist. You will also find that you will apply the same links to a number of different situations.

3   Vietnam's exports rose by 20% and its imports increased by 26% in 2021. In that year, the Vietnamese government increased the taxation on the importation of cars.

   a   Explain why exports are an injection into the circular flow.   [2]

   b   Consider the extent to which an increase in taxation may affect the circular flow.   [4]

> ### REFLECTION
>
> Were you able to show that you can explore how a change in taxation affects the circular flow in some depth? If, after checking the answer, you think you needed to provide more links, try answering a similar question such as 'Consider the extent to which an increase in saving may affect the circular flow'.

16.4 Equilibrium and disequilibrium income

1   When is a country's income in equilibrium?

2   What are the **four** sectors of an open economy?

3   a   Explain what would cause a country's income to move from disequilibrium to equilibrium.   [2]

   b   Describe the relationship between injections and leakages when a country's income is in disequilibrium.   [2]

16.5 Links between injections and leakages

1   Which injection and which leakage are generated by government activity?

2   a   Identify the difference between an injection and a leakage.   [2]

   b   Consider whether a decrease in injections will lead to a decrease in leakages.   [4]

Answer the following essay question. In answering Question 3(a), you may find it useful to first list the injections and leakages in a rough plan. Question 3(b) is a relatively technical question. Time should be spent carefully thinking through your answer before you start writing it. So, again, you may find it useful to write a brief plan.

3   a   Explain the difference between injections and leakages in the circular flow of income **and** consider whether leakages are likely to be high or low in a low-income country.   [8]

   b   Assess how an increase in investment may affect the circular flow of income.   [12]

REFLECTION

How confident do you feel that you have produced answers to the two parts of Question 3 that are accurate and cover the relevant points in a relevant and logical way? Consider asking an A Level Economics student if they can think of any way you could improve your answer.

SELF-ASSESSMENT CHECKLIST

Let's revisit the Knowledge focus and Exam skills focus for this chapter. Decide how confident you are with each statement.

Now I can	Show it	Needs more work	Almost there	Confident to move on
define the circular flow of income	Draw the circular flow of income.			
explain the difference between the circular flow of income in a closed economy and in an open economy: the flow of income between households, firms and the government and the international economy	List the different flows, injections and leakages in a closed and an open economy.			
analyse the impact of injections and leakages on the circular flow of income	Produce a revision card which states how injections and leakages affect the amount of income and spending which flow around the economy			
identify the difference between the country's income being in equilibrium and being in disequilibrium	Describe the relationship between injections and leakages when a country's income is in equilibrium and when it is in disequilibrium			
show that I can evaluate my progress	Assess your performance on Question 3(b) in Section 16.3.			
show that I can interpret information in tables.	Produce a table showing the injections and leakages in a closed economy without a government sector, in a closed economy with a government sector and in an open economy with a government sector.			

17 Aggregate demand and aggregate supply analysis

Analysis, including AD/AS analysis, may initially seem difficult, and you may be anxious that you will not be able to apply in it in the exam. Do not worry; you will be surprised at how often you will be able to use AD/AS analysis. As you get familiar with the analysis, your confidence will grow.

On the questions in this chapter and in exams, you should take into account the number of marks awarded in deciding how long you should spend answering a question. In Paper 1: AS Level Multiple Choice, the time allowance is one hour, and the number of marks is 30. In Paper 2: AS Level Data Response and Essays, the time given is two hours, and the marks awarded are 60. This works out at a maximum of two minutes per mark. It is a maximum as you have to allow time to read the information provided and the questions. So, for example, in answering the Exam skills question in Section 17.2, you should spend approximately 18 minutes in total.

17.1 Aggregate demand

1 What are the **four** groups who purchase a country's products?

UNDERSTAND
THIS TERM

- aggregate demand

« RECALL AND CONNECT 1 «

Who makes the decisions of what to produce in:

a   the private sector

b   the public sector?

17.2 Determinants of the components of aggregate demand

1 What are the **two** ways that households can spend more than their income?

2 Why may a fall in the rate of interest reduce saving but increase investment?

Think carefully about how you allocate your time here. For example, you should be spending approximately four minutes on answering Q3(b) and the same amount of time on Q3(c). These are approximate times.

3 When workers lose their jobs, they usually spend less. If the number of people without jobs reaches high levels, even those who stay employed may lower their spending. Firms may also reduce their investment.

   a   Explain:
      i   why workers who lose their jobs may spend less   [1]
      ii   why some workers who lose their jobs may not spend less.   [2]
   b   Explain why some workers who stay employed may spend less when
       other workers lose their jobs.   [2]
   c   Explain why firms may invest less when workers lose their jobs.   [2]

REFLECTION

How long did it take you to answer Question 3? Did you find that you rushed your answers or did you spend too long on answering Question 3(a)(i), for example? When you answer the Exams skills question in Section 17.4, it may be useful to have a watch or a mobile phone in front of you on the desk.

UNDERSTAND
THESE TREMS

- consumer expenditure
- dissaving
- saving
- investment
- government spending
- net exports
- exchange rate

4 Name **four** goods a government may purchase when it spends money on education.

5 Households in a country become richer. Why may this reduce net exports?

17.3 The aggregate demand curve

1   What are **two** reasons why a fall in the price level will cause an extension in aggregate demand?

2   What is a similarity and a difference between a shift in a demand curve and a shift in the aggregate demand curve?

> ### « RECALL AND CONNECT 2 «
>
> What is the difference between government spending and taxation in terms of the circular flow?

17.4 Aggregate supply

1   How is an increase in short-run aggregate supply illustrated on a diagram?

2   Give **two** causes of a decrease in short-run aggregate supply.

3   How do the views of Keynesian and new classical economists differ on whether an economy will produce at full capacity in the long run?

4   What is the shape of the LRAS curve according to:

   a   Keynesian economists

   b   new classical economists?

5   What effect would a decrease in population be likely to have on aggregate demand and aggregate supply?

> **UNDERSTAND THESE TERMS**
>
> - aggregate supply (AS)
> - short-run aggregate supply (SRAS)
> - long-run aggregate supply (LRAS)
> - average cost
> - supply-side shocks
> - Keynesians

There is quite a lot of information included in Table 17.1. Do not be put off by this. Calmly check what the information is showing. You may not be familiar with the term 'school life expectancy (years)', but this is explained in the footnote.

6

Country	School life expectancy (years)*		Size of labour force (millions)	
	2000	2021	2000	2021
Cuba	9	14	4.5	5.1
Japan	11	15	68	66.5
Tanzania	4	9	15	29.0

Table 17.1: School life expectancy and the size of the labour force in three selected countries

*School life expectancy (years) is the total number of years of schooling a child can expect to receive.
Source: CIA World Factbooks 2000 and 2022.

a   Assess, on the basis of the information in the table, which country may have experienced the most rapid increase in aggregate supply between 2000 and 2021. [6]

b   Consider the extent to which it would be useful to have information on the change in investment in these three countries to have a more complete picture about what happened to aggregate supply in the period shown. [4]

> **REFLECTION**

How confident did you feel in applying your knowledge of the causes of changes in aggregate supply in answering these questions? Are there any aspects you think you could still improve on?

« RECALL AND CONNECT 3 «

What will happen to aggregate demand if injections into the circular flow increase?

17.5 Macroequilibrium and disequilibrium

1   Which combination of shifts in aggregate demand and aggregate supply would result in a rise in the price level and a fall in real output?

> **REFLECTION**

How did you go about working out your answer to Question 1? What type of diagram could you have used? Drawing diagrams is a useful way of finding out what is happening when AD and/or AS change.

2   What are the **two** conditions that have to be met for macroequilibrium to occur?

3   If an economy is operating at full capacity, what would be the effect of an increase in aggregate demand on real output, the price level and employment?

Note that in answering a data response question on a particular country, you will not normally be expected to have prior knowledge on that country. In Question 4, the information you need to know about Fiji is supplied in the data. However, you will be expected to know major economic trends, such as the growth of China as a major economy.

4

> **Fiji's economic performance in 2021**
>
> Fiji's economy had mixed performance in 2021. The country's output fell in that year by 4%. This was largely because of a fall in tourism. Tourism accounts for a large proportion of Fiji's export revenue. The country had negative net exports in 2021. Wages did rise that year but by less than productivity. Consumer expenditure fell on some products but rose on others, including cars.

a   Explain **one** measure of a country's output.   [2]

b   Identify **two** components of aggregate demand mentioned in
    the paragraph.   [2]

c   Explain why Fiji's short-run aggregate supply may have decreased in 2021.   [3]

≪ RECALL AND CONNECT 4 ≪

What is a similarity and what is the difference between equilibrium in a market and macroeconomic equilibrium?

SELF-ASSESSMENT CHECKLIST

Let's revisit the Knowledge focus and Exam skills focus for this chapter.
Decide how confident you are with each statement.

Now I can	Show it	Needs more work	Almost there	Confident to move on
define the meaning of aggregate demand (AD)	Describe what 'aggregate demand' means.			
explain the components of aggregate demand	Identify the **four** components of aggregate demand and examine their main influences.			
analyse the determinants of aggregate demand	Produce a table showing the main influences on the **four** components of aggregate demand.			
explain the shape of the aggregate demand curve	Identify the relationship between changes in the price level and AD and the reasons why the AD curve slopes down from left to right.			
analyse the causes of a shift in the aggregate demand curve	Produce a mind map showing why the AD curve may shift to the left or right.			

CONTINUED

define the meaning of aggregate supply (AS)	Describe what 'aggregate supply' means.			
analyse the determinants of aggregate supply	List the influences on aggregate supply.			
explain the shape of the aggregate supply curve in the short run (SRAS) and the long run (LRAS)	Produce a revision card explaining why the SRAS curve slopes upwards from left to right and the two shapes of the LRAS curve.			
explain the causes of a shift in the AS curve in the short run (SRAS) and in the long run (LRAS)	Produce a mind map on the reasons why the AS curve may shift to the left or right.			
identify the difference between a movement along and a shift in aggregate demand and aggregate supply	Explain the difference between the cause of a movement along AD and AS curves and the causes of a shift in the curves to a fellow student.			
explain how equilibrium is established in the AD/AS model and how the level of real output, the price level and employment are determined	Produce a revision card with a definition of macroeconomic equilibrium and a diagram showing AD = AS.			
discuss the effect of shifts in the AD curve and the AS curve on the level of real output, the price level and employment	Produce a mind map showing the impact of changes in AD and AS on the macroeconomy.			
show that I can reduce anxiety about economic analysis by practising	Draw AD/AS diagrams to show the possible effects of an increase in AD, a decrease in AD, an increase in AS, a decrease in AS and an increase in both AD and AS.			
show that I can manage distribution of my time in the AS Level Economics papers.	Identify how long you would spend on answering a question which has four marks.			

18 Economic growth

EXAM SKILLS FOCUS

In this chapter you will:

- further practise answering 'state' questions

- show you can understand the connections between concepts within your answer to an exam question.

The command word 'state' means to express in clear terms and is associated with objective AO1 Knowledge and understanding. For example, in an exam question you may be asked to state two advantages of a change in an economic variable. In such a case, each one is likely to gain one mark. In answering 'state' questions, you need to identify the points accurately, but you do not have to explain them.

It is important that you recognise what concepts you need to apply in answering the higher mark exam questions. You should provide links between concepts. In doing this you should not jump stages. For example, if you were explaining why a country has recently been increasing its output more slowly than in previous years, keep the words 'how' and 'why' in mind. If you mention that the number of workers in the country has declined, explain **why** this occurred and **how** this affects output.

18.1 Economic growth

1 A country's output increases, but its GDP per head falls. What would explain this?

2 Give **two** reasons why a country's output may stay the same but it may experience economic development.

≪ RECALL AND CONNECT 1 ≪

How is a country's output labelled on an AD/AS diagram?

REFLECTION

Could you answer this question without checking? The more AD/AS diagrams you draw, the more they will come almost naturally to you.

18.2 Measurement of economic growth

1 What would it mean if:

a a country's economic growth rate was 4% in 2024?

b its economic growth rate falls from 4% in 2024 to 3% in 2025?

18.3 Nominal GDP and real GDP

1 Why may using nominal GDP figures give a misleading impression of changes in output?

Question 2(a) starts with the command word 'state'. Remember your answer to this question can be brief.

2 A country's nominal GDP rose from $500 billion to $530 billion. In the same period, the price index rose from 100 to 106.

a State what type of prices real GDP is measured in. [1]

b Explain how nominal GDP is converted into real GDP. [2]

c Calculate the percentage change in real GDP. [2]

18.4 Causes and consequences of economic growth

1   What has to exist for an increase in AD to result in an increase in a country's real GDP?

2   Economic growth can occur because of an increase in the quantity or quality of resources. Copy and complete Table 18.1, which looks at increases in the quantity and quality of resources.

Resource	Example of a cause of an increase in quantity	Example of a cause of an increase in quality
Capital	Net investment	
Enterprise		Improved higher education
Labour	Rise in the retirement age	
Land		Reduced water pollution

Table 18.1: Increases in the quantity and quality of resources

3   What is the opportunity cost of producing capital goods?

4   What effect would cutting down rainforests have on economic growth?

5

> **Economic growth and pollution**
>
> As low-income countries experience economic growth, they also tend to experience high levels of pollution. Industries tend to burn more fossil fuels, and farmers burn more fields. Households consume more products, drive more cars and throw away more waste. As income rises further, pollution sometimes falls. Production can become cleaner. Households may become more environmentally aware and firms may be set up to process recycled waste.
>
> One country that has experienced a significant increase in income in recent years is Mongolia. Mining of copper, gold and coal in the country has increased rapidly. Most Mongolian households burn coal to heat their homes. The country's capital, Ulaanbaatar, is one of the most polluted cities in the world. Air quality is particularly poor.

   a   Explain **one** benefit workers may gain from an increase in the output of coal in Mongolia.   [2]

   b   Identify **two** reasons why household waste may become less of a problem as income rises.   [2]

   c   Assess whether an increase in coal mining in Mongolia will result in more pollution.   [6]

> **REFLECTION**
>
> What skills did you apply in answering Question 5? Did you provide links in your answers to Questions 5(a) and 5(c)? How do you think you could have improved your answers?

In your answer to Question 6(a), do not just state what will happen to the AD curve but also explain why. In your answer to Question 6(b), do not forget to consider both sides and come to a conclusion.

6   a   Explain the components of aggregate demand **and** consider how a change in the price level will affect the aggregate demand curve.   [8]

      b   Assess whether economic growth will increase the quality of people's lives.   [12]

≪ RECALL AND CONNECT 2 ≪

What effect would an increase in injections into the circular flow of income have on economic growth?

SELF-ASSESSMENT CHECKLIST

Let's revisit the Knowledge focus and Exam skills focus for this chapter.
Decide how confident you are with each statement.

Now I can	Show it	Needs more work	Almost there	Confident to move on
explain the meaning of economic growth	Define what economic growth means.			
describe how economic growth is measured	Identify how economic growth is measured.			
explain the difference between growth in nominal GDP and real GDP	Convert nominal GDP of $500 billion, when the price level has risen from 120 to 125, into real GDP.			
analyse the causes of economic growth	Draw a diagram to show how an increase in AD may cause economic growth and another diagram showing how an increase in AS may cause economic growth.			
discuss the consequences of economic growth	Produce a table listing the advantages and disadvantages of economic growth.			
further practise answering 'state' questions	State one benefit of economic growth.			
Understand the connections between concepts within my answer and an exam question.	Produce a flow chart showing the possible links between increase spending on education and economic growth.			

19 Unemployment

KNOWLEDGE FOCUS

You will answer questions on:

19.1 Unemployment

19.2 The labour force

19.3 Level of unemployment and rate of unemployment

19.4 The stock and flow of unemployment

19.5 Measures of unemployment

19.6 The causes of unemployment

19.7 The consequences of unemployment

19.8 How significant is unemployment?

EXAM SKILLS FOCUS

In this chapter you will:

- show that you understand what knowledge you need to demonstrate

- further develop your understanding of the command words 'explain' and 'consider' and answer a question that asks you to 'explain' and 'consider'.

You need to ensure that your answers to exam questions are based on knowledge from the subject. When you read a question, think about what part or parts of the syllabus you have studied that you can draw on as the basis of your answer.

As mentioned in Chapter 3, the command word 'explain' means set out purposes or reasons, make the relationship between things evident, provide why and/or how links and support with relevant evidence. This description indicates that you need to go beyond just stating points. You should provide some detail in making clear, for example, reasons why something is likely to happen. The command word 'consider' indicates that you need to make a judgement, for example on whether it will always happen.

19.1 Unemployment

1 Which of the following groups are economically active:

- those who are too ill to work
- those in full-time education
- those who are unemployed
- those who look after their families full-time
- those who work in the public sector.

Explain your answer.

2 What effect would an increase in the number of economically active people have on a country's aggregate supply?

<table>
<tr><td>

UNDERSTAND THESE TERMS

- homemakers
- economically inactive
- labour force
- economically active

</td></tr>
</table>

REFLECTION

In making your decisions in Question 1, were you able to remember the meaning of economically active and economically inactive? Did completing this question help reinforce the understanding you have of the two terms? If you struggled to remember these terms, consider how you consolidated their meanings in your memory and why this may not have been effective.

≪ RECALL AND CONNECT 1 ≪

What effect is a decrease in unemployment likely to have on aggregate demand?

19.2 The labour force

1 What is the connection between the size of the labour force participation rate and the labour force?

Question 2 asks for two reasons. Remember that the command word 'explain' means that you have to go beyond just stating two reasons. Also note that there is no point giving more reasons than you are asked for. You will not gain any more marks for explaining a third reason. It might even lose you marks as you may examine each reason more briefly and with less thought than you would do by examining the required two reasons.

2 Explain **two** reasons why a country's labour force participation rate may increase **and** consider whether this will result in an increase in its labour force. [6]

How can you avoid confusing reasons why the labour force participation rate may increase with reasons why the labour force may increase? They are not the same thing. If necessary, check out the meaning of the 'labour force participation rate' and attempt the question again.

19.3 Level of unemployment and rate of unemployment

1   Why may the level of unemployment rise but the rate of unemployment fall?

Before answering Question 2, think carefully about what each term means.

2   A country has a population of 46 million, a working age population of 30 million and a labour force of 21 million, of whom 18 million are employed and 3 million are unemployed.

Calculate:

a   The labour force participation rate   [2]
b   The unemployment rate   [2]
c   The employment rate   [2]

19.4 The stock and flow of unemployment

UNDERSTAND THIS TERM

•   discouraged workers

1   What are **three** reasons why people may stop being unemployed?

2   A country has a labour force of 110 million. In what circumstance may 9 million unemployed be considered less of a problem than 5 million unemployed?

3

Country	Population (million)	Labour force (million)	Unemployment (%)
A	80	60	5
B	100	60	12
C	120	70	10
D	140	80	7.5

Table 19.1: Labour market information on four fictional countries

a   Calculate which country had the largest number of unemployed workers.   [2]
b   Calculate which country had the smallest number of employed workers.   [2]

19.5 Measures of unemployment

1   Which organisation's definition of unemployment does the labour force survey measure?

2   What are **two** disadvantages of the claimant count measure?

3   Copy and complete Table 19.2 on the advantages and disadvantages of the labour force survey measure.

Advantages	Disadvantages

Table 19.2: Advantages and disadvantages of the labour force survey measure

UNDERSTAND THESE TERMS

- claimant count
- labour force survey measure

19.6 The causes of unemployment

1   Which type of unemployment is likely to last the shortest period of time?

2   In each case, decide whether the following changes will cause frictional, structural or cyclical unemployment:

   a   a reduction in business and consumer confidence

   b   the switch to online banking

   c   the closure of coal mines

   d   a fall in net exports of a wide range of products

   e   an increase in the time people spend looking for the 'right' job

   f   a decrease in demand for bus travel.

Interpreting graphs and charts is a key skill of economists. You might consider making use of the world unemployment rate in Figure 19.1 in your answer to Q3(a). The question does not specifically mention the world unemployment rate, but it does provide a useful basis for a possible point.

3

Challenges that faced Sri Lanka 2019 – 2022

Between 2019 and 2022, the tourism industry in Sri Lanka lost thousands of jobs. The industry suffered a number of shocks. There were restrictions put on people entering the country in 2020 and 2021 due to the COVID-19 pandemic. In 2021 there was a financial crisis. The high inflation rate in the country and the queues for a number of products, including fuel, caused tourist numbers to fall further. The Sri Lankan government had tried to stimulate economic growth and reduce unemployment in 2020 by halving GST and lowering income tax. These measures lowered tax revenue but were not very successful in reducing unemployment.

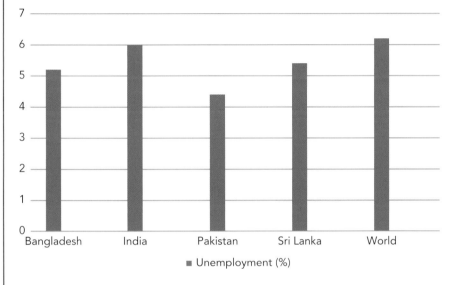

■ Unemployment (%)

Figure 19.1: Unemployment rates of selected countries 2021

Source: World Bank website

a   Compare Sri Lanka's unemployment rate with the other countries shown in Figure 19.1.   [2]

b   Identify **two** other pieces of information that would be useful to have to assess whether unemployment was more of a problem in Sri Lanka in 2021 than the other countries shown.   [2]

c   Explain what type of unemployment may occur if the Sri Lankan tourist industry continues to decline.   [3]

d   Assess whether a cut in tax rates will reduce unemployment.   [6]

REFLECTION

How confident are you now feeling in interpreting graphs? Is there anything you think you could have done which would have strengthened the quality of your answers?

19.7 The consequences of unemployment

1 What are **two** possible disadvantages of unemployment to a government?

2 Why may a short period of unemployment benefit workers?

3

> **Unemployment in South Africa**
>
> In 2021, South Africa's unemployment rate was 35%, although some economists estimated that it would be as high as 46% if discouraged workers were included. A relatively high proportion of those officially classified as unemployed had been out of work for more than a year. Unemployment is a major cause of poverty and homelessness in South Africa.

   a   State why discouraged workers are not included in unemployment figures. [2]

   b   Assess whether South Africa's unemployment will cause unemployment to remain high. [6]

19.8 How significant is unemployment?

1 Identify **three** pieces of information you would need in order to assess how harmful a rise in unemployment may be.

2 Is unemployment usually evenly spread?

3 Why may economic growth be accompanied by an increase in structural unemployment?

SELF-ASSESSMENT CHECKLIST

Let's revisit the Knowledge focus and Exam skills focus for this chapter. Decide how confident you are with each statement.

Now I can	Show it	Needs more work	Almost there	Confident to move on
define the meaning of economic growth	Describe what 'economic growth' means.			
explain the difference between the economically active and the economically inactive population	Identify the groups who are economically active and those who are not. Identify which groups are in the labour force.			
explain the difference between the level of unemployment and the rate of unemployment	Compare changes in the level of unemployment and the rate of unemployment for your own country.			

CONTINUED

calculate the rate of unemployment	Calculate the unemployment rate if 2 million workers are unemployed out of a labour force of 40 million.			
explain how unemployment is measured	Identify a difference in how the claimant count and labour force measure unemployment.			
consider the difficulties of measuring unemployment	Explain to another student the difficulties of measuring unemployment and which measure may give a more accurate figure.			
analyse the causes and types of unemployment: frictional, structural, cyclical, seasonal and technological	Produce a revision card on the different types of unemployment.			
discuss the consequences of unemployment	Produce a mind map on the advantages and disadvantages of unemployment.			
show that I understand what knowledge I need to demonstrate	Identify some groups who are economically active.			
further develop my understanding of the command words 'explain' and 'consider' and answer a question that asks me to 'explain' and 'consider'.	Explain what you think is the main type of unemployment in your country and consider whether this type of unemployment is likely to increase in your country in the future.			

20 Price stability

EXAM SKILLS FOCUS

In this chapter you will:

- show that you can recognise high-quality answers to calculation questions

- show that you understand the command word 'give' and answer a 'give' question.

In calculation questions, a high-quality response is one which uses the right information and method, is accurate and shows workings (workings are not required for one-mark questions).

'Give' means to produce an answer from a given source or recall/memory. The command word is linked to AO1 Knowledge and understanding. Questions which have this command word will require short answers. For example, if you are asked to give reasons for something, the answer may consist of just a few words.

20.1 What is price stability?

1   Table 20.1 shows the inflation rate in four fictional countries. Which pattern of inflation rates in Table 20.1 is most likely to meet the government aim of price stability?

	Inflation %				
	2023	2024	2025	2026	2027
Country A	2	8	−2	12	2
Country B	3	4	2	3	4
Country C	1	−5	1	5	1
Country D	2	3	8	15	2

Table 20.1: Inflation rates in four fictional countries 2023–2027

20.2 Inflation, deflation and disinflation

1   What happens to the value of money during inflation?

2   What is the difference between creeping inflation and deflation?

3   What does it mean if a country's inflation rate falls from 7% to 5%?

Do not rush your response to Question 4. It may initially seem straightforward, but you need to consider the questions and the bar chart carefully.

UNDERSTAND THESE TERMS
• price stability
• inflation rate
• inflation
• hyperinflation

4

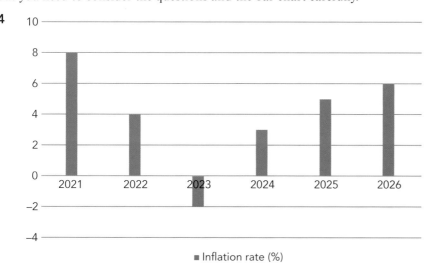

■ Inflation rate (%)

Figure 20.1: Inflation rate 2021–2026

Look at Figure 20.1. Explain in which year:

a   the price level was lowest   [2]

b   there was deflation   [2]

c   there was disinflation   [2]

d   the price level was highest.   [2]

How did you find answering Question 4? Were any parts harder than you first thought? If you got any parts wrong, you could try designing a question on economic growth rates asking when the country's output was at its lowest and highest and when the country might have experienced a recession. You could try this out on another student.

20.3 Calculating the inflation rate

1   The price level is 150 in September 2024 and 170 in September 2025.

    a   What was the inflation rate?

    b   Which method have you used?

2   The average price level rises from 108 in 2025 to 112 in 2026. What is the inflation rate?

UNDERSTAND THESE TERMS

- annual average method
- year-on-year method

20.4 Measurement of inflation and deflation

1   What is the relationship between the consumer price index and the cost of living?

2   What are weights in the consumer price index based on?

20.5 The difficulties of measuring changes in the price level

1   In a consumer price index, why does the weight attached to food tend to fall over time?

UNDERSTAND THIS TERM

- consumer price index (CPI)

In answering Questions 2 and 3, think carefully about the method you should use and make sure you follow the instruction to show your workings. Remember you can use a calculator. This may save you time and increase your accuracy.

2   Table 20.2 shows the amount households spend on different categories of products and the percentage change in the price of those categories in one year. Calculate, showing your workings, the inflation rate.   [3]

Product	Percentage of household expenditure	Percentage price change
Clothing	10	5
Electricity	10	20
Entertainment	5	–4
Food	15	30
Housing	20	10
Transport	12	25
Other	28	5

Table 20.2: The percentage of household expenditure spent on different product categories and changes in the prices of these product categories

3   In calculating a country's CPI, there are three categories of goods, X, Y and Z. The CPI in 2025 was 100 and in 2026 it was 113. Between 2025 and 2026, the price of X rose by 8%, the price of Y by 4% and the price of Z by 20%. Table 20.3 shows possible weights attached to the three categories of products. Calculate, showing your workings, which combination of weights would have increased the CPI by 13%.   [4]

	Good X	Good Y	Good Z
A	¼	½	¼
B	½	½	0
C	¼	¼	½
D	0	½	½
E	½	0	½

Table 20.3: Possible weights of three categories of products

REFLECTION

How did answering these Exam skill questions help you understand how the CPI is constructed? Why not try constructing a similar question for other students to attempt?

4   Why may a CPI overestimate the inflation rate?

20.6 The differences between money values and real data

UNDERSTAND THESE TERMS

- money values
- real data

1 What would it mean if real wages have increased by 3%?

2 The real rate of interest is –2%. If the inflation rate is 11%, what is the money rate of interest?

Question 3(a) uses the command word 'give'. Here all you need to do is to write the name of the country that you think experienced hyperinflation. You do not have to explain why you have selected this country.

3

Country	Consumer prices % change on a year ago
Argentina	60.1
Egypt	9.7
India	2.9
Malaysia	6.0
South Africa	5.8

Table 20.4: Change in consumer prices in 2022

a Give the name of the country which experienced hyperinflation in 2022. [1]

b Explain whether it is possible to judge whether prices were higher in Egypt than in Malaysia in 2022. [3]

≪ RECALL AND CONNECT 1 ≪

What is the difference between real and money GDP?

20.7 The causes of inflation

UNDERSTAND THESE TERMS

- cost-push inflation
- wage-price spiral
- demand-pull inflation
- monetarists

1   How is cost-push inflation illustrated on an AD/AS diagram?

2   What type of demand is referred to in demand-pull inflation?

3   What type of inflation may be caused by a large increase in the money supply?

4

> **Inflation in the Philippines**
>
> The inflation rate in the Philippines increased from 4% in 2021 to 7% in 2022. The Philippines relies heavily on imported food and fuel. Due to global shortages, the price of diesel fuel doubled, and the price of some food items, including cereals, increased by even more in 2022. Spending on food accounted for 40% of household expenditure in the Philippines. In response to the rising prices, the government of the Philippines raised the country's minimum wage.

a   Explain whether the main cause of inflation in the Philippines in 2022 was cost-push inflation or demand-pull inflation.   [3]

b   Calculate the weighting of food in the consumer price index of the Philippines in 2022.   [1]

c   Assess whether a rise in wages will enable workers to buy more goods and services.   [6]

≪ RECALL AND CONNECT 2 ≪

a   Why may an increase in AD not increase the price level?

b   What is the main aim of a minimum wage?

20.8 The consequences of inflation

UNDERSTAND THESE TERMS

- menu costs
- shoe leather costs
- fiscal drag
- inflationary noise
- total cost

1   Why is demand-pull inflation likely to be less harmful than cost-push inflation?

2   Why may inflation cause further inflation?

3   When are menu costs likely to be highest?

4   Why might a government benefit from inflation?

5

> ### Turkish government unusual approach to rising inflation rate
>
> In July 2022, Turkey's inflation rate rose to 80% while unemployment fell to 10%. To reduce the inflation rate, the Turkish government took the unorthodox approach of reducing the rate of interest. This was criticised by many economists who claimed that this would cause the inflation rate to go higher and that if inflation continued, it would cause an increase in unemployment.
>
> The high inflation rate was causing households and firms to find it difficult to interpret rises in the price of particular products They were not sure whether price increases reflected changes in the demand and supply conditions in particular markets or just inflationary pressures. This uncertainty was expected to reduce investment.

   a Explain why a cut in interest rates may cause inflation.   [2]

   b Consider the extent to which inflationary noise may discourage investment.   [4]

   c Assess whether inflation will cause unemployment.   [6]

In answering Question 6(a), it would be useful to give examples of those groups who are economically inactive. In answering Question 6(b), it does not matter whether you conclude that inflation or unemployment may cause more harm as long as you support your conclusion with relevant analysis.

6 **a** Explain the difference between people who are economically inactive and those who are unemployed **and** consider whether unemployment figures are always accurate.   [8]

    b Assess whether an economy will be harmed more by inflation or unemployment.   [12]

20.9 Extension: The causes and consequences of deflation

1 What is a key cause of 'good' deflation?

2 Why may it be difficult to stop 'bad' deflation?

SELF-ASSESSMENT CHECKLIST

Let's revisit the Knowledge focus and Exam skills focus for this chapter.
Decide how confident you are with each statement.

Now I can	Show it	Needs more work	Almost there	Confident to move on
define the meaning of 'inflation', 'deflation' and 'disinflation'	Describe what 'inflation', 'deflation' and 'disinflation' mean.			
calculate the rate of inflation	Calculate the rate of inflation if a country's price index rises from 130 to 142.			
explain how changes in the price level are measured by the consumer price index	Find out the weights in your own country's CPI.			
consider the difficulties of measuring changes in the price level	Produce a revision card on the stages of producing a weighted price index, identifying a difficulty at each stage.			
explain the difference between money values and real data	Explain to another student the difference between real and money wages.			
analyse the causes and types of inflation: cost-push and demand-pull inflation	Produce a table that contrasts demand-pull and cost-push inflation.			
analyse the consequences of inflation	Produce a mind map showing the consequences of inflation.			
recognise high-quality answers to calculation questions	Write a three-mark explain question on the calculation of a weighted price index and write a mark scheme for it.			
understand the command word 'give' and answer a 'give' question.	Give **one** cause of inflation.			

Exam Practice 4

This section contains both past paper questions from previous Cambridge exams and practice questions. These questions draw together your knowledge on a range of topics that you have covered up to this point and will help you prepare for your assessment.

For Question 1(a) read the question, the example student response and the commentary provided. Then, in Question 1(b), write an improved answer to the question, using the guidance in the commentary to help you.

1   a   Explain, with the help of a diagram, what is meant by equilibrium national income **and** consider how this equilibrium changes when there is an increase in aggregate demand.   [8]

Adapted from Cambridge International AS & A Level Economics (9708) Paper 21 Q3a, November 2016

Example student response	Examiner comments
Equilibrium national income is the level of national income where aggregate demand equals aggregate supply. The diagram shows AD = AS. 	**AO1 Knowledge and understanding** The answer does show some awareness of the meaning of equilibrium national income and how the equilibrium might change when there is an increase in AD. *2/3* **AO2 Analysis** The labelling of the diagrams is micro rather than macro. The diagrams do, however, show aggregate demand and aggregate supply being equal. *1/3*

Example student response	Examiner comments
An increase in AD will cause the equilibrium to change. Higher AD may cause the price level to rise and output to increase. 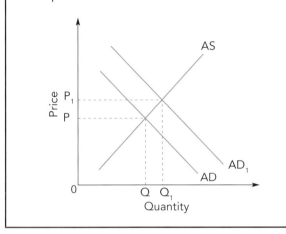	**AO3 Evaluation** The answer does recognise that the price level may rise and output (national income) may increase. It is interesting to note that 'price level' is written in the answer, but there is 'price' on the axes of the diagrams. The answer might also have mentioned that the effect on the price level and national income output may differ in the long run. *1/2* *Total: 4/8 marks*

b   Write an improved answer to Question 1(a).

Here is another past paper question which you should attempt.

2   Explain how a rise in the rate of interest might cause a shift in an economy's aggregate demand curve **and** consider whether investment is likely to be the largest component of aggregate demand.   [8]

   *Adapted from Cambridge International AS & A Level Economics (9708)
      Paper 22 Q4a, November 2014*

The following question has an example student response and commentary provided. Work through the question first, then compare your answer to the example student response and commentary.

3   Explain, using production possibility curves, the impact on an economy of a rise in the unemployment rate and an increase in the working population **and** consider how their impact differs.   [8]

   *Adapted from Cambridge International AS & A Level Economics (9708)
      Paper 21 Q4a, November 2017*

Example student response	Examiner comments
A rise in unemployment means that the economy is not producing as much as it could. They will be more unused resources. The economy will produce inside the production possibility curve as shown in the diagram below. 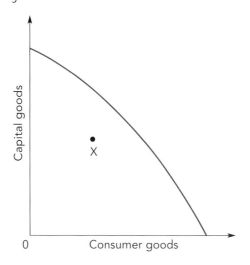 An increase in the working population means that there are more workers available. As a result, the economy can produce more, so the curve shifts to the right. 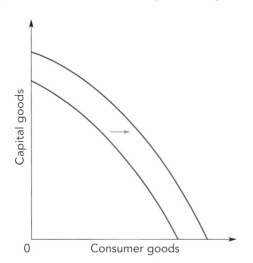 The increase in unemployment means the economy is producing inside the PPC whereas an increase in the working population shifts the PPC.	**AO1 Knowledge and understanding** The answer does show knowledge of PPCs, what unemployment means and what the working population is. *3/3* **AO2 Analysis** The student does not show that the production point moves further inside the PPC as a result of a rise in unemployment. The student does, however, explain that an increase in the working population will increase the amount the economy is capable of producing and does shift the PPC to the right. *2/3* **AO3 Evaluation** The student tries to make a judgement about the difference between the two changes. However, they do not clearly state that a rise in unemployment will cause a movement further inside the curve. They also do not clearly state that the reason the PPC shifts to the right is because of an increase in resources. *1/2* *Total: 6/8 marks*

Now that you have read the example student response to the previous question, here is a similar practice question which you should attempt. Use the guidance in the commentary to help you as you answer the question.

4   Explain, using production possibility curves, the effect of a fall in the unemployment rate and advances in technology **and** consider whether a country's production possibility curve is likely to shift to the left or the right over time.   [8]

For Question 5(a) read the question, the example student response and the commentary provided. Then, in Question 5(b), write an improved answer to the question, using the guidance in the commentary to help you.

5   a   Assess the causes of an increase in aggregate demand and whether such an increase will always cause inflation. Use diagrams to support your answer.   [12]

Adapted from Cambridge International AS & A Level Economics (9708) Paper 21 Q4b, November 2017

Example student response	Examiner comments
More consumer expenditure and more investment can result in higher spending in an economy. People may spend more on luxury goods and services. The government may spend more on education and healthcare and firms may spend more on capital goods. An increase in aggregate demand will cause inflation. The diagram shows a shift to the right of the AD curve. Higher spending encourages firms to raise their prices.	**AO1 Knowledge and understanding** The answer shows an incomplete knowledge of the components of aggregate demand. **AO2 Analysis** The answer does not analyse the causes of an increase in aggregate demand. Such an analysis and consideration of the possible shape of an LRAS curve would have enabled the likely effect to be evaluated. The diagram is, nevertheless, clear and accurately labelled, showing a possible effect of an increase in AD. *AO1 and AO2: 4/8* **AO3 Evaluation** There is no evaluation. *0/4* *Total: 4/12 marks*

b   Write an improved answer to Question 5(a).

Here is another past paper question which you should attempt. Use the guidance in the commentaries in this section to help you as you answer the question.

6   Assess whether it is the behaviour of producers, consumers or
     governments that is most likely to cause inflation.   [12]

**Adapted from Cambridge International AS & A Level Economics (9708)
     Paper 22 Q4b, June 2011**

21 Government macroeconomic policy objectives

Learning is about improving understanding and improving the application of that understanding. You can learn from every task you undertake. The important thing is to reflect on your progress and think about strategies to improve your performance.

'Comment' means to give an informed opinion. It is most commonly linked to AO3 Evaluation. If you are asked, for example, to consider whether some change is likely to be beneficial, consider both why it may be beneficial and why it may not be and come to a conclusion on its likely overall effect.

21.1 Price stability

≪ RECALL AND CONNECT 1 ≪

How is inflation measured?

1   What would be the risk of aiming for zero inflation?

2   How might an inflation target influence firms' behaviour?

In Question 3(c) the command word 'comment' requires you to consider both sides and to make an informed judgement about whether increasing the inflation target will cause a rise in the inflation rate.

3

Inflation targeting

New Zealand's government was the first government to set an inflation target for a central bank. Now many governments operate an inflation target. Achieving a low and stable inflation rate can promote investment. As well as preventing a high rate of inflation, a government is likely to want to avoid deflation. A fall in the price level can increase the real value of debt.

Knowing where to set the inflation target can be difficult. It has to be achievable, not too high and not too low. The New Zealand government, which still has an inflation target of 2%, is unlikely to raise it to, for instance, 8%.

a   Explain why achieving a low and stable inflation rate can promote investment. [3]

b   Explain how a fall in the price level can increase the real value of debt. [3]

c   Assess whether increasing an inflation target from 2% to 8% will cause a rise in the inflation rate. [8]

REFLECTION

What did you learn from undertaking Question 3? How could you use what you have learned to improve your performance on future questions?

21.2 Low unemployment

1   What effect is a reduction in unemployment likely to have on tax revenue?

In answering questions based on data, it is important to take that data into account. For instance, when you check the answer to Question 2(d), you will find it is not a general question on the effects of lower unemployment. It is another 'comment' question. This question only has four marks, so the same depth is not required as in Question 3(c) in Section 21.1, but you should still consider both why it may be beneficial, given the data, and why it may not and make a judgement.

2

Changes in unemployment, economic inactivity and wages

In July 2022, the labour force in Country A was 35 million. The country's unemployment rate fell to 3.6%. This was the lowest unemployment rate since 1974. However, while the unemployment rate fell, the economically inactive rate rose to 21.7%. Economic inactivity rose to nine million, partly as a result of rising numbers of long-term sick leaving the labour force. Shortages of workers pushed up nominal wages, but wages had increased by less than inflation since 2009.

---

   a   Calculate the number of unemployed workers in Country A in July 2022. [1]

   b   Explain what happened to real wages in Country A between 2009 and July 2022. [2]

   c   Identify **two** economically inactive groups not mentioned in the information provided. [2]

   d   Comment on whether the fall in the Country A unemployment rate in July 2022 is likely to have benefited the Country A economy. [4]

REFLECTION

Did you answer Question 2's parts in the context of the data provided? Were there any concepts you were unsure about? Identify these and consider how you could increase your understanding of them.

« RECALL AND CONNECT 2 «

Identify **two** measures of unemployment.

21.3 Economic growth

1   What are **two** reasons why governments try to avoid their countries experiencing too high a rate of economic growth?

2   What are **three** influences on the economic growth rate a government is likely to aim for?

« RECALL AND CONNECT 3 «

Draw an AD/AS diagram to show an economy experiencing a recession.

SELF-ASSESSMENT CHECKLIST

Let's revisit the Knowledge focus and Exam skills focus for this chapter.
Decide how confident you are with each statement.

Now I can	Show it	Needs more work	Almost there	Confident to move on
explain a government's macroeconomic policy objective of price stability	List the benefits and challenges of aiming to achieve price stability.			
explain a government's macroeconomic objective of low unemployment	Produce a table showing the benefits and challenges of aiming to achieve low unemployment.			
explain a government's macroeconomic objective of economic growth	Produce a revision card on the benefits and challenges of aiming to achieve economic growth.			
know what to do next to improve	Draw up a brief plan to improve your understanding of government macroeconomic policy objectives.			
understand the command word 'comment' and answer a 'comment' question.	Produce two sets of cards, one with a number of command words, including 'comment', and one with their definitions. Ask another student to match them.			

22 Fiscal policy

EXAM SKILLS FOCUS

In this chapter you will:

- show that you can present knowledge clearly and coherently

- show that you understand what knowledge you need to demonstrate.

It is important that you write in a way that both uses appropriate terms and is also clear to understand. Each point should follow on logically from the previous one. In essays, it is important that you explain the points you make rather than just asserting them.

It is important to be able to recognise what knowledge you need to be able to draw on to answer exam questions. Read a question carefully and consider carefully what is the relevant knowledge you can use in your answer.

22.1 Fiscal policy and the budget

UNDERSTAND THESE TERMS

- fiscal policy
- automatic stabilisers
- cyclical budget deficit
- structural budget deficit

1 Why may a government aim for a budget deficit?

2 Why is a structural deficit a cause for concern?

In Question 3, you can answer parts a and b on the basis of the information given and of a knowledge of the government budget position. Question 3(c) requires you to draw on your understanding of a possible relationship between gross domestic product (GDP) and government spending.

3 A government spends $80 billion and receives 20% of GDP in tax revenue.

    a Calculate at what level of GDP the government would have a balanced budget. [2]

    b Calculate what would be the budget position if the GDP is $500bn. [2]

    c Explain **one** reason why government spending may increase as GDP increases. [2]

≪ RECALL AND CONNECT 1 ≪

How do taxes influence the circular flow of income?

22.2 The national debt

UNDERSTAND THIS TERM

- national debt

1 What is the connection between the budget position and the national debt?

2 What are the disadvantages of a high national debt?

A logical and coherent structure to answering Question 3(b) would be to write a brief paragraph on why the purchase of South African bonds might be recommended on the basis of the information given. This could be followed by a brief paragraph on why the purchase of US government bonds might be recommended, again, on the basis of the information given. Finally, you could write a concluding paragraph on other factors that could be considered.

3

The significance of national debt

As a result of the COVID-19 pandemic, government spending increased in many countries while tax revenue fell. This increased many countries' national debt. For example, South Africa's national debt to GDP ratio increased to 75%, and the USA's national debt to GDP rose to 133%.

Some economists argue that governments should not be concerned about rising national debt as economic growth and inflation would reduce the national debt-to-GDP ratio in the future. Other economists, however, argue that governments should be worried. Interest rates rose in 2022, and there will be pressures on many governments in the future to spend more on healthcare and state pensions. They point out the importance of maintaining other governments', financial institutions' and individuals' confidence in a government's ability to service and repay national debt.

---

a   Explain how economic growth and inflation can reduce the national debt-to-GDP ratio.   [3]

b   Assess, from the information given, whether you would advise someone to lend to the South African government or to the US government.   [6]

REFLECTION

How did you decide what relevant economics could be applied in your answer to Question 3(b)? The data and Question 3(a) may have helped you.

≪ RECALL AND CONNECT 2 ≪

Is interest paid to foreign holders of government bonds an injection or a leakage from the circular flow of income?

22.3 Taxation

1   Who is responsible for paying indirect taxes?

2   Why may an increase in income tax reduce the inflation rate whereas an increase in a general sales tax may increase the inflation rate?

3 Copy and complete Table 22.1:

	Regressive tax	Proportional tax	Progressive tax
Amount of tax paid as income rises			Increases
% of income paid as income rises		Stays constant	
Effect on mrt of a rise in income			
Relationship between art and mrt			
Example		Flat tax	
Effect on distribution of income			

Table 22.1: A comparison of regressive, proportional and progressive taxes

4 A country has an income tax system which imposes 0% tax on the first $15 000 earned, 10% on the next $10 000 earned, 25% on the next $10 000 and 50% on income over $35 000.

    a Calculate:

        i the amount of tax someone earning $20 000 would pay. [1]

        ii the art and mrt a person who earns $40 000 would pay. [3]

    b Explain whether the tax system is progressive, proportional or regressive. [2]

UNDERSTAND THESE TERMS

- specific taxes
- tax avoidance
- tax evasion

≪ RECALL AND CONNECT 3 ≪

Sin taxes may be imposed on demerit goods. Why do governments try to discourage the consumption of demerit goods?

22.4 Government spending

1   What is an example of current government spending and what is an example of capital government spending on a state-run fire service?

2   Why are transfer payments a form of non-exhaustive government spending?

3   What are **two** reasons why a government may decide to increase its spending?

≪ RECALL AND CONNECT 4 ≪

What is the difference between public and merit goods?

22.5 Expansionary and contractionary fiscal policy

UNDERSTAND THESE TERMS

- expansionary fiscal policy
- contractionary fiscal policy
- discretionary fiscal policy

1   What are the **two** main reasons why corporate tax revenue may rise? How are these reasons related to automatic stabilisers and discretionary fiscal policy?

2   Why might contractionary fiscal policy increase the inflation rate?

All your answers should be based on your understanding of economics and should make use of economic terms and analysis. You should not base your answers on general knowledge. For example, you cannot provide a good answer to Question 3(c) unless you understand how an increase in income tax can affect, for inflation. It would not be sufficient to write about how an increase in income tax may be unpopular.

3

India's 2022–23 budget plans

India's finance minister, Nirmala Sitharaman, announced in the 2022–23 budget plans to spend more on infrastructure. This involved more spending on highways, cargo terminals, subsidies for solar panel production and affordable housing. However, interest payments would remain the highest item of government spending. Interest payments have accounted for a quarter of government spending for some time. In 2022–23, it was expected to rise to 27% of all government spending.

The government also expected tax revenue to rise, although it was forecast that there would be a budget deficit equivalent to 6.4% of GDP. With an unemployment rate of 8.2%, the government did not plan to increase income tax rates. It did announce a tax on virtual digital assets. Income from the transfer of cryptocurrencies and non-fungible tokens would be taxed at a rate of 30%.

UNDERSTAND THESE TERMS

- current government spending
- capital government spending
- exhaustive government spending
- non-exhaustive government spending

a Explain **one** possible opportunity cost of government spending on interest payments. [2]

b Explain whether the Indian government was planning to increase or reduce aggregate demand in 2022–23. [3]

c Assess whether an increase in income tax would benefit an economy. [8]

SELF-ASSESSMENT CHECKLIST

Let's revisit the Knowledge focus and Exam skills focus for this chapter. Decide how confident you are with each statement.

Now I can	Show it	Needs more work	Almost there	Confident to move on
define the meaning of fiscal policy	Describe what 'fiscal policy' means.			
define the meaning of a government's budget	Describe what is included in a government's budget.			
explain the difference between a government budget deficit and a government budget surplus	Describe the relationship between government spending and taxation in both cases.			
explain the meaning and significance of the national debt	Outline how the national debt arises and how it may influence government policy.			
explain the difference between indirect and direct taxes	Outline, with an example, the difference between indirect and direct taxes.			
explain the difference between progressive, regressive and proportional taxes	Produce a revision card on how the percentage of tax paid determines whether taxes are progressive, regressive or proportional.			
explain rates of tax: marginal and average rates of tax (mrt, art)	Calculate mrt and art if income rises from $400 to $500 and the tax paid rises from $50 to $100 and decide what type of tax this is.			
analyse the reasons for taxation	Explore the reasons why governments impose taxes.			

CONTINUED

explain the difference between current and capital government spending	Give an example of current and capital spending.			
analyse the reasons for government spending	Give **four** aims of government spending.			
explain the difference between expansionary and contractionary fiscal policy	Outline the difference between expansionary and contractionary fiscal policy.			
discuss, using AD/AS analysis, the impact of expansionary and contractionary fiscal policy on equilibrium level of national income, the level of real output, the price level and employment.	Draw an AD/AS diagram showing the effects of expansionary fiscal policy on the macroeconomy and an AD/AS diagram showing the effects of contractionary fiscal policy on the macroeconomy.			
present knowledge clearly and coherently	Produce a brief plan to a question on fiscal policy; e.g., analyse how expansionary fiscal policy could reduce unemployment.			
understand what knowledge I need to demonstrate.	Apply relevant economic theory in answering the question for which you have produced a plan.			

23 Monetary policy

EXAM SKILLS FOCUS

In this chapter you will:

- show that you can recognise the progress you are making

- learn to reduce test anxiety by taking part in revision with other students.

As you work through your course, you will find that your understanding and skills in answering exam questions develop. You will gain satisfaction from the progress you are making. The progress will not always be smooth, but you will have a number of opportunities to apply the same concepts to different situations. To improve performance, people in a range of activities practise and practise some more. For example, footballers practise taking penalties. They know how well they are doing not only by the number that they score but also how confident they feel in taking penalties.

One way of reducing test anxiety is to make revision fun. Revising with another student may be more enjoyable and more productive than revising on your own. You could, for example, produce a quiz on a topic for other students.

23.1 What is monetary policy?

1 Why are fiscal policy and monetary policy sometimes known as demand-side policies?

2 Which institution usually operates monetary policy?

≪ RECALL AND CONNECT 1 ≪

Why is price stability an aim for governments throughout the world?

UNDERSTAND THESE TERMS

- central bank
- commercial banks
- monetary policy

23.2 The tools of monetary policy

1 What is the repo rate?

2 How do commercial banks create money?

3 What are the **two** key reasons why a central bank might impose credit regulations?

≪ RECALL AND CONNECT 2 ≪

What is the real rate of interest?

UNDERSTAND THESE TERMS

- interest rates
- money supply
- credit regulations

23.3 The difference between expansionary and contractionary monetary policy

1 Copy the following text and fill in the missing words.

Expansionary monetary policy aims to increase aggregate _____. A _____ bank may _____ the rate of interest or _____ the money supply to encourage an increase in consumer expenditure and investment. Higher spending may encourage firms to expand and _____ more workers. As well as reducing unemployment, it may increase _____, but it runs the risk of causing _____ inflation.

In contrast, contractionary monetary policy may be used to increase price _____. Tighter _____ regulations may be used and the interest rate may be _____. Such a policy may be adopted when the economy is operating close to _____ capacity.

23.4 The impact of expansionary and contractionary monetary policy

1 Why might a rise in the rate of interest reduce demand-pull inflation?

2 What are **two** reasons why a reduction in the interest rate may not increase consumer expenditure?

Question 3 will help you to assess the progress you are making in interpreting line graphs.

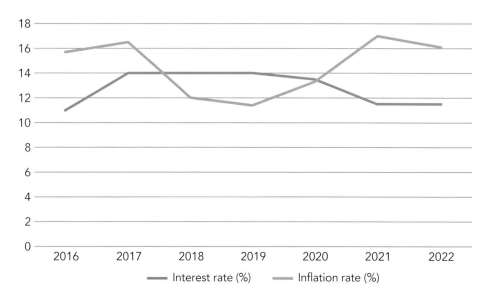

Figure 23.1: Nigerian interest rate and inflation rate 2016–2022

3 **a** Identify the period of time when the Nigerian central bank appeared to have operated an expansionary monetary policy. [2]

    b Assess the relationship between changes in the interest rate and inflation rate. [6]

23.5 The effectiveness of monetary policy

1   Why might commercial banks not keep to limits on bank lending?

2   Why might a rise in the interest rate reduce economic growth?

You may find Question 3(a) relatively straightforward. Do not worry if you find Question 3(b) and Question 3(c) more challenging. You will learn from answering the questions and thinking about how different groups can be affected by inflation and the relationship between the interest rate and house prices. You may find it useful to do some research on how different groups in your country have been affected by inflation and how interest rate changes have affected house prices.

You could also produce a quiz on monetary policy. You could try this out on two of your fellow students who could compete against each other.

3

> **Causes and consequences of interest rate rises in Australia in 2022**
>
> Between July and September 2022, the Reserve Bank of Australia raised the interest rate three times. The central bank was concerned about the accelerating inflation rate. In September the inflation rate had reached 6.1%. This was outside the country's inflation rate target of 2–3%. Australians experienced a number of problems resulting from the increase in the cost of living. However, some were also worried about the fall in house prices which occurred after the interest rate rises.

a   Identify **two** monetary policy tools the Reserve Bank of Australia could have used to reduce inflation.   [2]

b   Explain why Australian households may have suffered as a result of inflation **and** consider whether all Australians would have suffered.   [4]

c   Assess whether an increase in the interest rate may reduce house prices.   [6]

In answering Question 4(b), remember to refer to the diagram in the text of your answer.

4   a   Explain what is meant by contractionary monetary policy **and** consider what is likely to be the aim of contractionary monetary policy.   [8]

b   Assess, using an AD/AS diagram or diagrams, whether expansionary fiscal policy will increase economic growth.   [12]

REFLECTION

How confident were you in answering these questions? Look back at your answers and consider whether you interpreted the command words correctly and make sure you included relevant economics in your answers. You might also want to consider whether you could use any of the information included in your answers in a quiz.

SELF-ASSESSMENT CHECKLIST

Let's revisit the Knowledge focus and Exam skills focus for this chapter.
Decide how confident you are with each statement.

Now I can	Show it	Needs more work	Almost there	Confident to move on
define the meaning of monetary policy	Describe the meaning of 'monetary policy'.			
explain the main tools of monetary policy, including interest rates, the money supply and credit regulations	Produce a table showing how monetary policy may affect national output, price level and employment.			
explain the difference between expansionary and contractionary monetary policy	Outline the difference between the two types of policy.			
discuss, using AD/AS analysis, the impact of expansionary and contractionary monetary policy on equilibrium level of national income, the real level of output, the price level and employment	Draw an AD/AS diagram to show the effect of expansionary monetary policy on the macroeconomy and an AD/AS diagram to show the effect of a contractionary monetary policy.			
recognise the progress I am making	Explain to another student the difference between monetary policy and fiscal policy.			
learn to reduce test anxiety by taking part in revision with other students.	Produce a revision activity that is enjoyable for another student to complete.			

24 Supply-side policy

EXAM SKILLS FOCUS

In this chapter you will:

- further practise answering questions with the command word 'consider'

- show that you understand the command word 'analyse' and answer an 'analyse' question.

'Consider' means to review and respond to given information. This involves interpreting information and thinking carefully before making a decision.

The command word 'analyse' means to examine in detail to show meaning, identify elements and the relationship between them. Analysis is a high-order thinking skill that goes beyond the straightforward recall of knowledge. The high-order thinking skill of analysing involves providing links of reasoning. These links may be connected by words including 'because', 'causing', 'leads to' and 'results in'.

24.1 Supply-side policy objectives

1 Copy and complete Table 24.1.

	Fiscal and monetary policies	Supply-side policy
Operates on		The supply side of the economy
Aggregate demand/ aggregate supply	Increase or decrease aggregate demand	
Productive capacity		Increases productive capacity
Production possibility curve	Moves a point within a curve to a new position	

Table 24.1: Comparison of government policies

REFLECTION

How did Question 1 make you think about the diagrams you could use to illustrate the effects of fiscal, monetary and supply-side policies?

2 What is the difference between short-run and long-run aggregate supply?

24.2 Supply-side policy tools

1 Why is a cut in corporation tax likely to increase investment?

2 Why might immigration increase productive capacity?

If an exam question asks you to 'identify', remember that no extra marks would be given for explanation.

3 Identify **three** supply-side policy tools that increase government intervention and **three** supply-side policy tools that decrease government intervention.   [6]

≪ RECALL AND CONNECT 1 ≪

What are the **two** main tools of fiscal policy?

24.3 The impact of supply-side policy tools on the macroeconomy

1   How might trade union reform reduce disruption to output?

Question 2(a) has the command word 'consider'. This indicates that you need to think about the information and make a judgement. Question 2(b) has the command word 'analyse'. This indicates that you need to develop links between the points you make. Analysis does not require you to evaluate. In this case, you do not have to assess reasons why support for technological improvement may **not** improve Brazil's macroeconomic performance or the extent to which the policy tool may be successful. You may find that an AD/AS diagram may strengthen your analysis.

2

2021	Brazil	World average
Economic growth rate	4.6%	5.8%
Inflation rate	8.3%	3.4%
Unemployment rate	14.4%	6.2%
Current account balance as % of GDP	−1.7%	–

Table 24.2: Macroeconomic data on selected countries

Source: World Bank website

   a   Consider the extent to which Table 24.2 suggests Brazil's macroeconomic performance was below average in 2021. [3]

   b   Analyse, using the data in the table, how government support for technological improvement could improve Brazil's macroeconomic performance. [8]

REFLECTION

How well do you think you did in interpreting the command words 'consider' and 'analyse'? Look back at your answer to Question 2(a) and check that you came to a decision based on the evidence provided. Also check that your answer to Question 2(b) provided relevant links between points.

3   **a**   Identify an opportunity cost of a government investing in the rail network. [1]

   b   Explain how investment in the rail network can benefit firms. [3]

≪ RECALL AND CONNECT 2 ≪

Why do governments seek to keep unemployment low?

24.4 The effectiveness of supply-side policies

1   Copy and complete the mind map in Figure 24.1, which covers the main features of supply-side policy.

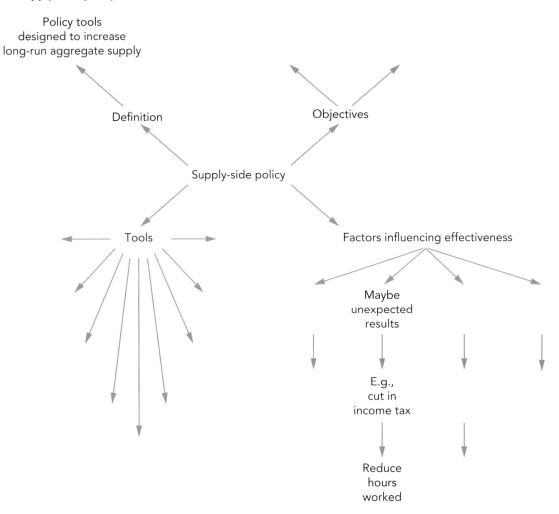

Figure 24.1: Supply-side policy

2   Why might a cut in corporation tax increase corporation tax revenue?

3

Vertical farming

Research is being undertaken in new methods of farming and farming equipment in universities throughout the world. The UAE and USA are two of the leading countries in the development of vertical farming. Dubai, for example, currently has the world's largest vertical farm. With both private sector investment and government subsidies, a number of other countries are developing vertical farming.

Vertical faming involves growing fruit and vegetables in rows on top of each other, often in inner city buildings and using advanced technology. The location means that the fruit and vegetables grown can get to consumers quickly. Growing crops in vertical rows, the use of advanced technology and the elimination of the effects of changes in weather conditions are resulting in high yields. Output per resource unit is reaching record levels. Significantly less water and labour is used, although with extensive use of artificial lighting, a large amount of energy is used.

a   Identify, using evidence from the information given, **two** ways a government can promote technological development.   [2]

b   Explain what evidence there is in the information above that productivity is higher in vertical faming than traditional farming.   [2]

c   Assess whether vertical farming is likely to increase in the future.   [6]

SELF-ASSESSMENT CHECKLIST

Let's revisit the Knowledge focus and Exam skills focus for this chapter.
Decide how confident you are with each statement.

Now I can	Show it	Needs more work	Almost there	Confident to move on
define the meaning of supply-side policy in terms of its effects on LRAS curve	Describe how supply-side policy seeks to shift the LRAS curve to the right.			
explain the objectives of supply-side policy (to increase productivity and productive capacity)	Produce a flow chart showing how **one** supply-side policy tool could increase productivity and output.			
analyse the tools of supply-side policy, including training, infrastructure development and support for technological improvement	Outline how **three** supply-side policy tools could increase macroeconomic performance.			

CONTINUED

discuss, using AD/AS analysis, the impact of supply-side policy on equilibrium national income, the level of real output, the price level and employment	Produce a table comparing the effectiveness of **three** supply-side policy tools.			
further practise answering questions with the command word 'consider'	Describe the meaning of 'consider' to another student.			
understand the command word 'analyse' and answer an 'analyse' question.	Produce an analyse question on the use of education as a supply-side policy tool.			

Exam practice 5

This section contains both past paper questions from previous Cambridge exams and practice questions. These questions draw together your knowledge on a range of topics that you have covered up to this point and will help you prepare for your assessment.

For Question 1(a) work through the question first, then compare your answer to the example student response and commentary. For Question 1(b) read the question, the example student response and the commentary provided. Then, in Question 1(c), write an improved answer to Question 1(b), using the guidance in the commentary to help you.

1   a   Explain, with the help of diagrams, a movement along an aggregate supply curve and a shift in the aggregate supply curve. Consider how these changes differ. [8]

Adapted from Cambridge International AS & A Level Economics (9708) Paper 21 Q4a, November 2019

Example student response	Examiner comments
A movement along an aggregate supply curve is caused by a change in the price level. If the price level rises, aggregate supply will extend. The country's producers will be willing and able to supply more at a higher price level. The diagram shows that a rise in the price level from P to P_1 causes AS to extend from Y to Y_1. 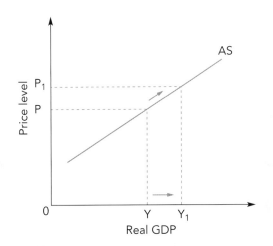 An aggregate supply curve may shift to the right or the left. A shift to the right indicates an increase in aggregate supply. The diagram shows AS increasing to AS_1.	**AO1 Knowledge and understanding** The answer does show an awareness of a movement along an AS curve, a shift in an AS curve and how the diagrams are labelled. *3/3* **AO2 Analysis** The changes are shown accurately on the diagrams, and there is relevant written analysis. *3/3* **AO3 Evaluation** There is some clear assessment of the difference. However, it would have been strengthened by an example of a cause of a shift in the aggregate supply curve. *1/2* *Total: 7/8 marks*

Example student response	Examiner comments
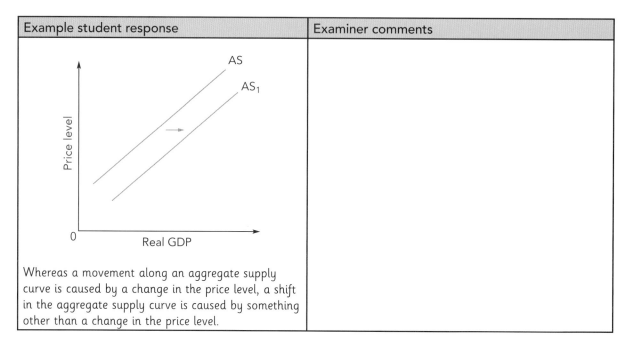 Whereas a movement along an aggregate supply curve is caused by a change in the price level, a shift in the aggregate supply curve is caused by something other than a change in the price level.	

b Assess whether supply-side policy tools are likely to be effective in increasing employment in an economy. [12]

Adapted from Cambridge International AS & A Level Economics (9708) Paper 21 Q4b, November 2019

Example student response	Examiner comments
Supply-side policy may increase or decrease the aggregate supply. To reduce unemployment, a government may spend money on education. It could, for example, train more teachers so that class sizes decrease. If education is successful, structural unemployment could decrease. When students leave school and university, they may be more productive and skilled. This could make them more geographically and occupationally mobile. Their greater skills and greater ability to find jobs may increase employment. However, more government spending on education may not always work. The government may provide more money for teachers to be employed but the teachers recruited may not be very good. The skills of workers may rise, but if there is a lack of demand for goods and services, there is also likely to be a lack of demand for workers. To increase employment during a recession it is likely to be more effective to use expansionary fiscal and monetary policies.	**AO1 Knowledge and understanding and AO2 Analysis** The answer does not start well. Supply-side policy does not aim to reduce aggregate supply. The answer only explores one supply-side policy tool, but the question asks for policy tools, so at least two policy tools should have been examined. The question is also about employment, and at the start of the answer, the student writes about unemployment. The student should have read the question more carefully. This would have enabled the student to write a more relevant answer. The answer would also have benefitted from greater depth and width. *2/8* **AO3 Evaluation** There is some clear evaluation, but it is limited as only one policy tool is examined. *2/4* *Total: 4/12 marks*

c Write an improved answer to Question 1(b).

Now that you have worked through Question 1, here is a similar practice question which you should attempt. Use the guidance in the commentaries in this section to help you as you answer the question.

2 a Explain, with the help of diagrams, a movement along an aggregate demand curve and a shift in the aggregate demand curve. Consider how these changes may differ.   [8]

   b Assess whether demand-side policy tools are likely to be effective in reducing unemployment in economy.   [12]

Questions 3(a) and 3(b) have example student responses and commentaries provided. For each part of the question, work through the question first, then compare your answer to the example student response and commentary. In Question 3(c) you will be asked to write a conclusion to the example student response provided in Question 3(b).

3 a Explain using aggregate demand and aggregate supply diagrams the distinction between cost-push inflation and demand-pull inflation **and** consider **one** cause of each.   [8]

   Adapted from Cambridge International AS & A Level Economics (9708) Paper 21 Q4a, March 2020

Example student response	Examiner comments
Cost-push inflation occurs as a result of increases in firms' costs of production. Higher costs of production will have a decrease in aggregate supply. The diagram shows that a decrease in aggregate supply will cause the price level to rise to P_1. 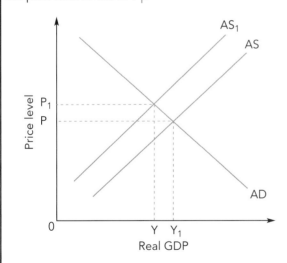 Cost-push inflation is accompanied by a fall in real GDP, at least in the short run.	**AO1 Knowledge and understanding** The answer shows good knowledge and understanding of both cost-push inflation and demand-pull inflation. However, an example could have been given of a cause of an increase in aggregate demand, for example, an increase in consumer expenditure due to a rise in consumers, confidence. 2/3 **AO2 Analysis** There is good analysis with accurate diagrams. 3/3

Example student response	Examiner comments
In contrast to cost-push inflation, demand-pull inflation is the result of increases in aggregate demand not matched by an increase in aggregate supply. The diagram shows the AD curve shifting to the right, causing the price level to rise to P_1. 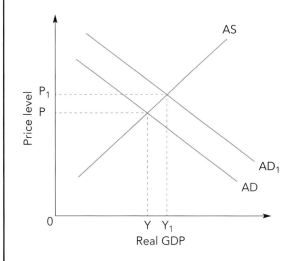 Demand-pull inflation is likely to be associated with an increase in real GDP, at least in the short run. Cost-push inflation may be caused by wages increasing at a faster rate than productivity. This will increase labour cost per unit. The two main causes of cost-push inflation are usually increases in wages and increases in fuel costs. Demand-pull inflation may be caused by an increase in any of the components of aggregate demand. So, whereas cost-push inflation results from an increase in one or more of the costs of production, demand-pull inflation results from an increase in one or more of the components of aggregate demand.	**AO3 Evaluation** A comparison is made between the causes and between possible effects on the price level and real GDP of the two types of inflation. *2/2* *Total: 7/8 marks*

b Assess whether monetary policy measures are always effective in correcting a high rate of inflation. [12]

Adapted from Cambridge International AS & A Level Economics (9708) Paper 21 Q4b, March 2020

Example student response	Examiner comments
The main monetary policy measures are changes in the interest rate, changes in the money supply and changes in credit restrictions. To reduce inflation, monetary policy will seek to reduce aggregate demand. An increase in the interest rate may reduce aggregate demand for a number of reasons. It can reduce consumer expenditure as it will cost more to borrow and it will be more rewarding to save. The higher cost of borrowing and higher return from saving may also discourage investment. In addition, firms may spend less on capital goods as they may expect consumer expenditure to be lower. Net exports may fall if the higher interest rate results in a rise in the exchange rate and so a rise in export prices and a fall in import prices. A higher rate of interest may also reduce government spending as it will be more expensive for the government to borrow to cover a budget deficit.	**AO1 Knowledge and understanding** The answer shows good knowledge and understanding of monetary policy. It identifies three relevant policy measures or tools. **AO2 Analysis** The answer provides clear and relevant analysis of how a higher interest rate, a reduction in the money supply and tighter restrictions on bank lending may reduce a high rate of inflation. *AO1 and AO2: 8/8* **AO3 Evaluation** The answer does consider why the measures may not always be effective. However, it would have benefitted from a concluding paragraph. *2/4* *Total: 10/12 marks*
A reduction in the money supply, or at least a reduction in the growth of the money supply and tighter restrictions on bank lending may also reduce aggregate demand by lowering consumer expenditure and investment.	
However, contractionary monetary policy may not correct a high rate of inflation. If households and firms are optimistic about the future, a rise in the interest rate may not reduce a rise in aggregate demand. Commercial banks may also seek to get round restrictions on bank lending.	
Monetary policy is a demand-side policy and is unlikely to be effective against cost-push inflation. Indeed, a higher interest may increase firms' cost of production. Although, it is possible that a higher interest rate which results in a higher exchange rate could reduce the cost of imported raw materials.	

c Write a conclusion to the answer in Question 3(b).

Here is another past paper question which you should attempt. Use the guidance in the commentaries in this section to help you as you answer the question.

4 Assess whether interest rate policy will prevent a rise in inflation [12]

Adapted from Cambridge International AS & A Level Economics (9708) Paper 42 Q5b, March 2009

Questions 5(a) and 5(b) have example student responses and commentaries provided. For each part, read the question, the example student response and the commentary provided. Then, in Question 5(c), write an improved answer to Questions 5(a) and 5(b), using the guidance in the commentaries to help you.

5 a Explain what is meant by deflation and use aggregate demand and aggregate supply diagrams to consider how it might arise in an economy. [8]

Adapted from Cambridge International AS & A Level Economics (9708) Paper 22 Q4a, June 2021

Example student response	Examiner comments
Deflation is a sustained fall in the price level. It means that the value of each unit of money rises. For example, each US dollar will buy more. Deflation is caused by a fall in aggregate demand. The diagram shows the AD curve shifting to the left. 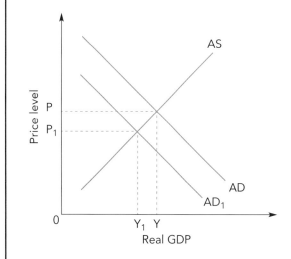 AD may decrease as a result of a decrease in household sending or firms' investment. It will cause national output to fall and unemployment to rise.	**AO1 Knowledge and understanding** The answer starts with a good definition. It then recognises that deflation may be caused by a decrease in aggregate demand. Note when using an abbreviation such as AD, it is useful to first include it in brackets after the word or words written in full. The answer shows an awareness of the appropriate labels. It does, however, not show an awareness that deflation may be caused by a decrease in aggregate supply. *2/3* **AO2 Analysis** There is some analysis based on one diagram. However, it is a partial answer. The use of the word 'diagrams' (plural) in the question should suggest to a student that there should be another diagram. *2/3* **AO3 Evaluation** The answer mentions a decrease in household spending or investment but does not examine why these may occur and does not examine why aggregate supply may increase. *0/2* *Total: 4/8 marks*

b Assess whether a government should use monetary policy
or fiscal policy to solve the problem of deflation in an economy. [12]

*Adapted from Cambridge International AS & A Level Economics
(9708) Paper 22 Q4b, June 2021*

Example student response	Examiner comments
A government could use monetary policy or fiscal policy to solve the problem of deflation in an economy. Either type of policy could increase aggregate demand. Monetary policy could do this by lowering the interest rate or by increasing the money supply. Fiscal policy would increase aggregate demand by cutting taxes or by increasing government spending. Expansionary fiscal policy or expansionary monetary policy could prevent the AD curve shifting to the left. A lower interest rate, for example, could encourage people to spend more and firms to invest rather than reducing their spending. There is a risk that if the policy tools adopted are too successful in reversing the fall in aggregate demand, inflation may replace deflation as a problem.	**AO1 Knowledge and understanding** The answer shows some awareness that it would be expansionary fiscal policy and/or expansionary monetary policy that would be used. **AO2 Analysis** The answer provides brief analysis of how such policy approaches may solve the problem of deflation. However, it does not fully analyse, for example, why lower taxes or a lower interest rate may encourage people to spend more. The inclusion of an AD/AS diagram might also have been useful. *AO1 and AO2: 4/8* **AO3 Evaluation** The answer recognises that the policy approaches could increase aggregate demand by too much. However, it does not answer the question in a sufficiently critical manner. It does not examine why expansionary demand-side policy may not work and it does not consider whether monetary policy or fiscal policy is more likely to be successful. *1/4* *Total: 5/12 marks*

c Write an improved answer to Questions 5(a) and 5(b).

Here is another practice question which you should attempt. Use the guidance in the
commentaries in this section to help you as you answer the question.

6 Assess whether the use of fiscal policy is the only effective means
of stimulating economic growth. [12]

25 The reasons for international trade

KNOWLEDGE FOCUS

You will answer questions on:

25.1 Absolute and comparative advantage

25.2 The benefits of specialisation and free trade (trade liberalisation)

25.3 Exports, imports and the terms of trade

25.4 Limitations of the theory of absolute and comparative advantage

EXAM SKILLS FOCUS

In this chapter you will:

*   show that you understand when it is useful to give numerical examples

*   show that you can select the questions you can perform best on.

There may be occasions when a numerical example may help your explanation or analysis. It is important to remember that such examples should not be too long.

You have a choice of one question out of two in both Sections B and C of Paper 2: AS Level Data Response and Essays. You should read the questions carefully and you must consider both the **a** and **b** parts. It might be tempting to answer, for example, Question 2 where you think you will do well on the **a** part. However, if you think you would struggle with the **b** part but could do reasonably well on both parts of Question 3, that may be the better option.

25.1 Absolute and comparative advantage

UNDERSTAND THESE TERMS

- factor endowment
- absolute advantage (used in the context of international trade)
- opportunity cost ratio
- comparative advantage (used in the context of international trade)

---

1 Why do countries trade internationally?

2 A country has large deposits of gold. The diagram shows the domestic market for gold and the world supply of gold. The country's gold producers initially only sell on the home market. The country and its gold producers then engage in international trade.

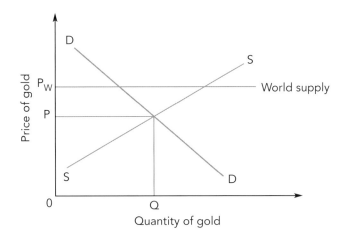

Figure 25.1: The domestic and international market for gold

a Would the country export or import gold?

b Which groups would gain and which groups will lose as a result of the country engaging in international trade?

3 Table 25.1 shows the production possibilities of two products in two countries.

Country Y		Country Z	
Product A	Product B	Product A	Product B
0	96	0	72
8	72	3	54
16	48	6	36
24	24	9	18
32	0	12	0

Table 25.1: Production possibilities in two fictional countries

a   Which country has the absolute advantage in producing Product A and Product B?

b   In which product does Country Y have a comparative advantage?

c   What would be an acceptable exchange rate between the two countries?

REFLECTION

Did you get any part of Question 3 wrong? If you did, think carefully about the specific actions you could take to build up your understanding of absolute advantage and comparative advantage.

《 RECALL AND CONNECT 1 《

What are **three** influences on where firms buy their raw materials from?

25.2 The benefits of specialisation and free trade (trade liberalisation)

1   How may firms benefit from free trade?

2   How does a trading possibility curve diagram differ from a production possibility diagram?

《 RECALL AND CONNECT 2 《

How may free international trade affect consumer surplus?

25.3 Exports, imports and the terms of trade

UNDERSTAND THESE TERMS

- imports
- exports
- terms of trade

---

1 Copy and complete Table 25.2 on the causes of a favourable movement in the terms of trade. Use a different word or term each time.

Export prices	Import prices
	decrease
	decrease
increase	unchanged
increase by more	
	decrease by more

Table 25.2: Combination of price movements that would cause a favourable movement in the terms of trade

2 Copy and complete the following combination of flow charts:

Rise in global incomes

↓

Higher _____ for country's exports

↓

Rise in terms of trade ratio

↓

Favourable movement in the terms of trade

↓

May be accompanied by a rise in output and employment

Higher costs of production

↓

Higher _____ rate

↓

_____ in terms of trade ratio

↓

_____ movement in the terms of trade

↓

May be accompanied by a _____ in output and employment

≪ RECALL AND CONNECT 3 ≪

What effect will a fall in price have on revenue if demand is price-inelastic?

25.4 Limitations of the theory of absolute and comparative advantage

1 What are **two** reasons why a country may not switch resources to producing a product that it finds it has a comparative advantage in?

2 What type of unemployment may arise as a result of countries adapting to a change in comparative advantage?

Before answering Question 3, think about whether it would be helpful to include any numerical examples in your answers. While it would be possible to use a numerical example in Question 3(b)(i), the question only has two marks and absolute advantage can be explained without an example. In contrast, in answering an essay question on absolute and comparative advantage it would be helpful to use a numerical example. But remember not to devote too much time giving long examples. One simple table with two countries and two products is often sufficient. Remember this when you answer Question 5(a) in Section 27.6.

3

> ### The growth of Vietnam's textile and clothing industry
>
> Vietnam's textile and clothing industry has grown more than 10% a year over the last decade. It is one of the country's largest industries and is a major contributor to the country's exports and impressive economic growth rate.
>
> There are a number of reasons for the industry's success. It has a large supply of skilled and relatively low-cost labour, and the firms in the industry have invested heavily in the latest capital equipment. Government policies have also tended to favour the industry, making it easy to set up new firms.
>
> The industry does, however, face a number of challenges. These include competition including in its largest export market, the USA. Its main competitors are firms in Bangladesh, China and the European Union.

    a   Explain **one** advantage Vietnam has in textile and clothing production.   [2]

    b   Explain:

        i   how an economist would assess whether China or Vietnam has the absolute advantage in textile and clothing production.   [2]

        ii   whether Vietnam should stop producing textiles and clothing if it is found that China does have an absolute advantage.   [3]

    c   Assess whether Vietnam's output of textiles and clothing will fall in the future.   [6]

REFLECTION

If you were given a choice between answering this question and Question 3 in Section 24.4 in the previous chapter, which would you choose? Remember you should consider how you would perform on all the question parts.

    4   **a**   Explain why governments aim for price stability **and** consider whether price stability will achieve international competitiveness.   [8]

        b   Assess, using an AD/AS diagram or diagrams, whether supply-side policy would be effective in reducing inflation.   [12]

SELF-ASSESSMENT CHECKLIST

Let's revisit the Knowledge focus and Exam skills focus for this chapter.
Decide how confident you are with each statement.

Now I can	Show it	Needs more work	Almost there	Confident to move on
explain the difference between absolute and comparative advantage	Describe the difference between absolute and comparative advantage.			
explain the benefits of specialisation and free trade (trade liberalisation), including the trading possibility curve	List the advantages of specialisation and free trade.			
explain how the terms of trade are measured	Calculate the terms of trade if the index of export prices is 96 and the index of import prices is 120.			
analyse the causes and impact of changes in the terms of trade	Produce a mind map on how changes in the terms of trade can affect an economy.			
discuss the limitations of the theories of absolute and comparative advantage	Identify **four** reasons why countries do not always base their output and trade on absolute and comparative advantage.			
understand when it is useful to give numerical examples	Produce a table with two countries and two products showing the difference between absolute and comparative advantage.			
select the questions I can perform best on.	Discuss with another student which past paper questions you would select from Paper 9708/22 November 2023.			

26 Protectionism

EXAM SKILLS FOCUS

In this chapter you will:

- show that you can reduce test anxiety by including breaks in your revision

- show that you can navigate synoptic questions.

Anyone can get anxious over performance and progress. One reason that this happens is because you get tired. It is important that you build breaks into your work. Quite often, having a break and then coming back to a question when you are feeling fresher enables you to think more clearly.

Synoptic questions are ones where you need to bring together your knowledge from different areas of your course. Navigating synoptic questions involves other skills. For example, it requires you to understand what knowledge you need to draw on and how topics are linked.

26.1 Protectionism

1   What is the aim of protectionism?

2   What is free international trade?

3   How does price elasticity of demand influence the effectiveness of import tariffs?

≪ RECALL AND CONNECT 1 ≪

a   What is the formula for price elasticity of demand?

b   What are the **five** degrees of price elasticity of demand?

26.2 Tools of protection and their impact

1   Why are import tariffs regressive?

2   Why is the granting of export subsidies sometimes called unfair competition?

3   Complete the answers for the following crossword in your notebook.
    You might find it useful to have a break when you have finished this.

Across

1   A term for taxes on imports (6,6).

4   During a trade war it is unlikely any country will win.
    What are they more likely to do? (4).

7   Restriction of competition from foreign industries (13).

9   What a trade ban aims to do to imports (4).

10 The number of types of taxes on imports or exports (3).

13 A fixed sum tax on imports or exports (8).

15 A product sold to another country (6).

16 The answer to the question 'Are voluntary export restraints a form of trade
    protection?' (3).

17 A tax on imports or exports (6).

19 What foreign firms may decide to do to import taxes on their products to stay price
    competitive. (6).

21 What trade restrictions may do to the range of products available to
    consumers (5,6).

23 The answer to the question, 'Is there any country which does not impose trade
    restrictions?' (2).

26 What will increase if a tax is imposed on the import of raw materials (4).

28 The most extreme form of limit on imports or exports (7).

30 The type of revenue that may be increased as a result of a trade restriction (3).

31 A description of an import tax that is late in being paid (7).

32 Restrictions on the purchase of foreign currency (8,7).

Down

1   The ability to produce a product at a lower opportunity cost than others (11,9).

2   What a government seeks to do to foreign industries during a trade war (7).

3   The industries that trade restrictions are designed to protect (8).

5   The currency of the European Union (4).

6   A term for excessive administrative burden (3,4).

8   A government tool to increase the price competitiveness of the country's firms (7).

11 Consumers (6).

12 The type of products trade restrictions may seek to ban (7).

14 The degree of PED needed to make a tax on imports reduce import
    expenditure (7).

18 The international exchange of goods and services without any trade
    restrictions (4,5).

20 Prevent the import or export of a product (3).

22 What a government may be trying to do to another country if it cuts off all trade
    with it (7).

24 A trade restriction may be imposed on a foreign monopoly.
    How many firms are there in a monopoly? (3).

25 The type of good a government may impose an export tax on to prevent
    famine (4).

27 A limit on imports or exports (5).

29 A good that is often protected (5).

26.3 The arguments for protectionism

1   What are the **three** types of industry that a government may try to protect?

2   Why may dumping by foreign firms harm a country's consumers?

3   What is the risk of imposing trade restrictions to retaliate against another country's trade restrictions?

4   Why may a government find it difficult to remove trade restrictions?

5   What type of unemployment may be avoided if declining industries are protected?

6   How may imposing import tariffs improve the terms of trade?

26.4 The arguments against protectionism

1   What disadvantages may firms experience as a result of trade restrictions?

2   Why may protectionism lower world output and living standards?

In Question 3(a)(ii), think about a microeconomic concept that you can draw on in your answer and, in Question 3(b), think about a government macroeconomic objective that might be threatened by the sudden removal of trade restrictions. Also, read the questions carefully to ensure, for example, that you pick up on the words 'not' in Question 3(a)(i) and 'sudden' in Question 3(b). When working on these kinds of questions, you may find it useful to underline key words when reading the case study.

3

> ### EU's international trade policy
>
> The European Union is the world's largest importer of agricultural products. Some of the products it imports it has both absolute and comparative disadvantages in due to its natural conditions, particularly its climate. The largest single exporter of agricultural products to the EU is Brazil. Among the products it sells to the EU are coffee, fruit and tobacco.
>
> The EU has imposed large tariffs on agricultural products, but in recent years it has been reducing them. Brazil, with its South American trading partners, has been in negotiations with the EU to reduce trade restrictions. Brazil is currently one of the most protected markets with high tariffs and high quotas.

   a   Explain why the EU:

      i   should not impose trade restrictions on coffee imports from Brazil.   [2]

      ii   should impose trade restrictions on tobacco imports from Brazil.   [2]

   b   Assess whether a country would benefit from the sudden removal of trade restrictions.   [6]

> ### REFLECTION
>
> Were there any of the Question 3 parts that you think you could have answered better? You might find it useful to mark your answers.

SELF-ASSESSMENT CHECKLIST

Let's revisit the Knowledge focus and Exam skills focus for this chapter.
Decide how confident you are with each statement.

Now I can	Show it	Needs more work	Almost there	Confident to move on
define the meaning of protectionism as it relates to international trade	Describe the meaning of 'protectionism'.			
explain the different tools of protection: tariffs, import quotas, export subsidies, embargoes and extensive administrative burden ('red tape')	Produce a revision card with the tools of protection and their definitions.			
analyse the impact of the different tools of protection	Produce a table contrasting the effects of **three** different tools of protection on the macroeconomy.			
discuss the arguments for and against protectionism	Produce a mind map on the arguments for and against protectionism.			
reduce test anxiety by including breaks in my revision	Give yourself at least a ten-minute break after completing each section.			
navigate synoptic questions.	Identify **two** microeconomic concepts that could be used in the case for protecting an infant industry.			

27 Current account of the balance of payments

169 >

EXAM SKILLS FOCUS

In this chapter you will:

- show that you understand the level of depth required in your answers

- show that you can follow instructional text other than command words.

You should by now have become aware of the depth you need to go into in your answers. There are two key guides to this. One is the command words used, and the other is the number of marks awarded. You should, for example, provide more depth on an 'analyse' question with six marks than one with four marks.

You may be asked to provide an example or a diagram in your answer. Examples are most commonly asked for in questions with the command words 'define', 'identify', 'give', 'state' and 'explain'. Diagrams are most commonly asked for in 'analyse' and 'assess' questions.

27.1 What is a country's balance of payments?

1   What are credit items in the balance of payments?

UNDERSTAND THESE TERMS

- balance of payments account
- capital account
- financial account

≪ RECALL AND CONNECT 1 ≪

How might trade restrictions influence the value of credit and debit items in a country's balance of payments?

27.2 Where they will appear in the current account of India's balance of payments

1   Copy and complete Table 27.1, showing where each of the items will appear in India's current account of the balance of payments and whether they are credit or debit items.

	Where they will appear in India's balance of payments				Credit or debit	
	Trade in goods	Trade in services	Primary income	Secondary income	Credit item	Debit item
The sale of Indian information technology services to France						
The purchase by Indian firms of machinery from Germany						
Interest paid by an Indian firm on a loan from a Bangladeshi bank						
The receipt of profit from a branch of an Indian multinational corporation to its headquarters in India						
The sale of tickets to Sri Lankan passengers on a flight operated by an Indian airline						
Financial aid provided by the Indian government to a nearby country which has suffered from widespread flooding						

Table 27.1: Credit and debit items in India's current account of the balance of payments

27.3 Balance and imbalances (deficit and surplus) in the current account of the balance of payments

1 What does a current account deficit mean?

2 What would it mean if a county has a trade in goods and services surplus but a current account deficit?

《 RECALL AND CONNECT 2 《

What influences the products a country exports and imports?

27.4 Current account balance calculations

1 If the secondary balance is –$20 billion, the primary balance is $32 billion, the trade in services balance is $40 billion and the trade in goods balance is –$55 billion, what is the current account balance?

2 From the following information (using New Zealand dollars), set out New Zealand's 2020 current account balance, calculating New Zealand's imports of goods balance, trade in goods balance, primary income balance and inflow of secondary income.

New Zealand's current account balance 2020

Exports of goods $59 587 million, imports of goods $56 389 million, exports of services $18 281 million, imports of services $17 274 million, inflow of primary income $8 863 million, outflow of primary income $14 639 million, outflow of secondary income $3220 million, secondary income balance –$873 million and current account balance –$2444 million.

<< RECALL AND CONNECT 3 <<

What is the difference between a trade in goods and services deficit and a government budget deficit?

27.5 Causes of imbalances in the current account of the balance of payments

1   Why may economic growth result in an increase in a trade in goods deficit?

2   What are **three** causes of a lack of international competitiveness?

3   Why might a country experience a fall in its inflation but a rise in a current account deficit?

4   What is the difference between a cyclical current account surplus and a structural current account surplus?

<< RECALL AND CONNECT 4 <<

a   What is meant by a high income elasticity of demand?

b   What effect may the granting of subsidies to domestic producers have on a country's trade deficit?

27.6 Consequences of imbalances in the current account on the economy

1   Why is a current account deficit sometimes described as people living beyond their means?

2   What effect would an increase in a country's current account surplus have on its aggregate demand?

3   How do economists measure the significance of current account deficits and surpluses?

You should be able to answer Question 4(a) in approximately two minutes.
It is assessing knowledge recall. You should spend approximately six minutes
on Question 4(b), which requires some depth. Question 4(c) requires more depth.
It has the second-highest mark and a high-order command word. You should spend
approximately 12 minutes on this question, some of which will be thinking time.
You may not have thought before about the link between an increase in a country's
savings ratio and its current account balance. However, the analytical skills you have
developed should enable you to think through what the links might be. Question 4(d)
also has a high-order command word and again requires thinking skills. It carries eight
marks, which means that you should spend 16 minutes on it. Note that it also has the
instruction to use an AD/AS diagram. You need to ensure that this is clear, accurate
and referred to in your text.

4

China, India and USA

India usually has a trade in goods deficit. In 2020, this deficit fell largely
because of a decrease in the country's GDP. Its trade in services deficit
also fell. This was also influenced by the fall in the country's real GDP but
was also the result of an increase in export revenue earned by the country's
software services. A major contributor to the country's secondary income
balance was workers' remittances.

The current account balance of all three countries was influenced by a range
of factors over the period shown. One factor was the countries' savings ratios.
China had a significantly higher savings ratio than India and an even higher
one than the USA.

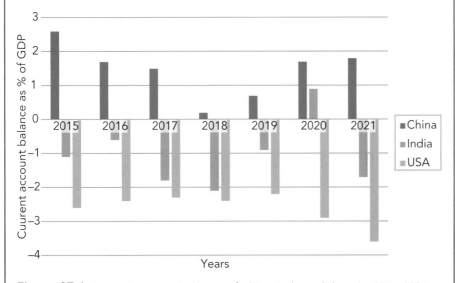

Figure 27.1: Current account balances of China, India and the USA 2015–2021

Source: TradingEconomics.com website for China

a Identify which balance in the current account is not mentioned in the
information. [1]

b Compare the current account balances of China, India and the USA
over the period shown. [3]

c   Consider whether an increase in a country's savings ratio
    will always improve a current account balance.   [6]

d   Assess, using an AD/AS diagram, the effect of an increase in exports
    of services on a country's real GDP.   [8]

REFLECTION

Using diagrams and words to assess changes involves using your brain in
two different ways. How well do you think you did on the last question here?
To what extent could you draw the diagram from memory? How happy were
you with the use of the diagram in your assessment?

In answering Question 5(a), remember the advice in Chapter 25: keep your example
simple. You need to show that you understand the concept, rather than that you can
deal with difficult numbers.

5   a   Explain, with an example, the difference between absolute and
        comparative advantage **and** consider the extent to which comparative
        advantage explains the pattern of international trade.   [8]

    b   Assess whether an economy will benefit from a surplus on the current
        account of its balance of payments.   [12]

SELF-ASSESSMENT CHECKLIST

Let's revisit the Knowledge focus and Exam skills focus for this chapter.
Decide how confident you are with each statement.

Now I can	Show it	Needs more work	Almost there	Confident to move on
explain the components of the current account of the balance of payments	Identify an example of an item that would appear in each of the four components of the current account of the balance of payments.			
calculate the balance of trade in goods, in services and in goods and services and overall current account balance	Calculate the current account balance if the trade in goods balance is $20 billion, trade in services balance is −$5 billion, primary income balance is −$18 billion and secondary income balance is $11 billion.			
analyse the causes of imbalance in the current account of the balance of payments	Produce a table on the causes of a current account deficit and a current account surplus.			

CONTINUED

discuss the consequences of imbalance in the current account of the balance of payments for the domestic and external economy	Produce a flow chart showing how a current account surplus may increase employment.			
understand the level of depth required in my answers	Identify **two** indicators of how much depth is required in an answer.			
follow instructional text other than command words.	Find **two** examples of instructional text from past exam papers and answer one of the questions.			

28 Exchange rates

EXAM SKILLS FOCUS

In this chapter you will:

- practise using mark schemes to understand how to improve your answers

- show that you can improve your answers by regularly testing yourself.

Mark schemes provided by Cambridge Assessment International Education are a useful source of information. It is possible that they may provide you with points you have not thought about and may reinforce your understanding of the difference between, for example, knowledge and understanding, analysis and evaluation.

Testing your knowledge on a regular basis by undertaking revision activities throughout your course will reinforce your knowledge and develop your skills. For example, the more essays you write, the more you will develop the skill of producing a logically structured answer.

28.1 The exchange rate

1   If Indonesia's rupiah–dollar exchange rate changes from 15 000 rupiah = $1 to 14 000 rupiah = $1, has the Indian rupiah risen or fallen in value in terms of US dollars?

2   What would be the change in the price, in US dollars, of an Indonesian export valued at 308 000 rupiah as a result of the change in the exchange rate?

28.2 How a floating exchange rate is determined

UNDERSTAND THIS TERM
• floating exchange rate

1   What is the foreign exchange market?

2   Identify **three** reasons why someone in Pakistan may buy US dollars.   [3]

≪ RECALL AND CONNECT 1 ≪

What is meant by market forces?

28.3 Depreciation and appreciation of a floating exchange rate

UNDERSTAND THESE TERMS
• depreciation
• appreciation

1   What effect does an appreciation of its currency have on a country's export prices and import prices?

2   Draw **two** diagrams to show the two ways depreciation can occur.

3

> **Exchange rate change and the trade in goods and services balance**
>
> A country's exchange rate against the US$ is initially 50 pesos = $1. The country's firms export 50 million products at an average price of 100 pesos. The country imports 60 million products at an average price of $3.
>
> The value of the peso then depreciates to 80 pesos = $1. As a result, exports rise to 90 million and imports fall to 40 million.

Calculate:

a   the initial trade in goods and services balance before the depreciation   [2]

b   the new trade in goods and services balance after the depreciation.   [2]

In what ways do you think answering Question 3 has improved your knowledge of how changes in the exchange rate can affect the trade in goods balance? Are there any actions you could take to improve it further?

《 RECALL AND CONNECT 2 《

What are the **two** key causes of a fall in the price of a good or service?

28.4 The causes of changes in a floating exchange rate

1   Decide whether the following changes would be likely to cause an appreciation or depreciation in the value of the Canadian dollar and explain why.

Change	Appreciation or depreciation	Explanation
An increase in the value of Canadian exports		
An increase in Canadian firms' purchase of imported raw materials		
The US central bank raising the rate of interest		
An increase in the number of Indian firms setting up branches in Canada		
Speculation that the Canadian dollar will fall in value in the future		

Table 28.1: Causes of an appreciation or depreciation in the value of the Canadian dollar

UNDERSTAND THIS TERM

•   hot money flows

《 RECALL AND CONNECT 3 《

What effect will a depreciation in the value of its currency have on a country's terms of trade and its balance of trade?

28.5 The impact of exchange rate changes on the domestic economy

 1 Which firms may gain from an appreciation in the exchange rate?

2 In what circumstances would a depreciation in the exchange rate not increase a country's output?

After answering Question 3, find a past exam paper (e.g., Paper 9708/21 May/June 2019) which contains a question based on a diagram. Answer it and then check the mark scheme to see if there were any points you missed.

3

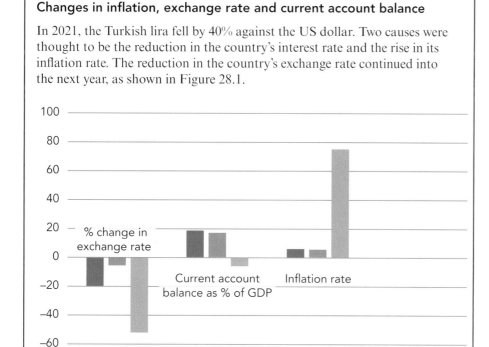

Changes in inflation, exchange rate and current account balance

In 2021, the Turkish lira fell by 40% against the US dollar. Two causes were thought to be the reduction in the country's interest rate and the rise in its inflation rate. The reduction in the country's exchange rate continued into the next year, as shown in Figure 28.1.

Figure 28.1: Percentage change in exchange rate (against the US$), current account balance as % of GDP and inflation rate of three selected countries 2022

a Consider whether an increase in a country's inflation rate may reduce its exchange rate. [4]

b Assess, using Figure 28.1, why countries can have a different relationship between a change in the exchange rate and the current account balance. [6]

REFLECTION

Think through what you did first in answering Question 3(b). How might you change your approach to a diagram interpretation question in the future?

SELF-ASSESSMENT CHECKLIST

Let's revisit the Knowledge focus and Exam skills focus for this chapter.
Decide how confident you are with each statement.

Now I can	Show it	Needs more work	Almost there	Confident to move on
define the meaning of an exchange rate	Describe the meaning of an exchange rate.			
explain how a floating exchange rate is determined	Draw a diagram to show how a floating exchange rate is determined.			
explain the difference between depreciation and appreciation of a floating exchange rate	Define a depreciation and an appreciation of a floating exchange rate.			
analyse the causes of changes in a floating exchange rate	Identify **four** causes of a depreciation in a floating exchange rate.			
discuss, using AD/AS analysis, the impact of exchange rate changes on the domestic economy's equilibrium national income and the level of real output, the price level and employment	Draw an AD/AS diagram to show the effect of an appreciation in the exchange rate on the macroeconomy.			
practice using mark schemes to understand how to improve my answers	After answering a question on the exchange rate from a past exam question, check the answer and the mark scheme. Note down what you learn from doing this.			
improve my answers by regularly testing myself.	Produce a flow chart showing the sequence of changes between a depreciation in the exchange rate and a fall in a current account deficit.			

29 Policies to correct imbalances in the current account of the balance of payments

It is important not to rush **'assess'** questions. Assess questions require you to analyse economic information, arguments and theories and then to evaluate these. To answer an 'assess' question effectively, there are a number of stages that you should go through. You should first check carefully what the question is asking. You then should consider what information you need to draw on. After that, you should organise the information either just in your mind or by producing a brief plan. Considering how you will develop the points you have identified should help you make a judgement.

Preparation reduces test anxiety. Going into an exam knowing that you have prepared adequately for it will give you confidence. This preparation will come from undertaking active revision, including practising answers, throughout your course.

29.1 Government policy objective of stability of the current account

1   Why might a government aim for a balance on the current account of the balance of payments in the long run?

≪ RECALL AND CONNECT 1 ≪

What are **three** other government macroeconomic policy objectives?

29.2 The effect of fiscal policy on the current account

1   Why might an expansionary fiscal policy increase a current account deficit?

2   Why might a cut in government spending increase a current account deficit in the long run?

REFLECTION

How confident did you feel in your understanding of the terms used in this question? The more you use a concept such as current account deficit in revision activities, the more confident you are likely to become that you will be able to answer questions on the topic under exam conditions.

≪ RECALL AND CONNECT 2 ≪

How may a country's economy benefit from another country's expansionary fiscal policy?

29.3 The effect of monetary policy on the current account

1   Copy the following text and fill in the missing words.

Among the monetary policy tools that may be used to reduce a current account deficit are changes in the interest rate and changes in the _____ supply. There are, however, a number of difficulties with using monetary policy. There is, for example, some uncertainty about how a change in the interest rate will affect the current account balance. A rise in the interest rate, designed to reduce a current account _____, for example, may cause a rise in the _____ rate. This is because less money from abroad may be placed in the country's _____ institutions. This would increase demand for the country's currency. A higher _____ rate would increase _____ prices and decrease _____ prices. This may increase a _____ in goods and services deficit. It may also be difficult to increase the _____ supply. A higher interest rate may not result in a decrease in _____ lending if consumers are _____ about the future. It may, however, discourage investment, which could reduce the international _____ and _____ competitiveness of the country's products.

29.4 The effect of supply-side policy on the current account

1   How might deregulation reduce a current account deficit?

2   In what **two** ways does supply-side policy differ from demand-side policies on its effect on the current account balance?

《 RECALL AND CONNECT 3 《《

What effect may successful supply-side policy tools have on the exchange rate?

29.5 The effect of protectionist policy on the current account

1   Why may protectionist policy tools not reduce a current account deficit?

The skills you are required to show on a data response question tend to build up. You are likely to find parts d, e and f of Question 2 more challenging than parts a, b and c. Remember to provide a judgement based on analysis in your answer to Question 2(f).

2

> ### UK mini-budget September 2022
>
> On 26 September 2022, the UK government announced a mini-budget. The government stated its main aim was to increase the country's economic growth rate. To achieve this, the government announced some supply-side policy tools including increased spending on infrastructure projects and large tax cuts, including abolishing the top rate of income tax. The government also announced measures to help households and firms with high energy prices.
>
> The financial markets were concerned that these measures would increase the budget deficit significantly and would increase the national debt. The value of the UK pound fell to a record low, coming close to £1 = $1. This led to concerns about the risk of imported inflation and the expectation that the Bank of England, the UK's central bank, would increase the interest rate.
>
> The government claimed that by increasing economic growth, the budget deficit would be reduced and that lower tax rates could also improve the country's current account balance. However, due to the unfavourable response to its mini-budget, the government announced a few weeks later that it was not going to abolish the 45% top rate of income tax.

a   Explain why spending on infrastructure projects is a supply-side policy.   [2]

b   Give **three** benefits of economic growth.   [3]

c   Explain why lower tax rates could improve the current account balance.   [2]

d   Explain how a rise in the rate of interest may:

  i   reduce the fall in the exchange rate   [1]

  ii   increase the budget deficit.   [2]

e   Analyse how a fall in the exchange rate could result in imported inflation.   [4]

f   Assess whether a reduction in tax rates will reduce the exchange rate.   [6]

REFLECTION

How did you decide how much time to spend on Question 2?
What skills did you use in answering each of the question parts?

3   a   Explain, using an appropriate diagram or diagrams, how speculation may affect a floating exchange rate **and** consider whether speculation is the main influence on the value of a floating exchange rate.   [8]

   b   Assess the extent to which contractionary fiscal policy will reduce a deficit on the current account of the balance of payments.   [12]

4 Complete the answers for the following crossword in your notebook:

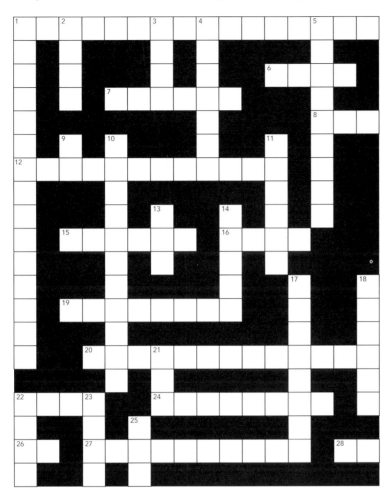

Across

1 The term for government policy tools that may be used to reduce a current account deficit by increasing productive capacity (6,4,6).

6 What may result from the build up of current account deficits (4).

7 A term for items that bring money into the country (6).

8 The currency of Albania (3).

12 A rise in a floating exchange rate (12).

15 The most widely traded currency (6).

16 What a government may do to fiscal policy to reduce a current account surplus (4).

19 A rise in this may increase demand for the currency (8).

20 Currency moved around the world in search of higher interest rates and rising exchange rates (3,5,5).

22 The effect on a current account deficit of an increase in import expenditure (4).

24 Money used in a country (8).

26 The answer to the question, 'Does investment appear in primary income?' (2).

27 The type of current account deficit that arises from domestic firms lacking international competitiveness (10).

28 The answer to the question, 'Do governments aim for current account instability?' (2).

Down

1 The component of the current account balance that covers transfers of money between countries not in return for goods and services (9,6).

2 The currency of a range of South American countries including Argentina (4).

3 What a government may be seeking to encourage households to do as a result of a rise in the interest rate (4).

4 The term for the trade in goods position if import expenditure exceeds export revenue (7).

5 The term for the situation when credit items do not equal debit items in the current account of the balance of payments (9).

9 The direction of movement of the exchange rate as a result of an increase in demand for the currency (2).

10 The action foreign governments may take as a result of the country's government imposing trade restrictions (11).

11 A reason why a firm may buy foreign currency (6).

13 The initials of a form of an indirect tax which may be increased to reduce consumer expenditure (3).

14 What people working abroad may do with some of their wages (5).

17 The type of current account deficit that arises from changes in income at home and/or abroad (8).

18 Another name for a declining industry (6).

21 The initials for name of the group of people at the Reserve Bank of India who set the interest rate (3).

22 The currency of South Africa (4).

23 What a government may do to monetary policy to reduce a current account surplus (4).

25 A cultural item that may be exported or imported (3).

≪ RECALL AND CONNECT 4 ≪

a How might exchange control reduce imports?

b Why might import tariffs increase the inflation rate?

SELF-ASSESSMENT CHECKLIST

Let's revisit the Knowledge focus and Exam skills focus for this chapter.
Decide how confident you are with each statement.

Now I can	Show it	Needs more work	Almost there	Confident to move on
explain the government policy objective of stability of the current account	List **three** reasons why governments try to achieve stability of the current account.			
analyse the effect of fiscal, monetary, supply-side and protectionist policies on the current account	Produce a table on the effect of fiscal, monetary and supply-side policies on the current account balance.			
further develop my understanding of the command word 'assess'	Produce a brief plan for an answer to the question: Assess whether a government should try to reduce a current account deficit.			
reduce test anxiety by being well prepared.	Check that you have covered all the objectives in your revision plan.			

Exam practice 6

This section contains both past paper questions from previous Cambridge exams and practice questions. These questions draw together your knowledge on a range of topics that you have covered up to this point and will help you prepare for your assessment.

Questions 1(a) and 1(b) have example student responses and commentaries provided. For each part, read the question, the example student response and the commentary provided. Then, in Question 1(c), write an improved answer to Questions 1(a) and 1(b), using the guidance in the commentaries to help you.

1 a An economy is facing the shutdown of its steel making industry as a result of cheap imports.

Explain what is meant by 'protectionism' and describe **two** ways in which this steel industry could be protected. Consider how these may affect government revenue. [8]

Adapted from Cambridge International AS & A Level Economics (9708) Paper 22 Q4, March 2022

Example student response	Examiner comments
Protectionism means stopping imports. There are a variety of ways a government could do this. It could put tariffs on imports to make them more expensive and so people will be less likely to buy them. The government could also impose a quota on imports. A quota is a limit on the amount that could be imported. The government could even impose an embargo on imports. This is a complete ban on imports.	**AO1 Knowledge and understanding** The definition of protection is limited. The answer does show an awareness of a number of ways of protecting domestic industries. The question, however, only asks for two. Writing about more than two wastes time. As noted below, this time could have been used better.
A government could also make it difficult for foreign firms to sell to the country by requiring them to meet high quality standards and having to fill out complex paperwork.	*2/3*
Governments may come to agreements to restrict their imports. A government might also discourage imports by subsidising its domestic industries.	**AO2 Analysis**
Subsidies do not directly raise government revenue. Indeed, they increase expenditure rather than raise revenue. However, if they succeed in increasing the output of domestic industries, there may be more corporation tax revenue. Tariffs can also increase tax revenue. However, the more successful they are in reducing imports, the less tax revenue they will raise.	If the student had concentrated on analysing two ways, there could have been more depth of analysis. *1/3*

Example student response	Examiner comments
	AO3 Evaluation
	Here the student does concentrate on two ways and provides relevant evaluation.
	2/2
	Total: 5/8 marks

b Assess the advantages and disadvantages of protecting an industry such as steel **and** consider whether the protection will be of overall benefit to this economy. [12]

Adapted from Cambridge International AS & A Level Economics (9708) Paper 22 Q4b, March 2022

Example student response	Examiner comments
Protecting an industry can increase its output. Higher output can reduce unemployment which can raise living standards.	**AO1 Knowledge and understanding**
Protection may increase net exports. The resulting higher aggregate demand may, however, cause demand-pull inflation.	There is some limited awareness of possible effects on output and employment. The answer, however, does not identify the main arguments for protecting particular industries.
If an economy produces a higher output, there may be more pollution and congestion.	
Industries may not employ more workers if they raise their output by using more capital goods. Living standards will not increase if there is pollution and congestion.	**AO2 Analysis**
Tariffs will increase prices for households and may limit their choice of goods and services. Quotas will also limit their choices. Government subsidies to exporters may result in fewer goods and services being sold on the home market.	There is some limited explanation of how protection may disadvantage consumers. The analysis, however, is not well thought out. It does not adequately link higher AD and output.
	AO1 and AO2: 2/8
	AO3 Evaluation
	There is no relevant evaluation. In the third paragraph the student tries to evaluate whether higher output is a benefit to an economy rather than specifically if protection is a benefit.
	0/4
	Total: 2/12 marks

c   Write improved answers to Questions 1(a) and 1(b).

Here is another past paper question which you should attempt. Use the guidance in the commentaries in this section to help you as you answer the question.

2   Assess, with examples, how trade protection may affect consumers and producers in an economy and whether, on balance, protection can be justified.   [12]

Adapted from Cambridge International AS & A Level Economics (9708) Paper 22 Q4b, June 2013

Question 3 has example student responses and commentaries provided. For each part of the question, work through the question first, then compare your answer to the example student response and commentary.

3   a   Explain what is meant by a rise in an economy's terms of trade. Consider how a change in an economy's exchange rate and its domestic price level might cause this to come about.   [8]

Adapted from Cambridge International AS & A Level Economics (9708) Paper 22 Q4a, March 2018

Example student response	Examiner comments
The terms of trade concerns the price of exports and imports. A rise in the terms of trade occurs when export prices increase and import prices fall. If export prices increase, exports will be able to buy more imports. A rise in the country's exchange rate will increase export prices, in terms of foreign currency, and reduce import prices, in terms of the domestic currency. A rise in the domestic price level will mean that the country is experiencing inflation. This will raise export prices. If other countries are experiencing a lower rate of inflation, import prices may rise by less than export prices.	**AO1 Knowledge and understanding** The definition of the terms of trade needed to be stronger. It would have been useful to include the formula for the terms of trade. The comment that 'exports will be able to buy more imports' could have been clearer in terms of, for example, the same quantity of exports could now be exchanged for a greater quantity of imports. *1/3* **AO2 Analysis** The answer does provide some examination of how a change in the exchange rate and domestic price level may affect export and import prices. *2/3*

Example student response	Examiner comments
	AO3 Evaluation The answer does not link the change in export and import prices to the terms of trade. *0/2* *Total: 3/8 marks*

b Assess whether a rise in an economy's terms of trade is likely to be of overall benefit to that economy. [12]

Adapted from Cambridge International AS & A Level Economics (9708) Paper 22 Q4b, March 2018

Example student response	Examiner comments
A rise in an economy's terms of trade will largely benefit an economy. Higher export prices will mean that export revenue will rise. Lower import prices will reduce import expenditure. More export revenue and less import expenditure will reduce a current account surplus or increase a current account deficit. A rise in net exports will increase national income and may raise the country's economic growth rate. Higher output can increase employment and reduce unemployment. However, an increase in net exports may cause demand-pull inflation if the economy is operating close to full capacity.	**AO1 Knowledge and understanding** There is some understanding of how a rise in an economy's terms of trade will affect export and import prices. **AO2 Analysis** There is limited analysis based on how higher export revenue and lower import expenditure may affect the current account balance and how higher net exports may affect inflation. There is, however, no consideration given to how a rise in the terms of trade could result in lower export revenue and higher import expenditure. *AO1 and AO2: 2/8* **AO3 Evaluation** There is insufficient analysis to establish relevant evaluation. *0/4* *Total: 2/12 marks*

Here is another practice question which you should attempt. Use the guidance in the commentaries in this section to help you as you answer the question.

4 **a** Explain what could cause a depreciation in a country's exchange rate. Consider how a depreciation would affect the country's terms of trade. [8]

   b Assess whether a depreciation in a country's exchange rate will increase employment. [12]

Question 5 has example student responses and commentaries provided. For each part of the question, work through the question first, then compare your answer to the example student response and commentary.

5 **a** Explain, with the aid of a diagram, the impact of a subsidy to domestic producers of a product on the export revenue from that product. Consider the influence of price elasticity. [8]

Adapted from Cambridge International AS & A Level Economics (9708) Paper 21 Q4a, November 2020

Example student response	Examiner comments
A subsidy given to domestic producers is a government payment designed to encourage them to increase their output. It may be given as an attempt to increase exports. It acts in a similar way to a decrease in costs of production. The diagram shows that a subsidy of YZ per unit, would result in an increase in supply from SS to S_1S_1. Price falls from P to P_1 and the quantity traded rises from Q to Q_1. In this case, price falls by a greater percentage than the rise in quantity demanded. 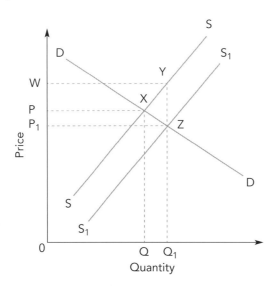 If all the product is exported, export revenue would rise from OPXQ to OP_1ZQ_1. The firms' total revenue would actually increase to $OWYQ_1$. Of this, OP_1ZQ_1 would come from foreign consumers and P_1WYZ would come from the government.	**AO1 Knowledge and understanding** There is good knowledge shown of the meaning of a subsidy given to producers and the meaning of export revenue. *3/3* **AO2 Analysis** There is some strong analysis. There is a particularly good use of diagrams. The question asks for a diagram, but the student provides two diagrams. This is actually useful as it makes a clear contrast between the effect of a subsidy in the case of elastic and inelastic demand. However, the student might also have considered the influence of price elasticity of supply. The contrast between the amount or revenue received from the government and the market is interesting and does not lose marks.

Example student response	Examiner comments
The diagram shows elastic demand. The more elastic demand is, the less firms have to lower price to increase their sales and the more export revenue they can gain. The second diagram shows the effect of a subsidy when demand is inelastic. 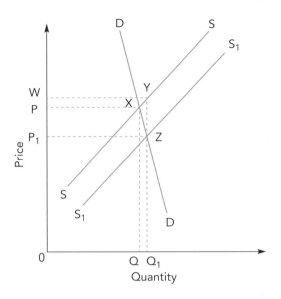 In this case, domestic producers will again receive more revenue in total but this time as price falls by a greater percentage than the rise in the quantity demanded, export revenue falls from OPXQ to OP$_1$ZQI. So, while a subsidy would be expected to increase the volume of exports whether demand is elastic or inelastic, export revenue would only increase if demand is elastic.	However, the focus of the question is on export revenue, so the diagrams could have been simpler, and time could have been saved. The answer does not consider the influence of price elasticity of supply. If supply is price inelastic, price is likely to fall by a greater percentage than the rise in quantity traded and so export revenue may fall. *3/3* **AO3 Evaluation** The student does show the significance of price elasticity of demand on the outcome. There is a good conclusion, although again there could have been a brief reference to PES. *1/2* *Total: 7/8 marks*

b Assess whether supply-side policy tools are an effective way of correcting a deficit on an economy's current account of the balance of payments. [12]

> ***Adapted from Cambridge International AS & A Level Economics (9708) Paper 21 Q4b, November 2020***

Example student response	Examiner comments
Supply-side policy tools aim to increase long run aggregate supply. There is a range of supply-side policy tools that can be used to achieve their objectives of increasing productivity and productive capacity. These include education and training, cuts in income tax and privatisation. Education and training can increase workers' skills. They should be able to work more quickly, work with more advanced technology and make fewer mistakes. This should increase labour productivity with workers producing more units per hour. This can lower costs of production and enable domestic products to be sold at a lower price. A more educated and better trained labour force may also produce better quality products. A rise in price and quality competitiveness should result in a rise in demand for exports and a fall in demand for imports. This could raise export revenue and reduce import expenditure.	**AO1 Knowledge and understanding** The question refers to supply-side policy tools in the plural, so an understanding of at least two policy tools is needed. The answer reveals a clear understanding of three policy tools. However, cuts in income tax did not add much. The current account could have been defined.

Example student response	Examiner comments
Cuts in income tax can increase the incentive to enter the labour force and increase the number of hours each individual worker works. A rise in the quantity of workers may reduce the need for imports. For example, a country may be importing food as it does not have enough workers to exploit a given quantity of land.	This could have provided the basis for consideration that it includes more than just trade in goods and services.
Privatisation can increase efficiency as firms would now be subject to market forces. They would no longer be supported by government financial support. There may be more competition in the industry, with a number of firms, rather than one state-owned monopoly. A more efficient industry may keep prices low and quality high. It may also be more responsive to changes in consumer demand. Such changes can again increase export revenue and lower import expenditure, with both foreign and domestic consumers buying more of the country's goods and services.	**AO2 Analysis** There is clear analysis of why the supply-side policy tools both may and may not reduce a current account deficit. *AO1 and AO2: 7/8*
Supply-side policy has the potential to correct a current account deficit as its policy tools are aimed at improving labour and product market performance, and so productivity and productive capacity.	**AO3 Evaluation**
However, raising productivity may not increase net exports if the country's trading partners are experiencing a recession. In such a situation, demand for exports may not increase and their trading partners may put more effort into selling their products in the country.	There is some clear, supported judgement throughout the answer and in the concluding paragraph at the end. There might also have been consideration of the impact that trade restrictions might have on the outcome.
There is no guarantee that increased government spending on education and training will increase the quality of the education and training. The education and training may also not be in the areas needed in the long run.	*3/4*
Cuts in income tax may reduce the quantity of labour available. This is because workers may decide to work fewer hours. They may be able to do this because they may now be able to receive the same income while enjoying more leisure hours.	*Total: 10/12 marks*
Privatisation does not guarantee more competition or greater efficiency. It is possible that the industry may become a private sector monopoly. Such a monopoly may push up prices, restrict supply and become complacent.	
Nevertheless, as the key to correcting a current account deficit is usually considered to be raising price and quality competitiveness, supply-side policy tools have the potential to correct a current account deficit. They are likely to be more effective during a period of global growth and if they are carefully targeted.	

Here is another practice question which you should attempt. Use the guidance in the commentaries in this section to help you as you answer the question.

6   a   Explain the **four** components of the current account of the balance of payments. Consider whether the value of credit items have to equal the value of debit items on the current account of the balance of payments.   [8]

  b   Assess whether a government should increase direct taxes to reduce a deficit on the current account of the balance of payments.   [12]

30 Utility

195 >

KNOWLEDGE FOCUS

You will answer questions on:

30.1 Utility and diminishing marginal utility

30.2 The equi-marginal principle

30.3 Derivation of an individual demand curve

30.4 Limitations of marginal utility theory and assumptions of rational behaviour

EXAM SKILLS FOCUS

In this chapter you will:

- show that you can manage the distribution of your time in the A Level Economics papers

- show that you can draw out connections in knowledge from prior learning.

An important exam skill is keeping to time. In Paper 3: A Level Multiple Choice the time allowance is 1 hour 15 minutes and the number of marks is 30. This works out at 2 minutes 30 seconds per mark. In Paper 4: A Level Data Response and Essays the time given is two hours, and the marks awarded are 60. This works out at two minutes per mark. It is crucial to check how many marks a question is worth before you answer it so that you know roughly how much time to spend and how much detail is required. As you work through the Exam skills questions in this chapter, have a look at the marks allocated to the questions and think about how much time you should spend on each.

As you learn more economic theory, you will need to refresh your memory of certain topics that you have learned before. This is because more sophisticated concepts are often built on strong foundational knowledge. For example, this chapter on utility is closely related to your prior learning of demand curves. It is important that you highlight these connections in your notes because it will allow you to make stronger analytical points by showing that you understand each small step in your chain of reasoning.

30.1 Utility and diminishing marginal utility

UNDERSTAND THESE TERMS
• utility
• marginal utility
• law of diminishing marginal utility

1 Explain how marginal utility and total utility are related.

Study Table 30.1. It shows the total utility received by a consumer who drinks several cups of coffee in a day.

Cups of coffee	Total utility	Marginal utility
1	20	
2	35	
3	45	
4	50	
5	52	

Table 30.1: Total and marginal utility for coffee consumption

2 Calculate the marginal utility for each cup and fill in the right-hand column in a copy of the table. [2]

3 With reference to law of diminishing marginal utility, explain the shape of the total utility curve. [4]

30.2 The equi-marginal principle

1 Copy the following text and fill in the blanks.

consumers   marginal   price   total

The equi-marginal principle states that _____ will choose a combination of goods to maximise their _____ utility. This will occur where the consumer will consider both the _____ utility of goods and the _____.

2 List the assumptions that the equi-marginal principle is based on.

30.3 Derivation of an individual demand curve

1 Explain how an individual consumer's demand curve for a product is derived **and** consider how this may be linked to its market demand. [4]

2

> **Gas prices**
>
> Natural gas is used throughout Country A. Nine out of every ten households have a gas connection and use a gas boiler. Natural gas is the country's main source of heating and cooking. The average Country A household uses 1 200 kilowatt hours of gas per month.
>
> Between January 2021 and January 2022, Country A gas prices increased from $0.04 per kilowatt hour to $0.14 per kilowatt hour (a rise of 250%). However, the quantity demanded fell relatively little.
>
> A recent report argued that many households could easily reduce their gas bills in one of the following ways:
>
> • Reduce their gas consumption. The study found that homeowners would frequently leave their heating on when they left the home or keep their 'hot water' on for many hours beyond what was needed.
>
> • Consumers were not switching between gas suppliers to take advantage of lower prices and cost savings. This is sometimes called 'consumer inertia'.

With reference to the law of diminishing marginal utility and the data, explain:

a how an individual consumer's demand curve for a product is derived and

b why the demand curve for gas is likely to be price inelastic. [8]

A common error that students make is that they do not answer all the elements of a question. In Questions 1 and 2, there were two parts to the question.

In the first essay, you need to explain how an individual demand curve is derived and how it is linked to a market demand curve. Did you complete both parts?

In the second, the two parts were more explicit: explain (a) how an individual demand curve is derived and (b) why the natural gas is inelastic. Did you complete both parts?

A good tip here is to highlight or underline all of the command words in a question. Do you think this is a strategy you could use?

30.4 Limitations of marginal utility theory and assumptions of rational behaviour

≪ RECALL AND CONNECT 2 ≪

a   Define the term 'rational choices'.

b   Give **two** examples of rational behaviour from your learning of the AS Level Economics content.

1   List the assumptions that the law of diminishing marginal utility is based on.

Read the case study in Section 30.3 again before you to try to answer Question 2. This time, however, try to set yourself a time limit to write your response. An appropriate challenge would be one minute of reading time and 15 minutes writing time.

2   With reference to the data, comment on **two** limitations to the usefulness of the law of diminishing marginal utility in understanding gas markets in Country A.   [8]

If you did not finish writing your answer, then switch to a different colour pen or font (if you are typing) until you have completed your answer.

How did it feel writing to time? Does your answer reflect your best work? Can you identify any strategies that might improve your writing speed?

SELF-ASSESSMENT CHECKLIST

Let's revisit the Knowledge focus and Exam skills focus for this chapter.
Decide how confident you are with each statement.

Now I can	Show it	Needs more work	Almost there	Confident to move on
define the meaning of total utility and marginal utility	Define both 'total utility' and 'marginal utility' accurately.			
calculate total utility and marginal utility	State the formulae to calculate TU from MU and vice versa.			
explain diminishing marginal utility	Write an explanation of the law of diminishing utility in two sentences only.			
explain the equi-marginal principle	Write an explanation of the law of the equi-marginal principle in two sentences only.			
derive an individual demand curve	Explain how an individual demand curve can be derived from the law of diminishing marginal utility.			
evaluate the limitations of marginal utility and its assumptions of rational behaviour	Write an essay highlighting the usefulness and the limitations of the law.			
manage the distribution of my time in the A Level Economics papers	Write the answer to a 12-mark question in 24 minutes.			
draw out connections in knowledge from prior learning.	Create a glossary of technical words from this chapter. Reflect on the effectiveness of this task as a way of improving your own understanding.			

31 Indifference curves and budget lines

The use of diagrams is a truly unique feature of economics as a subject. From your first introduction to the subject, you will have been exposed to diagrams and told to use them in your own writing as much as possible. Diagrams are an effective way to demonstrate your understanding of economic theory, so it is important to use them effectively.

The command word 'demonstrate' means to show how or give an example. It requires that you show how you have arrived at your answer or give an example. You should clearly show that your answer is drawn on evidence or theory. This command word is not used frequently, and when it is, it tends to be used with short-answer questions that ask you to respond to data in some way.

31.1 Indifference curves

1   What does the slope of the indifference curve show?

2   What does a higher indifference curve mean?

3   Why can indifference curves for the same goods not cross each other?

31.2 Budget lines

1   What is meant by the term 'budget line'?

2   Figure 31.1 shows the budget line for a consumer who is choosing what combination of goods to buy. They could afford to buy 20 units of Good X, 10 units of Good Y or a different combination that lies on the budget line.

Being able to shift a budget line in different scenarios is an important skill. This is an AO2 Analysis skill.

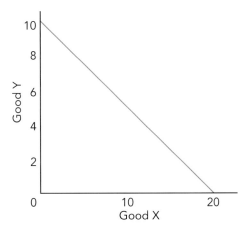

Figure 31.1: A budget line

Redraw Figure 31.1 in the following four different scenarios. Assume that both Good X and Good Y are normal goods.

a   The price of Good X increases.

b   The price of Good Y decreases.

c   Income increases.

d   Income decreases.

REFLECTION

Diagrams are important in economics. Have a look at your diagrams again now and go through the following checklist:

- Are the axes clearly labelled (Good X and Good Y)?

- Are the lines straight?

- Is there an arrow to signify movement?

How confident are you in labelling all of the lines on your diagrams?

Other common errors that students make are:

- The diagrams are drawn too small for it to be possible to see what they are showing.

- The diagrams are not drawn neatly enough to see what they are showing.

- The student fails to refer to their diagram in the text. Therefore, they are not actually using the diagram as part of their analysis.

What strategies can you put in place that will ensure that you do not make these common errors?

≪ RECALL AND CONNECT 1 ≪

It is important that you can also draw these curves if the good is an inferior good or a Giffen good.

a   Define income elasticity of demand.

b   What is an inferior good?

c   What is the difference between a Giffen good and an inferior good?

3   You could attempt the diagrams again for each both inferior goods and Giffen goods. Or you could complete Table 31.1 to check your understanding of what they would look like.

Copy Table 31.1. In each blank space, state what is the impact on the demand for Good X: increase or decrease?

	Good X Is ...		
	Normal	Inferior	Giffen
Price of Good X rises			
Income rises			

Table 31.1: The impact on demand of price/income changes for different types of goods

In Paper 4: A Level Data Response and Essays, it is possible to get a 20-mark question on indifference curves and budget lines. In those cases, it will be important to draw the diagrams and also to explain them.

How easy did you find it to draw the diagrams?

Can you complete the drawings with numbers on the axes?

How confident do you feel about explaining the shift by using the concepts of income and substitution effects, which is covered in the next section?

31.3 The income and substitution effects of a price change

UNDERSTAND THESE TERMS

- substitution effect
- income effect

In this chapter, the main focus is on using diagrams in your answers. The following questions will assess that. A lesser focus, however, is to ensure that you understand the command word 'demonstrate'. This command word does not tend to appear a lot, but if it does, you should be ready.

1   Use indifference curve analysis to demonstrate how an increase in income might affect a consumer's demand for a normal good and an inferior good.   [6]

2   Use indifference curve analysis to demonstrate how a price decrease might affect a consumer's demand for a normal good and a Giffen good.   [6]

31.4 Limitations of the model of indifference curves

1   Explain **three** limitations to indifference curve analysis.

SELF-ASSESSMENT CHECKLIST

Let's revisit the Knowledge focus and Exam skills focus for this chapter.
Decide how confident you are with each statement.

Now I can	Show it	Needs more work	Almost there	Confident to move on
define the meaning of an indifference curve and a budget line	Distinguish between the concepts of an indifference curve and a budget line.			
explain the causes of a shift in the budget line	Explain the four main shifts and illustrate them on a diagram.			
analyse the income, substitution and price effects for normal, inferior and Giffen goods	Refer to the different effects in the diagrams that you drew previously.			
evaluate the limitations of the model of indifference curves	List at least **three** limitations to the theory.			
understand how to use diagrams in my answers	Identify a past paper question that requires a diagram to be drawn. Draw that diagram with accuracy and then peer-assess with another student.			
understand the command word 'demonstrate' and answer a 'demonstrate' question.	Explain to another student what the command word 'demonstrate' means.			

32 Efficiency and market failure

EXAM SKILLS FOCUS

In this chapter you will:

- show that you can apply economic theory to real-world case studies

- show that you can demonstrate the links between different concepts in an answer.

As you move into the A Level Economics content, you will find that using the data becomes more important. Indeed, one of the key skills in economics is to apply a particular economic concept to a real-life scenario. You may be given a scenario (in the data), or you may be asked to apply the concept to a well-known scenario. Students often make a common error of forgetting to apply their concept even though the question specifically asks them to.

You will frequently come across questions that ask you to explain or consider the links between different economic concepts. This means that you must demonstrate a precise knowledge of separate concepts before presenting a clear and cohesive chain of analysis that explains how those concepts might be connected. This requires you to have a strong level of knowledge across the syllabus at all times.

32.1 Introduction to efficiency

UNDERSTAND THESE TERMS

- economic efficiency
- productive efficiency
- allocative efficiency

32.2 Conditions needed for productive efficiency

« RECALL AND CONNECT 1 «

The concept of Pareto optimality can be illustrated on a PPC.

a   Define the term 'PPC'.

b   Explain why most PPCs are drawn as a curve rather than a straight line.

1   With the help of a diagram, explain how productive efficiency can
be illustrated on a PPC.   [5]

32.3 Conditions needed for allocative efficiency

1   With the help of a diagram, explain how allocative efficiency can
be achieved in a competitive market.   [5]

32.4 Pareto optimality

UNDERSTAND THIS TERM

- Pareto optimality

« RECALL AND CONNECT 2 «

Like productive efficiency, the concept of Pareto optimality can also be
illustrated on a PPC.

a   How would you illustrate the concept of opportunity cost on a PPC?

b   Describe the differences between a PPC with increasing opportunity
costs and a PPC with constant opportunity cost.

1   With the help of a diagram, assess whether every point on or under the PPC must be Pareto optimal. [20]

Question 2 is good example of a question that is explicitly asking you to articulate a link between concepts. A top tip is to define both concepts at the start of your answer before making a link between them. Given that there are five marks available, the question is not looking for a 'yes' or 'no' answer. You may want to consider whether these concepts:

- are complementary in some way
- are synonymous
- are negatively correlated
- are connected at certain time or not others
- have no relationship whatsoever.

2   Assess whether the concepts of allocative efficiency and Pareto optimality are linked. [5]

REFLECTION

'Linking' questions can be quite tricky, especially if your understanding of one of the concepts is not particularly strong.

How can you improve your understanding of all concepts of the syllabus? How could you test yourself on the links between different concepts in the syllabus?

32.5 Dynamic efficiency

UNDERSTAND THIS TERM

- dynamic efficiency

1   What might dynamic efficiency look like for different firms?
    Try this matching activity.

Firms	
a	Car manufacturer
b	Hospitality (hotels)
c	Picture frame manufacturer
d	Finance

Efficiencies	
i	Self-service check-in
ii	App-based service
iii	3D printing technology
iv	Computer aided design

One top tip is to read the questions before you read the data. If you do this, then you can make a note of useful quotes, facts and figures to use in your essays later on. You are allowed to write, highlight and make notes on your question sheet, which can be very helpful. Just remember that the question paper is not marked.

2

> **Passenger air travel during COVID-19**
>
> In 2021, due to the COVID-19 pandemic, the estimated number of airline passengers across the world amounted to just over 2.2 billion people. This was a 50% loss in global air passenger traffic compared to 2019.
>
> Since late 2022, however, the aviation industry has been recovering more quickly than anyone might have imagined. This has put a strain on operations, and many airports, particularly in emerging markets, are looking at ways to manage.
>
> In South Africa, for example, the government has recently announced that it will invest in technologies such as biometric solutions (fingerprint and facial recognition) and e-gates to speed up passenger transit in the country's airports. Meanwhile, Dubai International Airport is said to be prioritising self-service initiatives such as self check-in and self-bag drop to ease congestion.

With the help of a diagram, assess whether dynamic efficiency will help to reduce costs in the aviation industry quickly. [20]

REFLECTION

Consider your own practice:

*   Did you read the questions before the data?
*   Did you highlight quotes, facts and figures from the data?

3   Explain what is meant by dynamic efficiency, productive efficiency and Pareto optimality. Assess whether they are all linked. [20]

32.6 Market failure

1   What were the **four** causes of market failure when you studied it in Chapter 13?

2   What are the **two** new additional market failures that are listed in Chapter 32?

SELF-ASSESSMENT CHECKLIST

Let's revisit the Knowledge focus and Exam skills focus for this chapter.
Decide how confident you are with each statement.

Now I can	Show it	Needs more work	Almost there	Confident to move on
define the meaning of productive efficiency and allocative efficiency	Define both 'productive efficiency' and 'allocative efficiency' accurately.			
explain the conditions needed for productive efficiency and allocative efficiency	State the rules for finding productive efficiency and allocative efficiency on a diagram.			
explain Pareto optimality	Explain the concept using a PPC diagram of dynamic efficiency.			
define the meaning of dynamic efficiency	Define the concept and give examples.			
define the meaning of market failure	Define the concept of market failure.			
explain the reasons for market failure	List **five** causes of market failure.			
apply economic theory to real-world case studies	Answer a past paper question, which is linked to a case study. Use facts, figures and quotes from the case study in your answer.			
demonstrate the links between different concepts in an answer.	Write a chain of analysis that links **two** key concepts stated in a question. For example, discuss whether a firm that achieves productive efficiency will always be dynamically efficient as well.			

33 Private costs and benefits, externalities and social costs and benefits

KNOWLEDGE FOCUS

You will answer questions on:

33.1 Externalities

33.2 Types of costs and benefits

33.3 Negative and positive externalities of production and consumption

33.4 Asymmetric information and moral hazard

33.5 Use of costs and benefits in analysing decisions

EXAM SKILLS FOCUS

In this chapter you will:

- show that you understand how to write an essay worth 20 marks in Paper 4: A Level Data Response and Essays

- understand how thinking aloud can support metacognitive practice.

The purpose of the 20-mark questions in Paper 4: A Level Data Response and Essays is to provide you with an opportunity to demonstrate your ability across a range of objectives: knowledge and understanding, analysis and evaluation. Because these questions are worth so many marks, you must make sure that you answer all parts of the question, write in considerable depth and use detailed chains of analysis to explain why things are happening. A diagram will often be required.

Metacognitive practice has been shown to be an effective way to improve your own learning. One strategy that is frequently used as part of a wider metacognitive strategy is 'thinking aloud'. Like it sounds, this means that you will verbally talk about your thought processes as you are conducting a task. That strategy will be simulated in this chapter.

33.1 Externalities

UNDERSTAND THESE TERMS

- externality
- third party
- negative externality
- positive externality

Read the following case studies and answer the questions.

Case Study A

An individual buys a ticket to see a band play at a local venue. The local venue charges her $30 for a ticket. She has a great night. Across the road, a young couple with a small baby cannot sleep because the noise from concert venue is so loud every night.

1   Identify the first, second and third party in Case Study A.

2   State what type of externality is present.

Case Study B

A high-profile author writes a series of fantasy books that are based on his local neighbourhood. Millions of people buy his books and are inspired by the stories. Many residents are happy because the presence of such a high-profile author and mass interest in their neighbourhood is driving house prices up.

3   Identify the first, second and third party in Case Study B.

4   State what type of externality is present.

33.2 Types of costs and benefits

UNDERSTAND THESE TERMS

- private costs (PC)
- private benefits (PB)
- external costs (EC)
- external benefits (EB)
- social costs (SC)
- social benefits (SB)

Re-read the case studies in Section 33.1 and answer the following questions.

1 Using examples from the data in Case Study A, outline the difference between a private cost and an external cost. [4]

2 Using examples from the data in Case Study B, outline the difference between a private benefit and an external benefit. [4]

33.3 Negative and positive externalities of production and consumption

1 Draw four diagrams:

 a negative externalities in production

 b negative externalities in consumption

 c positive externalities in production

 d positive externalities in consumption.

2 Consider the goods and services in the word box. Copy Table 33.1 and match the good or service with the type of market failure that it illustrates.

> tobacco healthcare junk food crude oil
> gardening education nuclear energy medical research

Type of externality	Example
Negative externalities in production	
Negative externalities in consumption	
Positive externalities in production	
Positive externalities in consumption	

Table 33.1: Examples of externalities

This is the first of two essay questions in this chapter. Before you answer the first question, read through the sample thought processes of a student sitting down to write the answer. You should still write your own answer, but you can use the thought processes to guide your writing if you wish.

Example student process

- I set my stop watch for 40 minutes.

- I read the title. I highlight the following words: 'assess', 'financial services', 'ever', 'positive externalities', 'negative externalities' and the number '20'.

- I quickly draw a rough essay plan.

- I will spend half of my essay outlining the economic concept of positive externalities and how it applies to financial services such as banking.

- It is not immediately obvious to me how banking is linked to positive externalities, so I complete a quick mind-map of everything I can think of to do with banking. Very quickly, my synoptic knowledge allows me to make a link between access to credit and spending money in the economy for the benefit of others (the multiplier effect). This 'benefit to others' can be linked to the concept of the third party.

- I will spend half of my essay outlining the economic concept of negative externalities and how it applies to financial services such as banking.

- I have lots of knowledge about the financial sector causing problems for the third party from my wider reading about the 2007–08 crisis.

- I have 37 minutes left. I start writing. I have a rough plan and I know that I need to draw both externality diagrams as I write. I know that I need a summary paragraph at the end, so I will try and think about what I should say as I'm writing.

- As I reach the final paragraph with 3 minutes to spare, I go back to the highlighted key words and make sure I have covered all of them. I still have not really considered the word 'ever', so I decide this will form the basis of my final judgement. Externalities (both positive and negative) are definitely present in banking, though I would argue there are more positive than negative ones for the majority of the time.

---

3   Assess whether the consumption of financial services (such as banking) ever leads to the impact of positive externalities or negative externalities on the third party.   [20]

REFLECTION

Did it help to read the student's thought processes? Make a note of your own thought processes the next time that you write an answer to a long essay question like this. How does your thought process differ? Do you think you could improve your thought processes in any way in order to improve the way in which you write answers?

33.4 Asymmetric information and moral hazard

Question 1 is a much smaller question, but you could try noting down your thought process.

1

> **The 2007-08 financial crisis**
>
> Prior to the 2007–08 financial crisis, the US government chose to deregulate its financial markets. The intent was to stimulate the housing market. As every economist knows, when house prices go up, people feel wealthier and they tend to spend more. This is known as the wealth effect.
>
> One of the unintended consequences of the deregulation policy, however, was that the housing prices increased too much. Mortgage lenders no longer had any effective regulation from the state. They were eager to tell potential customers about the upfront interest rates (which were low) but did not tell them about the high interest rates that would accumulate towards the end of the lending term.
>
> In 2007–08, thousands of US households began to default on their high mortgage repayments. This sent the financial sector into meltdown. Several high-profile banks such as Lehmann Brothers and Bear Sterns went bankrupt. The US president at the time, Barack Obama, decided that the best response was to bail out the banking system, which included the mortgage lenders, by giving them public (taxpayers') money to fund their debts. This led to criticism from many quarters that bankers would not learn their lessons.

Using the data, consider the difference between the terms 'asymmetric information' and 'moral hazard'. [5]

33.5 Use of costs and benefits in analysing decisions

1 State the **four** stages of a cost–benefit analysis.

2 State some of the limitations of using a cost–benefit analysis to make decisions.

3 Assess the usefulness to a government of conducting a cost–benefit analysis before beginning a new high-cost infrastructure project like building a new airport. [20]

SELF-ASSESSMENT CHECKLIST

Let's revisit the Knowledge focus and Exam skills focus for this chapter.
Decide how confident you are with each statement.

Now I can	Show it	Needs more work	Almost there	Confident to move on
define the meaning of a negative externality and a positive externality	Distinguish between the the terms 'negative externality' and 'positive externality'.			
define the meaning of private costs and benefits, external costs and benefits and social costs and benefits	Distinguish between the terms 'private costs', 'private benefits', 'external costs', 'external benefits', 'social costs' and 'social benefits'.			
calculate private costs and benefits, external costs and benefits and social costs and benefits	Create your own calculations questions that involve each of these concepts.			
analyse negative and positive externalities of production and consumption	Draw the diagrams for each of the **four** market failures.			
analyse the deadweight welfare losses arising from negative and positive externalities	Identify the deadweight loss on each of the **four** diagrams.			
explain asymmetric information and moral hazard	Define both terms.			
evaluate the use of costs and benefits in analysing decisions	State the stages of a cost–benefit analysis and some of the limitations.			
understand how to write an essay worth 20 marks in Paper 4: A Level Data Response and Essays	Find a 20-mark question from Specimen Paper 4 and write your answer.			
understand how thinking aloud can support metacognitive practice.	Write down what you are thinking before you write a long answer question.			

34 Types of cost, revenue and profit, short-run and long-run production

EXAM SKILLS FOCUS

In this chapter you will:

*   further develop your understanding of the command word 'describe'

*   learn three strategies that can support your use of technical economic vocabulary with accuracy.

The command word 'describe' means to state the points of a topic or give characteristics and main features. Often, the command word 'describe' will be used to assess your understanding of some quantitative data. You might be asked to describe a trend on a graph or the shape of a particular curve without necessarily needing to explain the connection. Alternatively, you could be asked to describe certain concepts. In this case, you should give appropriate knowledge of a particular topic or issue.

It is important to use technical vocabulary in all of your writing. Using technical terms with accuracy demonstrates a high level of understanding of content knowledge. Various metacognitive methods can be used to support your understanding of key terms, such as dual coding, writing in full sentences and creating memorable slogans.

34.1 Introduction to production

« RECALL AND CONNECT 1 «

a State the **four** factors of production.

b Describe the shape of a supply curve.

As you move forwards in your course, it is important that you reflect on the global nature of economics. All firms use the same factors of production, but the relative cost of those factors of production will change depending where you are in the world.

1 Identify some countries that illustrate the following situations:

    a countries where labour costs might be high/low

    b countries where the cost of extracting natural resources might be high/low

    c countries where it is relatively easy/difficult to access funds to start a new firm.

34.2 Short-run production function

REFLECTION

How confident are you about the terms in this chapter? A common mistake is to confuse two key terms: 'product' and 'productivity'. A strategy that you can use to help remember the difference is by writing out the term as part of a full sentence.

Using the strategy of writing in full sentences, can you think of **three** sentences that you could use the term 'product' in and **three** sentences that you could use the term 'productivity' in?

UNDERSTAND THESE TERMS

- total product
- marginal product
- law of diminishing returns
- average product

1 Copy and complete Table 34.1.

Labour	Total product	Average product	Marginal product
1	20		
2	50		
3	75		
4	96		
5	110		

Table 34.1: Total, average and marginal product values

2 State the formula for average product.

3 State the formula for marginal product.

A common mistake that students make with certain key terms is to confuse the law of diminishing marginal returns with the law of diminishing marginal utility. Unfortunately, they are very different. The former helps you derive the supply curve, whilst the latter helps you derive the demand curve.

One strategy you can use to help you remember the difference is dual coding. This means drawing a small picture next to the concept in your notes. The picture should be simple but memorable enough to stimulate an association with the concept.

4   Identify the point at which the law of diminishing marginal returns starts.

REFLECTION

Using the strategy of dual coding, what picture could you draw for the law of diminishing marginal returns? And how would you draw a picture for the law of diminishing marginal utility?

34.3 Short-run cost function

UNDERSTAND THESE TERMS

• fixed costs (FC)

• variable costs (VC)

The most important knowledge from this topic is knowing how to draw each diagram and the formulae for each.

1   Draw **one** graph showing total fixed cost, total variable cost and total costs.

2   Draw another graph showing average fixed cost, average variable cost, average total cost and marginal cost.

3   State the formula for each of following costs: total fixed cost, total variable cost, average fixed cost, average variable cost, average total cost and marginal cost.

4   Copy and complete Table 34.2.

Output	Total costs ($)	Average costs ($)	Marginal costs ($)
0	4000	NA	NA
100	4500		
200	4800		
300	5100		
400	5600		
500	6500		
600	8400		

Table 34.2: Total, average and marginal cost values

5   Describe the shape of the total cost curve.   [2]

6   Describe the nature of the marginal cost curve.   [2]

There are lots of exam questions that might ask you to explain the link between two or more concepts. The main point of such a question is to check for understanding across the syllabus and the depth of your economic knowledge. Do you know pieces of information in isolation from each other, or do you have an interconnected schema of the entire content?

For these types of questions, you should start by separating the terms and defining them individually. However, once the introduction is done, then you must try to outline how they might relate to each other. An obvious linking question on this topic would be to assess your understanding of the relationship between various curves.

7   Explain the link between diminishing marginal returns and the shape of a firm's short-run marginal cost curve and short-run average total cost curve.   [5]

8   Using diagrams, explain the link between the firm's average fixed cost curve, its average variable cost curve and its average total cost curve.   [5]

34.4 Long-run production function

≪ RECALL AND CONNECT 2 ≪

a   Define the short run.

b   Define the long run.

UNDERSTAND THESE TERMS

- increasing returns to scale
- decreasing returns to scale
- isocosts
- isoquant

1

Cobalt (DRC)

Cobalt is a chemical element. It is an essential component in the manufacture of lithium-ion batteries, which are used in electric vehicles (EVs). According to reports, cobalt mining in 2022 reached a record high. Over 200 000 tonnes of cobalt were mined globally.

The world's largest producer of cobalt is the Democratic Republic of Congo (DRC) in Africa. Estimates suggest that the country's cobalt industry (factor inputs) has increased by 40% in the last ten years. New mines have been opened, more machinery purchased and new labour employed and trained. Ten years ago, the country produced 60 000 tonnes. Today, that figure has doubled to 120 000 tonnes.

Despite all of this, however, the DRC remains one of the poorest countries in the world in terms of GDP per capita.

Using the data, explain the link between the long run and the concept of increasing returns to scale.   [7]

2 Copy the following text and fill in the blanks.

It is possible to derive the long-run production function for a firm by constructing an isoquant map using the principles of a production function. The isoquant map shows the different combinations of _____ and _____ that can be used to produce various levels of _____. The isoquant map consists of a collection of isoquants for different (higher) _____ levels of production. From this, it is possible to read off the respective combinations of _____ and _____ that could produce these _____ levels.

34.5 Long-run cost function

UNDERSTAND THIS TERM

- minimum efficient scale

1 Draw a long-run average cost curve using a series of short-run cost curves.

2 Copy and complete Table 34.3, matching the industry with whether it has a high or low minimum efficient scale (MES).

| hairdressing | nuclear power | tap water | train services |
| piano repair service | coffee shop |

Low MES	High MES

Table 34.3: Example of high and low minimum efficent scale

3 Decide whether each of the following statements are true or false.

a Competitive market structures are associated with a low MES.
b The LRAC is always U-shaped.
c The MES is found when the LRAC stops falling.

34.6 Internal and external economies and diseconomies of scale

1 Match each term with its correct definition.

Terms		Definition	
a	Internal economies of scale	i	Cost savings that occur as a result of the industry increasing in scale
b	Internal diseconomies of scale	ii	Cost savings that occur as a result of the firm increasing in scale
c	External economies of scale	iii	Cost rises that occur as a result of the industry increasing in scale
d	External diseconomies of scale	iv	Cost rises that occur as a result of the firm increasing in scale

2 Illustrate each of these concepts using a diagram:

  a internal economies of scale

  b internal diseconomies of scale

  c external economies of scale

  d external diseconomies of scale.

3 State **three** internal economies of scale and **three** internal diseconomies of scale.

In order to support your exam preparation, it is important that you try some of the questions under timed conditions. This is one such case. These questions relate to the case study you have already read in Section 34.4 (on cobalt production).

You should aim to complete these questions in 50 minutes (three minutes for reading and 47 minutes for writing).

4 Using the data, consider the difference between increasing returns to scale and economies of scale. [5]

5 As the cobalt industry in the DRC continues to increase, the price of producing cobalt will continue to decrease. Assess this view. [20]

REFLECTION

What are your reflections from this task? Did you manage to answer both questions in time?

Are you happy with the result? If not, is it because of content knowledge or timing issues? What will you do next time to make the task easier to complete?

34.7 Total, average and marginal revenue

Explain the relationship between revenue and PED.

It is important to remember the relationship between the different revenue curves so that you use technical terms with accuracy. And yet, with so much content to learn, it can be very difficult to remember the exact definitions and relationships. A third metacognitive strategy you can use (dual coding and using full sentences were looked at earlier) is to create memorable slogans. For example:

- The profit-maximising level of output occurs where the MC curve intersects with the MR curve.

- MR is similar to 'mister' in English.

- MC is similar to 'missy' in English.

- Therefore, this can be remembered as 'mister marries missy'.

REFLECTION

How could you use memorable slogans elsewhere in your course notes?

1   Copy Table 34.4 and fill in the blanks.

Concept	Explanation	Formula
Total revenue		
Average revenue		
Marginal revenue		

Table 34.4: Explanation and formulae for TR, AR and MR values

2   Table 34.5 shows the demand schedule for a monopolist.
Copy the table; calculate TR, AR and MR; and fill in the blanks.

Price	Quantity	TR	AR	MR
$200	1			
$180	2			
$160	3			
$140	4			
$120	5			
$100	6			

Table 34.5: Total, average and marginal revenue values

3   Identify the level of output at which PED is unitary.

34.8 Normal, subnormal and supernormal profit

1 Here are three scenarios for a firm. In each case:

   a calculate the level of economic profit

   b decide whether it is supernormal, normal or subnormal profit

   c state what the firm should do now as a result.

Scenario 1	Scenario 2	Scenario 3
Total revenue: $5 billion	Total revenue: $300 000	Total revenue: $48.12 million
Total cost: $2 billion	Total cost: $150 000	Total cost: $35.74 million
Normal profit: $0.5 billion	Normal profit: $200 000	Normal profit: $12.38 million

SELF-ASSESSMENT CHECKLIST

Let's revisit the Knowledge focus and Exam skills focus for this chapter.
Decide how confident you are with each statement.

Now I can	Show it	Needs more work	Almost there	Confident to move on
explain the short-run production function, including fixed and variable factors of production; total product, average product and marginal product; and the law of diminishing returns (law of variable proportions)	Draw the diagrams for TP, AP and MP. Relate them all to the law of diminishing marginal returns.			
calculate total product, average product and marginal product	Create your own calculation questions that involve TP, AP and MP.			

CONTINUED

Now I can	Show it	Needs more work	Almost there	Confident to move on
explain the short-run cost function, including fixed costs (FC) and variable costs (VC); total, average and marginal costs (TC, AC, MC); and the shape of short-run average cost and marginal cost curves	Draw the diagrams for FC, VC and TC.			
calculate fixed costs and variable costs and total, average and marginal costs	Create your own calculation questions that involve TC, FC and VC.			
explain the long-run production function, including no fixed factors of production and returns to scale	Define the long run and contrast it to the short run.			
explain the long-run cost function, including the shape of the long-run average cost curve and the minimum efficient scale	Draw a LRAC curve and identify the MES.			
analyse the relationship between economies of scale and decreasing average costs	Explain why economies of scale lead to falling unit costs, using examples.			
explain internal economies of scale and external economies of scale	List **three** economies of scale and **three** diseconomies of scale.			
explain internal diseconomies of scale and external diseconomies of scale	Explain the difference between the two concepts.			
define the meaning of total, average and marginal revenue	Define the meaning of TR, AR and MR.			
calculate total, average and marginal revenue	Create your own calculation questions involving TR, AR and MR.			

CONTINUED

define the meaning of normal, subnormal and supernormal profit	Explain the difference between the concepts normal, subnormal and supernormal profit.			
calculate supernormal and subnormal profit	Create your own calculation questions involving the different types of profit.			
develop my understanding of the command word 'describe'	Explain to another student what you need to do in a 'describe' question.			
learn three strategies that can support my use of technical economic vocabulary with accuracy.	State **three** strategies that can support your use of technical economic vocabulary with accuracy.			

35 Different market structures

EXAM SKILLS FOCUS

In this chapter you will:

- show that you can build a chain of analysis in order to achieve high AO2 Analysis marks

- understand how to build affective checks into your learning schedule in order to manage test anxiety.

When you answer longer questions like essays, the mark scheme uses a 'level marking' approach. This means that just being correct is not enough to get top marks. You will need to show that you understand the question deeply by making many detailed connections between different ideas. To do this, you should aim to write longer, more detailed answers that show how different parts of the question connect to each other. In other words, you do not settle for a short assertive statement but, instead, really focus on the detailed links between concepts.

The 'affective domain of learning' means how you feel when you are studying. It is important to pay attention to how you are feeling. All students should be encouraged to monitor their own emotions whilst learning as this can help to identify sources of stress and, as a result, lead to potential solutions.

35.1 Market structures and their characteristics

UNDERSTAND THESE TERMS

- perfect competition
- imperfect competition
- monopolistic competition
- oligopoly
- pure monopoly
- natural monopoly

≪ RECALL AND CONNECT 1 ≪

a Define the term 'market'.

b Define the term 'market mechanism'.

REFLECTION

You need to remember six definitions in a row for this section's Understand these terms box. How did this feel?

You should consider building affective checks into your learning schedule. This means that, at regular intervals, you should consciously ask yourself 'How is my learning making me feel at the moment?' If you recognise signs of test anxiety (e.g., headaches, excessive sweating, nausea), then you should seek support from close friends and family.

One method to alleviate any anxiety you feel about remembering definitions might be to create abbreviations and mnemonics. For example, all of the different types of market structures can be described in terms of four characteristics. They are:

- the nature of the **p**roducts and whether they are different (P)
- the extent to which all firms in the market have the same **i**nformation (I)
- the **n**umber of sellers (N)
- the **e**ase of entry into the market (E).

These four characteristics are worth remembering. It is easy to forget definitions and diagrams in exam situations, but remembering these four characteristics with the abbreviation PINE will allow you to try to work things out from scratch if necessary.

Now come up with an abbreviation or a mnemonic to help you remember another concept.

1   Copy and complete Table 35.1, describing each market structure in terms of the four characteristics in the table.

	Perfect competition	Monopolistic competition	Oligopoly	Monopoly
Number of sellers				
Nature of the product				
Barriers to entry				
Information				

Table 35.1: Characteristics of different market structures

2

> **Car washes (USA)**
>
> A car wash is a firm that employs labour and uses capital (tools, equipment, machines) for washing cars or other vehicles. There has been a large growth in the number of these firms globally over the last ten years. In the USA, for example, nearly eight million vehicles are washed in car washes per day.
>
> It is easy to set up a car wash: the rent is relatively cheap, the initial outlay for equipment is small and the wages for labour are low. The price of a car wash is often less than $10. At that price, lots of consumers are happy to pay for the service but, from a firm's perspective, it means that profit margins are small. Therefore, many car washes try to upsell their products. At some car washes, consumers are encouraged to buy a coffee or a snack whilst they wait, or they are encouraged to buy cleaning and maintenance products to take home with them.

Assess the extent to which the global car wash market is a good example of perfect competition. [20]

35.2 Barriers to entry and exit

It is important to have a strong understanding of all concepts and to have examples, where possible.

1 Copy and complete Table 35.2, with a description and an example for each barrier.

	Description	Example
Legal barrier		
Market barrier		
Cost barrier (high fixed cost)		
Cost barrier (predatory pricing)		
Cost barrier (limit pricing)		
Physical barrier		

Table 35.2: Examples of barriers to entry

35.3 Performance of firms in different market structures

In order to achieve high scores for your analysis paragraphs, it is important that you can build long chains of analysis. Let's take a look at an example focused on perfect competition.

Figure 35.6 in the coursebook shows how a firm in perfect competition can make supernormal profit in the short run but will reach an equilibrium point in the long run in which it makes normal profit.

UNDERSTAND THESE TERMS

- barriers to entry
- barrier to exit

If you are describing this process, you might say the following:

1   The firm is earning abnormal profit.
2   The supply curve for the industry shifts outwards (right).
3   The demand curve for the firm shifts downwards (left).
4   The firm makes normal profit.

The key for success in your course is to learn this process and, most importantly of all, to be able to explain *why* the process is happening the way it is.

For example:

1   The firm is earning abnormal profit.
2   The supply curve for the industry shifts outwards (right). Why? Because more firms enter the market. This is inevitable since there are low barriers to entry in perfect competition. The abnormal profit attracts those new firms.
3   The demand curve for the firm shifts downwards (left). Why? The supply curve shift puts downwards pressure on price. Since all firms in perfect competition are price takers, they must accept lower prices. They cannot charge higher prices because there are lots of firms in the market selling identical products; to do so would lead to a steep drop in sales.
4   The firm makes normal profit. Why? This is because the firm is now charging P = ATC.

This is now a sophisticated chain of analysis. Your answer demonstrates a strong understanding and a logical set of events that follow from each other. The whole thing is rooted in good economic theory.

Now it is your turn but with monopolistic competition. Take care to explain *why* at each stage of the process.

1   A firm is in monopolistically competitive market. With the help of a diagram, explain how the market reaches a long-run equilibrium when that firm earns abnormal profit in the short run.   [7]

REFLECTION

The *why* is crucially important. If nothing else, it differentiates you from many other students who have learned the process but do not understand why the process happens the way it does.

As an additional challenge, you should try to explain the same processes (perfect competition and monopolistic competition) but in reverse. That is, you should assume that the firm is making a loss in the short run. How (and *why*) does the market reach a new long-run equilibrium?

How confident are you are building chains of analysis like this?

UNDERSTAND THESE TERMS

- price competition
- non-price competition
- concentration ratio

2

> **Pay TV (Vietnam)**
>
> Pay TV is big business in Vietnam. In a population of 98 million, over 17 million households pay for some form of pay TV subscription.
>
> Despite growing interest in foreign subscription services like Netflix and Disney+, the most popular services are still domestically owned. According to recent reports, there 38 different providers of pay TV services in Vietnam, but the four largest Vietnamese providers hold over 80% of the total market share.
>
> There are worries that, over the next five years or so, Vietnamese providers will gradually fall out of favour. Foreign-owned services like Netflix and Disney+ have larger economies of scale and financial resources than their Vietnamese counterparts. On the other hand, consumers are likely to welcome the new challengers because there has been little price competition in this market for some time. Pay TV prices have risen well above the rate of inflation in Vietnam for many years.

a   Using the data, explain what is meant by a four-firm concentration ratio.   [2]

b   Explain why firms in oligopolistic markets tend to compete on non-price terms.   [6]

35.4 Comparison of monopoly with perfect competition

《 RECALL AND CONNECT 2 《

a   Define the term 'consumer'.

b   Define the term 'firm'.

In terms of comparing the performance of market structures, two common ways are through comparing the impact on efficiency or on economic agents.

Let's start by looking at the former (efficiency).

1   Copy and complete Table 35.3 by stating the impact of the market structure on that type of efficiency.

	Allocative efficiency	Productive efficiency	Dynamic efficiency	X-efficiency
Perfect competition				
Monopoly				

Table 35.3: Impact of 'efficiency' on different market structures

Being able to complete Table 35.3 shows your knowledge of market structure and types of efficiency. But a strong answer will also show understanding of why these market structures are (or are not) efficient.

For example, a student might say, 'Perfectly competitive markets are not dynamically efficient'. Another student might say, 'Perfectly competitive markets are not dynamically efficient. This is because firms in perfect competition are unable to make abnormal profit. Therefore, they do not have the funds to invest in research and development (innovation) that would enable them to become dynamically efficient. They have the incentive but not the money'.

Even though both answers are correct, the second student has a much stronger answer and will score more marks. Can you explain why?

Do you feel more or less confident about writing long answer questions now?

Another way to assess your understanding will be to ask you about the impact of the two market structures in terms of different economic agents.

2   Copy and complete Tables 35.4 and 35.5 by stating the impact of the market structure on that particular economic agent.

Monopoly		
Consumers	Advantage	
	Disadvantage	
Producers	Advantage	
	Disadvantage	

Table 35.4: Advantages and disadvantages of monopoly on consumers/producers

Perfect competition		
Consumers	Advantage	
	Disadvantage	
Producers	Advantage	
	Disadvantage	

Table 35.5: Advantages and disadvantages of perfect competition on consumers/producers

> **REFLECTION**
>
> To achieve high marks, it is vitally important that you can support your analysis with diagrams. Make sure that you can draw the perfect competition diagrams and monopoly diagrams.
>
> On a scale of one to five, how confident do you feel about drawing the diagrams for the different market structures?

3 It is often said that perfect competition is better for consumers, and monopoly is better for producers. Assess the extent to which this statement is true. [20]

35.5 Contestable markets

1 List **three** conditions of a perfectly contestable market.

2 List **three** desirable outcomes of a perfectly contestable market.

3 Explain how increased contestability can lead to improvement in x-efficiency. [8]

> **UNDERSTAND THESE TERMS**
>
> - contestable market
> - contestability
> - deregulation

> **SELF-ASSESSMENT CHECKLIST**
>
> Let's revisit the Knowledge focus and Exam skills focus for this chapter.
> Decide how confident you are with each statement.

Now I can	Show it	Needs more work	Almost there	Confident to move on
describe the market structures of perfect competition and imperfect competition (monopoly, monopolistic competition, oligopoly and natural monopoly)	List **three** characteristics of each market structure.			
explain the characteristics of the market structures in terms of the number of buyers and sellers, product differentiation, degree of freedom of entry and availability of information	Create an abbreviation or a mnemonic to help remember the important characteristics.			
explain barriers to entry and exit (legal, market, cost and physical)	List **three** examples of barriers to entry and exit.			

CONTINUED				
analyse the performance of firms in different market structures through: • revenues and revenue curves • output in the short run and in the long run • profits in the short run and in the long run • shutdown price in the short run and in the long run • deriving a firm's supply curve in a perfectly competitive market • efficiency and x-inefficiency in the short run and in the long run • price competition and non-price competition • collusion and the Prisoner's Dilemma in oligopolistic markets (including a two-player pay-off matrix)	Complete a series of multiple-choice questions (such as the digital ones that are provided with this book) that will assess your knowledge of the performance of firms in different market structures.			
define the meaning of a concentration ratio	Define the concept of concentration ratio.			
calculate a concentration ratio	Create your own question to calculate a concentration ratio.			
analyse the features and implications of contestable markets	List **three** impacts of a contestable market.			
build a chain of analysis in order to achieve high analysis (AO2) marks	Answer a past paper question that is greater than eight marks.			
build affective checks into my learning schedule in order to manage test anxiety.	Start a study journal in which you note down your feelings as you study.			

36 Growth and survival of firms

EXAM SKILLS FOCUS

In this chapter you will:

- show you understand the command word 'justify' and answer a 'justify' question

- practise the skill of writing efficiently.

The command word 'justify' means to support a case with evidence or argument. The command word is often used in conjunction with an additional command word like 'identify' or 'explain'. Its inclusion serves as an additional prompt to remind students that their answer (or justification) is supported by relevant evidence. It is important that you use facts, figures or quotes from the data when answering a question that asks you to justify your response.

Many students often report that they feel like they did not have sufficient time in an exam. One of the reasons for this is that they spend too long on questions that carry a relatively low number of marks. In essence, they are writing too much information that is unnecessary. During this chapter, you should aim to write answers that are efficient in terms of time.

36.1 Reasons for different sizes of firms

1 Economic theory generally assumes that all firms are driven to grow (get bigger). However, this is not always true.

Copy Table 36.1 and add the correct statement showing the reason to stay small or to get larger.

> to achieve economies of scale   to capture the resources of another firm
> the firm may involve specialist skills possessed by very few people
> to increase market share and become a monopoly
> the firm may want to offer the consumer a personal service
> a lack of money for investment   to achieve economies of scope
> limited economic activities of the market

Reasons to stay small	Reasons to grow

Table 36.1: Reasons for firms to stay small or grow

Read the following extract and then answer the questions.

2
> **Legal services (Australia)**
>
> Firm A is a long-established legal firm operating in Queensland, Australia. Firm A specialises in elder law. Elder law is a legal practice area specialising in issues faced by old people such as age-related illness, long-term care, housing and wills. There are only two members of staff at the company, which prides itself on the personal service it can provide to its clients. In recent months, the owners have been considering an offer from a rival firm (Firm B), which operates nationally, to merge companies.

Using the data, justify **two** reasons for Firm A choosing not to merge.   [4]

3 Using, the data, justify **two** benefits for Firm A from a merger.   [4]

REFLECTION

One of the ways in which a student might lose time on a short-answer question like this is failing to separate the ideas of 'types of growth' from 'benefits of growth'. As a result, they may add in unnecessary sentences that identify what type of growth this is (e.g., horizontal integration, external growth). This would not be credited by a mark scheme and is, unfortunately, a waste of time.

On a scale of one to five (five being totally confident), how confident are you in writing efficiently?

36.2 Internal and external growth of firms

1   Copy and complete Table 36.2. Identify whether the each of the statements is an example of internal or external growth.

> using retained profit to invest in new capital goods
> increasing market share through marketing
> acquisition of another (rival) firm
> acquiring a bank loan using company assets for collateral
> a horizontal merger with another firm   joint venture overseas

Internal growth	External growth

Table 36.2: Examples of internal and external growth

36.3 Integration

For the following questions, you should try to write to time.
Try to spend no more than 48 minutes (two minutes reading and 46 minutes writing).

1
Car manufacturing (Brazil)

A leading car manufacturer in Brazil is concerned that its sales are not quite as high as expected. Therefore, the owners have tasked a consultancy firm to recommend a couple of possible mergers to help support the long-term future of the company. The consultancy recommends a new Brazilian start-up company that manufactures lithium-ion batteries suitable for road vehicles. As an alternative, the consultancy also recommends an Indian car company, which is of similar size but produces cars for the Indian market.

Using the data, identify examples of both horizontal and vertical integration. Justify your answers.   [4]

2   Assess the likely effectiveness of both mergers and which one (if either) the Brazilian car company should choose.   [20]

36.4 Cartels

a　What is a cartel?

b　In which market structure would you most commonly find a cartel?

c　Give an example of a famous cartel.

1　Copy and complete the table below.

Three conditions for effective cartels	1
	2
	3
Three threats to a cartel's effectiveness	1
	2
	3

Table 36.3: Conditions for effective cartels and threat to a cartels' effectiveness

36.5 The principal–agent problem

Describe the different market structures in terms of the four key characteristics: number of firms, type of product, level of information and barriers to entry.

1　Copy the text below and fill in the blanks.

| a manager　　an owner　　best interests　　agent　　principal　　more |

The principal–agent problem occurs when one person (the _____) makes decisions on behalf of another person (the _____). In the case of business decision-making, the principal is generally considered to be _____ and the principal is considered to be _____. The agent, through a day-to-day involvement in the firm, has _____ information than the principal. This difference is an example of asymmetric information. The problem is that the principal does not know how the agent will act; the principal is also not sure that the agent will act in the principal's _____.

The reason that the principal–agent problem is covered in this section is that there is generally considered to be a link between the size of a firm and the likelihood of a principal–agent problem.

2   Explain what is meant by 'the principal–agent problem' and assess whether it is likely to be found in all market structures.   [20]

SELF-ASSESSMENT CHECKLIST

Let's revisit the Knowledge focus and Exam skills focus for this chapter.
Decide how confident you are with each statement.

Now I can	Show it	Needs more work	Almost there	Confident to move on
explain reasons for the different sizes of firms	List **three** reasons that a firm might choose to grow. List **three** reasons why a firm might choose to remain small.			
explain the difference between internal and external growth of firms	List **two** methods of internal growth and **two** methods of external growth.			
analyse the methods, reasons and consequences of integration (horizontal, vertical, conglomerate)	Distinguish between the different types of mergers, with examples.			
analyse the conditions and consequences for an effective cartel	List **three** conditions for an effective cartel. List **three** consequences of having a cartel.			
discuss the principal–agent problem	Define the principal–agent problem. Explain why the principal–agent problem is more likely to occur in uncompetitive markets.			
understand the command word 'justify' and answer a 'justify' question	Explain to another student what the command word 'justify' means.			
practise the skill of writing efficiently.	Go back through some of your previous answers from other chapters and try to edit your work by removing sentences that are unnecessary.			

37 Differing objectives and policies of firms

EXAM SKILLS FOCUS

In this chapter you will:

- show that you can write an outline essay plan

- understand the importance of building up a list of relevant real-world examples to use in your answers.

There are several uses for writing a short outline for an essay or long answer question. First, you might use it in an exam; you might spend a few minutes writing the plan before writing the essay out in full. Second, you can use outline essay plans as an effective revision tool. Some students attempt to learn full essays by rote, but it is more effective to use the key headings in your outline plan as a memory prompt for later use. By breaking down your learning into manageable chunks like this, outline essay plans can be a great revision tool for managing exam preparation in a less stressful way.

It is important that you have your own examples of all concepts. In exam questions, you may be asked to provide your own examples or you might choose to include your own examples as a way of supporting (or evaluating) your economic analysis. For example, a good evaluative point in any essay might be: 'This is not always the case; for example, …', and then you write about an anomaly that does not conform to the theory you just outlined. Therefore, you should keep a note of real-world examples throughout your course.

37.1 The traditional profit-maximising objective

It is very easy to remember the rule that the profit-maximising level of output for a firm is MC = MR. But students often find it very hard to explain why this is the case. Try these questions to help.

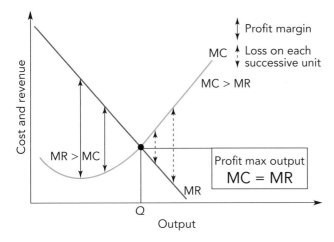

Figure 37.1: The profit–maximisation rule

1   Using Figure 37.1, explain:

   a   why any level of output before Q is not profit-maximising

   b   why any level of output after Q is not profit-maximising.

   Using your answers to these questions, it should be easier now to answer Question 2.

2   Explain why the profit-maximising level of output is MC =MR.

   It is very common to see evaluative questions about the business objectives of firms. Since such questions always require a counter-point, it is important that you learn a strong explanation (that you can remember) for why the theory says profit maximisation is at MC = MR.

3   Can you think of **three** reasons why a firm may not be producing at the profit-maximising level of output?

REFLECTION

It is important that you have examples of real firms that match these behaviours (profit-maximising and non-profit-maximising behaviours). Do you have **three** examples of profit-maximising firms? Do you have some examples of the **three** main non-profit-maximising behaviours that you identified previously?

An outline essay plan is a term which means a short outline for an essay or long answer question. Here is an example outline for the essay in Question 4:

- State the profit-maximising rule (MC = MR).
- Explain why it is the rule (profit is the reward for entrepreneurship).
- Draw diagram.
- Give example (Robert Kuok).
- Explain why profit-maximising behaviour might be disadvantageous to a firm.
- Give example (European gas firms).
- Explain another business strategy that a firm might employ (sales maximisation).
- Give example (Amazon).
- Write a conclusion.

4 Using examples, assess whether firms will always produce at the profit-maximising level of output. [20]

37.2 Other objectives of firms

1 Copy and complete Table 37.1. Write a description of each objective and state, when possible, where you would illustrate this point on a cost revenue diagram.

Objective	Description	Where to find it on a diagram?
Sales maximisation		
Revenue maximisation		
Profit satisficing		
Survival		

Table 37.1: Business objectives of the firm

2 With the help of a diagram, explain the difference between sales maximisation and revenue maximisation. [8]

To help write this answer, use the following outline essay plan:

- State business objectives.
- Define business objectives.
- Draw a diagram to illustrate the behaviour.
- Explain why this objective is illustrated on the diagram.
- Give an example.
- Repeat for the second objective.

37.3 Price discrimination

1 Can you describe **three** different types of price discrimination?

2 Can you describe **three** conditions for effective third-degree price discrimination?

Exam questions will often ask you to consider concepts from the perspective of different economic agents (such as consumers and producers).

3 Outline some of the advantages and disadvantages to both consumers and producers of third-degree price discrimination.

	Advantage	Disadvantage
Consumers		
Producers		

Table 37.2: Advantages and disadvantages of price discrimination

4 Assess, using examples, whether price discrimination is good for all economic agents. [20]

37.4 Other pricing policies

« RECALL AND CONNECT 1 «

Define the terms 'limit pricing', 'predatory pricing' and 'price leadership'

1 Match these pricing strategies with the most likely reason for it (the strategy) to be employed.

Terms		Strategies	
a	Limit pricing	i	Large firm reduces price because it feels threatened by a new entrant
b	Predatory pricing	ii	Small firm wants to avoid price competition with the dominant firm in the market
c	Price leadership	iii	Large firm in a contestable market chooses to lower price to create a new barrier to entry

37.5 Relationship between price elasticity of demand and a firm's revenue

1   Draw the relationship between the AR curve (demand curve) and the total revenue curve.

SELF-ASSESSMENT CHECKLIST

Let's revisit the Knowledge focus and Exam skills focus for this chapter.
Decide how confident you are with each statement.

Now I can	Show it	Needs more work	Almost there	Confident to move on
analyse the traditional profit-maximising objective of firms	Explain why profit-maximisation occurs at MC = MR.			
explain other objectives of firms, including survival, profit satisficing, sales maximisation and revenue maximisation	Illustrate each of these objectives on a cost revenue diagram.			
analyse price discrimination, including the conditions for effective price discrimination and the consequences of price discrimination	Explain the advantages and disadvantages of price discrimination.			
evaluate other pricing policies, including limit pricing, predatory pricing and price leadership	Outline what these **three** pricing policies are.			

CONTINUED

explain the relationship between price elasticity of demand and a firm's revenue for a downward-sloping demand curve and a kinked demand curve	Explain how total revenue, average revenue and PED are all related.			
write an outline essay plan.	Write an outline essay plan for your next essay or long answer question.			
understand the importance of building up a list of real-world examples to use in my answers.	Create a notebook with real-world examples for all the concepts in your course.			

Exam practice 7

This section contains practice questions. These questions draw together your knowledge on a range of topics that you have covered up to this point and will help you prepare for your assessment.

The following questions have example student responses and commentaries provided. For each question, work through the question first, then compare your answer to the example student response and commentary.

1   Assess the view that all firms should aim to grow in scale.   [20]

Example student response	Examiner comments
The size of the firm is often called its scale. This relates to the number of factor inputs – or factors of production – that a firm has, such as labour, capital, land.	**AO1 Knowledge and understanding** This is a decent introduction which shows a good understanding of 'scale'. It related to factors of production well.
Some firms will choose to grow (or, increase their scale) by increasing their factor inputs. There are various reasons for doing so. Firstly, the firm can achieve internal economies of scale. This is when unit costs fall as a result of an increase in scale. It is illustrated a movement along the LRAC curve, and might be accessed through purchasing economies (bulk buying), technical economies (division of labour) or financial economies (accessing loans at lower rates). Economies of scale are beneficial because they can lead to higher profit margins for the firm.	**AO2 Analysis** The answer is structured neatly. The first half is about the factors influencing a firm's growth. The student chooses to start with an analysis of economies of scale. The definition is correct and the examples are correct too. The answer could be improved with the drawing of the diagram, even though the student does refer to the LRAC curve. In addition, a real-world example of a firm increasing in scale and benefitting from economies of scale would have been useful.
Secondly, the firm might grow to access new markets and increase their likely sales. For example, a company based in one particular region may decide to open new stores in a different region in order to gain more customers. Some firms might even move abroad.	In total, the student offered three reasons why a firm might choose to grow. Each of the reasons is well explained and correct. That said, diagrams would have improved the answer.
Thirdly, a firm might grow in order to reduce the threat of competition. This normally happens when two rival firms merge. The new firm is likely to have a much larger market share and, as a monopoly, might be able to push up prices.	*AO1 and AO2: 12/14* **AO3 Evaluation**
Not all firms choose to grow though. Some firms might remain small for various reasons. For example, it may simply be that they do not have the funds available to invest and buy new capital goods. Secondly, there simply might not be enough demand (for this niche product) to cover and sustain any extra spending on growth. Finally, the firm may wish to stay small because the owners want to retain control of the business.	The second half of the answer is about reasons why a firm might stay small. In total, the student offered three factors why a firm might stay small – totalling six factors considered in total. The evaluative section is relatively brief (compared to the preceding analysis) and, again, diagrams and examples would have improved the answer greatly.

Example student response	Examiner comments
Growth can often mean that new owners come on board or there is a loss of coordination/communication that comes from diseconomies of scale. Overall, it is not true that all firms should aim to grow in scale. There are potentially many benefits to doing so like economies of scale and increasing sales, but it is certainly not the case all of the time, in every context.	The final paragraph offers a conclusion. It firmly answers the question ('it is not true') but then fails to justify that assertion with any link to preceding analysis ('it is not the case all of the time, in every context'). It sounds rather vague. 4/6 *Total: 16/20 marks*

2 Evaluate the view that in the absence of government regulation there are no limits on the ability of a monopolist to charge whatever price it wishes. [20]

Example student response	Examiner comments
A monopoly is a market structure which has the following characteristics: one large firm, a unique product, imperfect information and high barriers to entry. A common criticism of monopoly is that the firm (the monopolist) can charge high prices to consumers. By virtue of having a large market share, a monopolist will face a relatively inelastic demand curve. Combined with the fact that the monopolist is a price maker, the firm can charge higher prices in order to raise total revenue, and economic profit. The diagram below shows a monopoly in action. The firm produces at profit-maximising level of output, which is the point where MC = MR. The price is determined as such. This is much higher than if the firm was operating in perfect competition. In perfect competition, firms are price takers and productively efficient. Therefore, the price is the same as the average cost. This is not the case with monopoly. 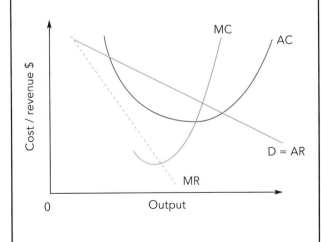	**AO1 Knowledge and understanding** There is good introduction that shows a good understanding of the keyword: monopoly. In addition, the second paragraph demonstrates strong understanding of the relationship between revenue and PED. **AO2 Analysis** The diagram is accurate. However, it does not show the price. Given that the question is focused on the price that monopolies can charge, this detail would have been useful. Equally, there is some comparison with the price under perfect competition. The answer could have been developed further with a perfect competition diagram. It also would have been good to see some link to the idea of government regulation because this is a key element of the essay title. *AO1 and AO2: 9/14* **AO3 Evaluation** The evaluation is very good indeed. The student offers four pieces of evaluation: reasons why monopolies cannot just charge whatever price they want (even without regulation). It is all explained in solid technical language. *6/6* *Total: 15/20 marks*

Example student response	Examiner comments
However, there are limits on how much a monopolist can charge. Firstly, it depends if the market is contestable. Even monopoly market structures can be contestable, and the threat of new entrants entering the market might mean that the firm lowers its price to the AC level.	
This is similar to the pricing strategy of limit pricing. If the monopolist is worried by the threat of new entrants, it will reduce its price to hinder new entrants from entering the market like a hit-and-run firm.	
A monopolist firm might also lower its prices if it is pursuing a different business objective. If the firm is sales maximising in order to build its market share even higher, then it may drop prices in order to encourage new customers.	
Even with none of these things, a monopolist can't simply raise prices forever. PED changes along a demand curve and at some stage towards the top right, PED will become elastic. At that stage, continuing to raise prices will actually lower the amount of revenue that the firm makes.	
In conclusion, there are definitely limits on how much a firm can charge. However, these limits might be quite high and so government intervention is probably necessary.	

3   Evaluate whether the three concepts of equity, allocative efficiency and Pareto optimality are all linked.   [20]

Example student response	Examiner comments
Allocative efficiency is the idea that price is equal to marginal cost; firms are producing those goods and services most wanted by consumers. In other words, that the economy is making the best possible use of available resources. Pareto optimality is the situation where it is impossible to make someone better off without making someone else worse off.	**AO1 Knowledge and understanding** Overall the essay demonstrates a good understanding of the concepts of allocative efficiency and Pareto optimality, as well as the relationship between them. However, the explanation of equity is somewhat brief and lacks detail.
Allocative efficiency and Pareto optimality are linked. Allocative efficiency can be illustrated on a PPC diagram. A given point on the PPC must be allocative efficient because it satisfies the condition that 'you are making the best possible use of available resources'. If more of both goods could be produced, there would be a gain in allocative efficiency. This is because there is an improvement in welfare.	**AO2 Analysis** The student effectively analyses the relationship between allocative efficiency and Pareto optimality by referring to a PPC diagram to illustrate their connection. The student explains why every point on the PPC is allocatively efficient and also Pareto efficient (the analysis and economic terminology are accurate and correct), but the analysis of equity is not as thorough. The student could also benefit from providing more examples or expanding upon their explanation. *AO1 and AO2: 8/14*

Example student response	Examiner comments
The same point on the PPC is also Pareto optimal. It is not possible to make someone better off without making someone worse off. This is because if we produce more of one good, it must be true that we are simultaneously reducing the output of the other good. Any point within the PPC is also not allocatively efficiency (we could use the resources better) and not Pareto optimal. Equity is the concept of fairness in economics. This is not linked to either of the two previous concepts. For example, Pareto optimality does not necessarily imply equity. It is easy to see a scenario in which Pareto optimality is achieved (it is impossible to make someone better off without making someone else worse off) but, simultaneously, that the current distribution of resources was inequitable and, for example, that low-income households had less welfare than high-income households.	**AO3 Evaluation** The student evaluates the link between allocative efficiency and Pareto optimality effectively by explaining how a given point inside the PPC diagram does not satisfy both conditions. However, the evaluation of equity is somewhat limited. It is true that the concept of equity is not linked to either concept, even though a similar concept (equality) would be, but this answer could be improved by discussing potential trade-offs between equity and other economic objectives. There is no conclusion. *3/6* *Total: 11/20 marks*

4   Evaluate the impact of horizontal integration on the new firm.   [20]

Example student response	Examiner comments
A horizontal merger occurs when two firms operating in the same industry or producing similar products combine to form a new entity. This type of merger can have significant impacts on the new firm. One possible impact of a horizontal merger is the new firm may take on more debt to finance the acquisition. This could potentially lead to financial instability if the new firm cannot generate enough revenue to service its debt obligations. However, if the merger results in improved efficiency and profitability, the new firm may be better equipped to repay its debt over time. Economies of scale are other potential benefits of a horizontal merger. By combining resources and streamlining operations, the new firm can achieve cost savings and improved efficiency. This could result in lower prices for consumers, as the new firm can produce and sell goods at a lower cost. Additionally, the new firm may have a stronger market position, which could allow it to negotiate better terms with suppliers or increase its pricing power. However, a horizontal merger can also lead to diseconomies of scale if the new firm becomes too large and unwieldy. This could result in increased bureaucracy, slower decision-making, and decreased flexibility. This will lead to a rightwards movement along the LRAC curve, which causes units costs to rise. In some cases, a horizontal merger could also lead to job losses as the new firm seeks to eliminate duplicate positions.	**AO1 Knowledge and understanding** The essay shows a strong understanding of the concept of a horizontal merger, including the potential impacts on the new firm and, towards the end, consumers and suppliers. The student has demonstrated their knowledge of key economic terms and concepts related to integration. **AO2 Analysis** In general, the analysis is excellent. The student offers several points of analysis, each of which is explained correctly. However, providing more specific examples or case studies could help to illustrate and support their arguments more effectively. *AO1 and AO2: 13/14* **AO3 Evaluation** Again, this is an excellent section. The essay has provided a well-reasoned evaluation of the potential impacts of a horizontal merger on the new firm. The student has considered the potential drawbacks of the merger and has evaluated its potential success based on a range of factors. The conclusion is well-written and reaches a reasonable judgement. *6/6*

Example student response	Examiner comments
Away from the firm, consumers may benefit from a horizontal merger if it leads to lower prices due to increased efficiency and cost savings. However, if the new firm becomes too dominant in the market, it may have the power to raise prices and reduce consumer choice. In this case, competition authorities may need to intervene to prevent antitrust violations. Suppliers may also be impacted by a horizontal merger. Some may lose contracts as the new firm consolidates its sourcing activities. However, the new firm may also provide new opportunities for suppliers to enter new markets or expand their operations. In conclusion, a horizontal merger can have both positive and negative impacts on the new firm. It may result in increased efficiency, cost savings, and a stronger market position. Ultimately, the success of a horizontal merger depends on the ability of the new firm to effectively integrate its operations and realise the benefits of the merger while minimising the negative impacts.	Note: The student could consider restructuring the essay to better separate and clarify their analysis and evaluation of each potential impact. *Total: 19/20 marks*

5 Assess the impact on other economic agents of a supermarket reducing its costs. [20]

Example student response	Examiner comments
Supermarkets may try to reduce their costs for a number of reasons such as to operate at a minimum average cost and achieve productive efficiency. Firstly, reducing costs could lead to lower prices which could increase consumer surplus. This would lead to an increase in market share and could give the firm future price-making power. Additionally, lower prices could serve as a barrier to entry for other firms, especially in highly contestable markets. Furthermore, reducing costs could lead to internal economies of scale, which could improve efficiency and reduce prices. However, it is important to be cautious about how firms are achieving these lower costs. If they do so by exploiting their workers, it could result in low wages and poor working conditions. This could have negative impacts on the employees, society, and the firm's reputation. Moreover, if firms focus too much on reducing costs by expanding and achieving economies of scale, they might go too far and end up with diseconomies of scale. In the short run, reduced profits could limit the finance available for expansion, and lead to less tax revenue for the government if profits and prices are lower.	**AO1 Knowledge and understanding** In general, the student demonstrates a good understanding of economic concepts. **AO2 Analysis** The student meets the rubric of the question and offers a decent number of advantages and disadvantages. In general, there is good use of technical language, but there are two main issues. First, the student really needs to develop some of their points. For example, the statement 'this could have negative impacts on the employees, society, and the firm's reputation' is a fair point but it needs explaining further. The student should explain why it is undesirable for society and the impact of the firm's reputation getting worse (e.g., falling sales). Second, the points are too vague. The question specifically asked about supermarkets, and yet there is barely any reference to supermarkets or the likely market structure that supermarkets are in (oligopoly).

Example student response	Examiner comments
Overall, the success of reducing costs depends on several factors such as the market structure, product and the methods used to achieve lower costs. If firms achieve lower costs by balancing the needs of all the stakeholders, it could lead to positive outcomes such as international competitiveness.	The answer is not relevant enough to the question asked to gain high AO2 Analysis marks.
	AO1 and AO2: 7/14
	AO3 Evaluation
In conclusion, while reducing costs may bring advantages such as lower prices and higher efficiency, firms need to balance these benefits with their social responsibilities towards employees and society as a whole. Only then can they achieve success in the long run while benefiting all the stakeholders.	The evaluation is also too vague and not well enough developed. The section that reads: 'overall, the success of reducing costs depends on several factors such as the market structure, product, and the methods used to achieve lower costs' is true but that should be the start of a chain of analysis and not a single statement. When the student writes 'it could lead to positive outcomes such as international competitiveness', it is important that they then explain why this could happen and why it would matter to the firm.
	2/6
	Total: 9/20 marks

Here are two more practice questions which you should attempt. Use the guidance in the commentaries in this section to help you as you answer the questions.

6 Assess whether the theory of perfect competition is relevant in the modern world. [20]

7 'Monopoly is a market failure and has no positive outcomes for the consumer.' Evaluate this statement. [20]

38 Government policies to achieve efficient resource allocation and correct market failure

EXAM SKILLS FOCUS

In this chapter you will:

- show that you understand all the elements needed when writing a high-quality essay

- understand how to create your own questions in order to improve metacognition.

Essay questions assess the full range of assessment objectives. In an essay, you need to demonstrate knowledge, technical analysis and evaluative comment in a coherent structure. A useful essay template for the topics in this chapter would be, first, demonstrate a strong understanding of the market failure problem. Second, explain how a particular policy can solve the market failure. Third, evaluate your own chain of analysis. Finally, you should show that you can compare the costs and benefits of two possible solutions before weighing up the merits of both with a well-reasoned judgement at the end.

An effective strategy that can support learning is to create your own questions. Creating questions is a high-value thinking skill. It engages your working memory in the short term, but it also supports your long-term memory. In this chapter, you are encouraged to create your own questions and to use them as part of a self-questioning process.

38.1 Government policies to correct negative and positive externalities

UNDERSTAND THESE TERMS

- regulations
- property rights
- pollution permit

《 RECALL AND CONNECT 1 《

Many of the methods of government intervention and their effects on markets were introduced in Chapter 13. Therefore, there is ample opportunity here, in Chapter 38, to revise some of those core concepts.

a Define the term negative externalities in production.

b Explain how an indirect tax works.

c Define the term positive consumption externalities.

d Explain how a subsidy works.

Exam questions may ask you to assess the relative merits of different policies.

1 Copy and complete Table 38.1, stating some of the advantages and disadvantages of different government interventions.

	Advantage	Disadvantage
Indirect taxes		
Regulations		
Property rights		
Pollution permits		
Subsidy		

Table 38.1: Advantages and disadvantages of different government interventions

Try to use the following outline essay plan to answer Question 2:

- What is the market failure?
- Draw the diagram.
- How does the first solution (indirect taxes) fix the market failure?
- Draw the diagram.
- Explain what the evaluations are to the preceding chain of analysis.
- How does the second solution (pollution permits) fix the market failure?
- Draw the diagram.

- Explain what the evaluations are to the preceding chain of analysis.

- Write a final paragraph which offers a well-reasoned judgement that answers the question.

2   Assess whether a government should impose an indirect tax or use a pollution permit scheme to reduce carbon emissions.   [20]

REFLECTION

It is important that you spend some time practising other combinations of this type of question. For example, the focus of the question may be negative consumption externalities or positive externalities. The policies may focus on property rights or subsidies.

To support you with some of that work, grade yourself on a scale of one to five (five = very confident) about your answers to the following essay questions:

- Assess whether a government should impose an indirect tax or a subsidy scheme to increase the consumption of electric vehicles.

- Assess whether the government should enforce property rights or a permit scheme to reduce the problem of over-fishing.

Can you create your own questions? A good question in this topic will normally ask which one of two specified policy solutions is better at fixing a particular market failure.

38.2 Other tools to correct market failure

≪ RECALL AND CONNECT 2 ≪

Define the term 'privatisation'.

UNDERSTAND THESE TERMS

- nationalisation
- 'nudge' theory

1   Copy and complete Table 38.2. State some of the advantages and disadvantages of some other government interventions.

	Advantage	Disadvantage
Nationalisation		
Privatisation		
Nudge theory		

Table 38.2: Advantages and disadvantages of more government interventions

2 Assess whether there is any benefit to nationalising public transport services such as buses and trains. [20]

REFLECTION

As before, you should try now to create your own questions based on this topic. A good question will ask whether one of the foregoing intervention strategies will be useful or beneficial in a particular market. For example: Evaluate the advantages and disadvantages of privatising energy markets, such as gas and electricity.

38.3 Government failure in microeconomic intervention

UNDERSTAND THIS TERM

- Government failure

1 State **three** main forms of government failure.

2 Assess whether government intervention can always be relied upon to reduce market failure. [20]

SELF-ASSESSMENT CHECKLIST

Let's revisit the Knowledge focus and Exam skills focus for this chapter. Decide how confident you are with each statement.

Now I can	Show it	Needs more work	Almost there	Confident to move on
explain how a range of tools can be used to correct the different forms of market failure, including specific and *ad valorem* indirect taxes, subsidies, price controls, production quotas, prohibitions and licences, regulation and deregulation, direct provision, pollution permits, property rights, nationalisation and privatisation, provision of information and behavioural insights and 'nudge' theory	Explain the term 'market failure' (with diagram if appropriate) and link **two** of the policy solutions to that definition.			
evaluate the effectiveness of the tools used to correct market failure	State some of advantages and disadvantages of different intervention strategies.			

CONTINUED				
define the meaning of government failure in microeconomic intervention	Define the term 'government failure'.			
explain the causes and consequences of government failure	State **three** causes of government failure.			
understand all the elements needed when writing a high-quality essay	List **five** things that must be present in a high-quality essay.			
understand how to create my own questions in order to improve metacognition.	Write **three** essay questions that are based on the content knowledge from this chapter.			

39 Equity and redistribution of income and wealth

KNOWLEDGE FOCUS

You will answer questions on:

39.1 Equity, equality and efficiency

39.2 Absolute and relative poverty

39.3 Policies towards equity and equality

EXAM SKILLS FOCUS

In this chapter you will:

- show that you can distinguish between economic terms that are closely related but technically different

- understand the importance of staying up to date with current affairs during your period of study.

In order to answer an exam question effectively, you must be able to discern the particular knowledge you need to demonstrate and apply. This is difficult, however, when there are several closely related concepts. In this chapter, for example, there are different measures of poverty and closely linked concepts such equity, equality and efficiency. For success in your course, you must be able to distinguish between closely related concepts.

One effective way to improve your analysis is to use current real-world examples. Too often, economics students learn abstract theory as if it were detached from real life. It is not. Students who follow current affairs news stories tend to find it easier to apply their knowledge to new case studies. This is because they are continually reading news events and, perhaps unconsciously, linking them to their learning. Exam answers can be improved by including up-to-date knowledge, and you may find it easier to make evaluative points in long answer questions because current events may not conform to standard theory.

39.1 Equity, equality and efficiency

1   Match these descriptions to the correct concept.

Terms		Descriptions	
a	Equity	i	if a society distributes its resources fairly among its people
b	Equality	ii	If a society uses its resources to produce maximum output
c	Efficiency	iii	If a society treats everyone in the same way.

2   Equality or equity? Identify whether these economic policies treat people equally or equitably.

   a   Government providing housing for unemployed and homeless people

   b   Government legislation that says firms must include women in their shortlist for job vacancies to help reduce the gender pay gap

   c   Access to free education regardless of income

   d   Means tested benefits

   e   Universal basic income

   f   Every individual paid exactly the same by the state

REFLECTION

Students often confuse equity and equality, and so it is important that you can distinguish between the two concepts. The focus of an exam question can be changed by linking it to equality rather than equity. Are you happy that you understand the difference? Can you create a couple of long-answer questions that focus on each concept?

39.2 Absolute and relative poverty

« RECALL AND CONNECT 1 «

Define the term 'absolute poverty'.

UNDERSTAND THIS TERM

   •   relative poverty

You need to learn the definitions of absolute poverty and relative poverty that are given in your coursebook. However, it is also important (for your own learning) to make sure that you check if there are any updates to these thresholds over the period of time that you are studying economics. Measures of poverty can change over time. Have you looked at the World Bank's website to check these measures?

Equally, it is important to have a general understanding of the term 'poverty' rather than just learning the measures. Poverty is a situation in which a household cannot afford to satisfy the basic wants and needs such as shelter, heat, water and food. It can also be useful to know some countries and regions that have high levels of poverty. Can you list **five** countries that suffer from high levels of poverty?

Other measures of poverty do exist. Even though you cannot be asked about them directly, it can useful to know some of them, for example, the multidimensional poverty index (MPI). Have you ever looked at MPI data?

39.3 Policies towards equity and equality

≪ RECALL AND CONNECT 2 ≪

a Using an example, distinguish between the terms 'income' and 'wealth'.

b Explain why income tax is considered progressive.

c Give **two** examples of transfer payments.

UNDERSTAND THESE TERMS

- means-tested benefits
- poverty trap
- universal benefits
- universal basic income
- negative income tax

1   Copy and complete Table 39.1. State some advantages and disadvantages of each of the following government interventions.

	Advantage	Disadvantage
Means-tested benefits		
Universal benefits		
Negative income tax		

Table 39.2: Advantages and disadvantages of different government interventions strategies to reduce inequalities

2   Assess whether there is a link between:

a   transfer payments and absolute poverty

b   negative income tax and equity.   [20]

REFLECTION

You may be asked in an exam to assess different methods of reducing poverty and/or income inequality. It is worth noting that many governments have had relatively limited success in reducing income inequality over time. It would be valuable to do some research here.

Can you list **two** countries that have tried means-tested benefits? Universal benefits? Negative income tax? To what extent have they been successful?

How often do you read the news to keep track of current affairs related to your study of economics?

SELF-ASSESSMENT CHECKLIST

Let's revisit the Knowledge focus and Exam skills focus for this chapter.
Decide how confident you are with each statement.

Now I can	Show it	Needs more work	Almost there	Confident to move on
explain the difference between equity and equality	Give **three** examples of economic policies that achieve equity and do the same for equality.			
explain the difference between equity and efficiency	Define 'efficiency'.			
analyse the distinction between absolute poverty and relative poverty	State the definitions for both ideas.			
describe the poverty trap	Define 'poverty trap'.			

CONTINUED

evaluate policies towards equity and equality such as negative income tax, universal benefits and means-tested benefits and universal basic income	List the advantages and disadvantages of each.			
distinguish between economic terms that are closely related but technically different	Identify some closely related concepts from previous chapters (e.g., Chapters 33 and 34) and write out (in full sentences) the differences between the concepts.			
understand the importance of staying up to date with current affairs during my period of study.	Create a scrapbook of news stories that are related to some of your recent learning.			

40 Labour market forces and government intervention

EXAM SKILLS FOCUS

In this chapter you will:

- recognise how to respond to a quotation question

- understand the importance of regular self-testing.

A common way to test your understanding of economic theory is to ask you to respond to a particular quotation or claim. Students can sometimes find these sorts of questions quite tricky, not because they have poor knowledge but because they find it hard to decode what the question is asking. One thing to remember is that exam questions must be based on the content in the syllabus. Therefore, you should always be thinking: Which part of the syllabus am I being tested on? While the focus of the question will be different in each case, you should continue with the best practice advice that you have been given so far: highlight the command word, look at the mark allocation and make sure you apply your answer to the context given.

During revision, it is important that you avoid a cramming process. Instead, aim for a longer lead time for exam preparation and break down the content into small, manageable chunks. In addition, you should increase the volume of testing opportunities. In this chapter, you will have the opportunity to practise several 'explain' questions; this should give you some idea of the frequency of testing that you should aim for.

40.1 The demand for labour

« RECALL AND CONNECT 1 «

Describe the law of diminishing marginal returns.

1 What is the formula for MRP?

2 Now have a look at Table 40.1. It shows a selection of data for a firm that sells coffee for $5 per cup. The workers are the baristas working in the café.

Calculate the MRP at every level of labour.

Workers	Total output (product)	Marginal output (product)	Price	MRP (price × marginal output)
1	30	30	5	
2	70	40	5	
3	112	42	5	
4	152	40	5	
5	182	30	5	
6	198	16	5	
7	199	1	5	

Table 40.1: Calculation of MRP

3 If the market rate for a barista was $80 a day, how many baristas would this café employ? Justify your answer.

4 Using the concept of MRP, explain why the demand curve of labour slopes downwards. [4]

40.2 The supply of labour

1 Copy the following text and fill in the gaps.

The supply of labour is the total number of hours that labour is _____ and _____ to work for a particular _____. It should be remembered that the labour market involves _____ and their willingness to participate (or otherwise) in the labour market. This decision usually depends upon the _____ that they are offered for their _____, although for some workers, the wage has only a minor influence on their decision of whether to work — other _____ factors have a stronger influence.

40.3 Wage determination in perfect markets

Students often confuse labour market diagrams with product market diagrams. It is essential that you label the axes of your labour market diagram correctly.

1   What is on the y axis and x axis in a labour market diagram?

2   Using a diagram, explain the impact of an increase in the demand for labour on the market wage and number of workers employed.   [5]

It is important that you can explain economic theory from different perspectives, such as when demand shifts right/left and the supply of labour shifts right/left. In an exam, the case study may not tell you which curve to shift. Instead, it will be up to you to read the case study and decide for yourself.

3   Can you state **three** reasons why the demand curve for labour may shift right?

4   Can you state **three** reasons why the supply curve for labour may shift right?

5

> **Albania and its EU membership**
>
> Albania has a population of under three million people. It is a relatively poor country in Europe, and its economy is dominated by the agricultural sector. For example, 24% of Albania's territory is agricultural land, and 40% of the population work in the agricultural sector.
>
> Albania applied for EU membership status in 2009 and was granted candidate status in 2014. This means that Albania may join the European Union trade bloc at some point in the near future. If it becomes a member, then all 450 million inhabitants of other EU countries will have the right to work in Albania. In addition, all Albanian citizens have the right to work in EU countries without the need for a visa. Many Albanians see EU membership as being bad for the labour market.

'EU membership is bad for the labour market'. Explain some of the negatives impacts of EU membership on the labour market for agricultural workers in Albania.   [7]

40.4 Wage determination in imperfect markets

1 Draw the diagrams for each of the following situations:

- trade union keeping wage above equilibrium
- monopsony keeping wage below equilibrium
- minimum wage keeping wage above equilibrium.

2 Copy and complete Table 40.2. State some advantages and disadvantages of each situation.

Clue: think about it from the perspective of different stakeholders.

	Advantage	Disadvantage
Trade union		
Monopsony		
Minimum wage		

Table 40.2: Advantages and disadvantages of trade unions, monopsony power and minimum wages

REFLECTION

It is always useful to learn the counter-arguments to the main economic theory. Imperfect labour markets are the counter-argument (evaluation) to the traditional labour market economics.

How well do you know the advantages and disadvantage in Table 40.2?

3 'Traditional economic theory of wage determination is useless because there are so many exceptions to the rules.' Assess the extent to which you agree with this assertion. [20]

40.5 Wage differentials

1 'Wages differentials are always caused by market forces.' Assess this statement. [20]

40.6 Transfer earnings and economic rent

1 Look at the following diagrams. Can you identify the areas of economic rent and/or transfer earnings in each diagram?

a

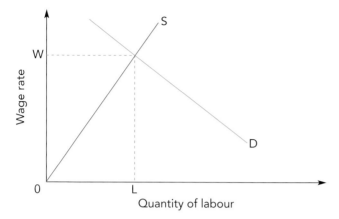

b

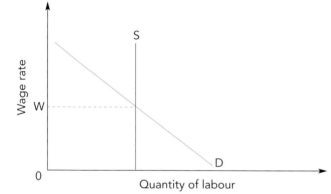

c

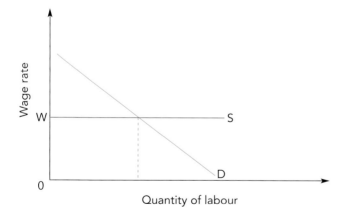

SELF-ASSESSMENT CHECKLIST

Let's revisit the Knowledge focus and Exam skills focus for this chapter.
Decide how confident you are with each statement.

Now I can	Show it	Needs more work	Almost there	Confident to move on
explain why the demand for labour is a derived demand	Explain how the demand for labour is a derived demand.			
define the meaning of marginal revenue product (MRP)	State the formula for MRP.			
calculate the marginal revenue product of labour and use marginal revenue product to derive an individual firm's demand for labour	State the formula for MRP.			
analyse the factors affecting demand for labour in a firm or in an occupation	Explain **two** reasons why the demand curve for labour might increase for gold miners, and explain **two** reasons why the demand curve for labour might decrease for farmers.			
analyse the causes of shifts in the demand curve and movements along the demand curve for labour in a firm or in an occupation	State **three** factors that shift the demand curve for labour.			
analyse the factors affecting the supply of labour in a firm or in an occupation, including wage and non-wage factors	State **three** factors that shift the supply curve for labour.			
analyse the causes of shifts in the supply curve and movements along the supply curve for labour in a firm or in an occupation	State **three** factors that shift the supply curve for labour.			

CONTINUED				
analyse wage determination in perfect markets, including equilibrium wage rate and employment in a labour market	Draw a labour market diagram.			
evaluate wage determination in imperfect markets, including the influence of trade unions, government and monopsony employers	State some advantages and disadvantages of each imperfection.			
explain the determinants of wage differentials by labour market forces	Explain why workers in the same industry might earn different wages.			
define the meaning of transfer earnings and economic rent	Distinguish between the concepts of transfer earnings and economic rents.			
evaluate the factors that affect transfer earnings and economic rent in an occupation.	Explain how the elasticity of supply for labour is related to transfer earnings.			
recognise how to respond to a quotation question	Ensure you can explain the reasoning behind a quote and then offer counter-arguments, For example: 'High minimum wages cause more economic problems than they fix.'			
understand the importance of regular self-testing.	Create a revision schedule which has a self-assessment check built into it.			

Exam practice 8

This section contains practice questions. These questions draw together your knowledge on a range of topics that you have covered up to this point and will help you prepare for your assessment.

The following questions have example student responses and commentaries provided. For each question, work through the question first, then compare your answer to the example student response and commentary.

1 After negotiation, the workers in an industry obtained higher wage rates from employers. The employers' spokesperson said that 'the cost of the deal would have to be met through improved productivity or by reductions in other costs'.

Assess whether this deal can be incorporated into the economic theory of wages **and** consider the possible outcome for employment of such a deal. [20]

Example student response	Examiner comments
Traditional economic theory suggests that wages are set by the market of supply and demand. For example, in a typical labour market there will be a pool of potential workers (supply) and a number of firms willing to hire people (demand).	**AO1 Knowledge and understanding** This is a good introduction on traditional economic theory on labour markets.
The demand curve is derived from the law of diminishing marginal returns. In the short run, if a firm tries to increase its output then the fixed factor of production will act as a constraint to the other variable factors of production. This means that the production process becomes less efficient. As a result, as the firms add each additional unit of labour to other fixed resources, the marginal output starts to decrease. This means that the MRP (marginal revenue product) or, the addition to total revenue as a result of employing one more worker, is falling. In other words, as the number of units of labour increases, the additional revenue that each one brings in decreases. And, therefore, the wage that the firm is willing to pay to that unit of labour decreases. Hence, the demand curve for labour is downward sloping.	**AO2 Analysis** There is excellent analysis throughout. The student frequently refers back to the original stem of the question. Where diagrams are used, they are accurately drawn. Two things to note are, first, the second paragraph is probably too long. The focus of the answer must be on a high negotiated wage and its impact. This student has spent a lot of time explaining traditional economic theory without (yet) starting to analyse those key elements of the question.
The supply curve is upwards-sloping because the number of people willing and able to work increases when the market wage increases. The intersection of supply and demand sets the market wage and the number of people employed in the market. This is because this is the point at which the MRP equals the desired wage.	
However, traditional economic theory does not help to explain situations such as trade unions and negotiated wages. In this scenario, workers in an industry obtained from employers higher wage rates. This can be illustrated in a diagram like the one below where the negotiated wage is fixed above the market equilibrium wage rate. Thus, traditional economic theory allows us to demonstrate the impact of such an event, even though is now an imperfect market.	

Example student response	Examiner comments
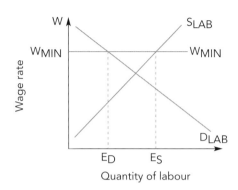 One positive outcome of the event is that workers are now being paid more. This will raise income and standards of living. However, there are lots of negatives. For example, the outcome on employment is that there is excess supply at the new negotiated (trade union) wage. More people want to work than the firm wants to hire. Unlike economic theory, the wage has been set by the negotiations and not by market forces. So, some level of unemployment has been created by this negotiation. Similarly, the employers' spokesperson said that 'the cost of the deal would have to be met through improved productivity or by reductions in other costs'. This is because an increase in wages will lead to an increase in the costs of production for a firm. This can be demonstrated in a simple demand and supply diagram with the supply curve shifting to the left. There is a contraction along the demand curve and, as a result, revenue and profit for the firm is likely to decrease. The firm may now have to find different ways to compensate for these increased costs. 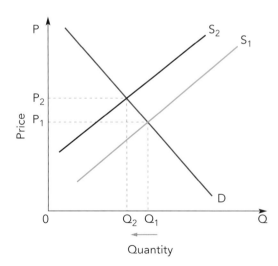 For example, they can reduce fixed costs by re-negotiating rental agreements or variable costs by finding new suppliers for raw materials. This may reduce working conditions for staff. Or, it may reduce the quality of the final product which may then reduce sales.	Second, the student could have used more diagrams. For example, instead of using supply and demand, the student could have used a cost–revenue diagram from their previous knowledge. That would allow the student to show the impact on supernormal profits more accurately. In addition, the link to MRP theory is great analysis, but the answer could have been improved with a diagram to illustrate the impact of upwards pressure on wages. Using analysis from the A Level part of your course (rather than the AS Level part) will demonstrate a higher level of skill. That said, this is a very good example of string analysis. *AO1 and AO2: 13/14* **AO3 Evaluation** Generally, the evaluation is excellent. The student brings in real-life examples like 'labour can be replaced by AI', an important current affairs issue. The conclusion feels a bit rushed. It tries to answer the question, but it is too short. *5/6* *Total: 18/20 marks*

Example student response	Examiner comments
In terms of the labour force, the firm may look to increase productivity in order to get more output per worker. This will help to offset wage rate rises. This means that workers might be expected to attend more training courses, work harder during the day and lose any breaks. If productivity increases then the MRP increases too. This is because each additional worker now brings in more revenue to the firm than before. This is beneficial for the firm. It will also lead to an increase in the demand curve for labour, since demand for labour is derived from MRP theory. Therefore, if demand increases then it may be the case that the 'new' wage actually represents a fair reward for the increased productivity of workers. Because workers are more expensive, the firms may now consider whether they should buy more capital goods (machines). Machines are an alternative to human labour. In conclusion, traditional economic theory can help us to analyse the impact of this negotiated wage. Even though workers are getting paid more, there are lots of negative outcomes such as unemployment, increased likelihood of being replaced by robots, worse working conditions and losing breaks.	

2   With the help of diagrams, assess the links between transfer earnings, economic rent, the elasticity of supply of labour and an individual worker's wage rate.   [20]

Example student response	Examiner comments
Transfer earnings are the amount that is earned by a factor of production in its best alternative use. Economic rent is a payment made to a factor of production above that which is necessary to keep it in. PES of labour is the responsiveness of supply to a change in wage. Transfer earnings are indicated by the area under the labour supply curve which is upward sloping. Economic rent, by contrast, is the area above the supply curve but underneath the equilibrium wage rate. 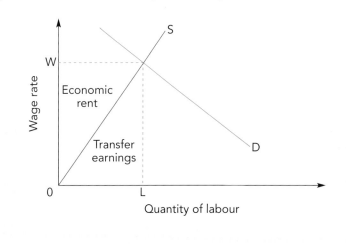	**AO1 Knowledge and understanding** The student demonstrates a strong understanding of all three key terms in the question. **AO2 Analysis** The second paragraph has an accurate diagram, which clearly shows the breakdown for economic rent and transfer earnings. This paragraph engages with the question entirely. It explains what happens when PES changes (in this case, becomes more inelastic) and why that happens. The diagram about perfectly inelastic supply also demonstrates strong understanding. *AO1 and AO2: 14/14*

Example student response	Examiner comments
From this diagram, it is clear that as PES becomes more inelastic, economic rent increases and transfer earnings decrease. This is because inelastic PES implies that the skills for this occupation are scarce. People are uniquely skilled, are highly qualified and add lots of value to the firm. Their wage is almost entirely economic rent because they are being rewarded for their very special skill set. If PES is perfectly inelastic, then the wage is entirely economic rent. 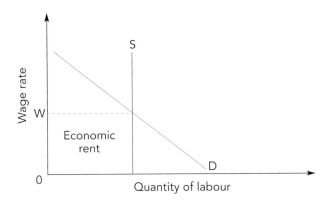 By contrast, if PES is relatively elastic then economic rent decreases and transfer earnings increase. This is because elastic PES implies that the skills for this occupation are relatively low. Many people are qualified for this job and are happy to do it, e.g., bus drivers. They are essentially being paid the minimum amount to keep them in the job but no more. If PES is perfectly elastic then the wage is entirely transfer earnings. 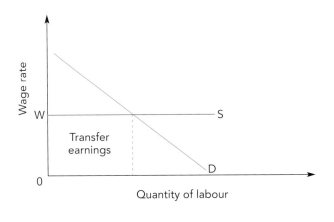	**AO3 Evaluation** The evaluation is excellent as well. Again, the student is fully answering the question. They have looked at all of the key terms, and they have drawn accurate diagrams throughout the essay to illustrate what is going on. However, the answer would have been improved by also including a conclusion. **5/6** Note: This is not a particularly long essay, but it does satisfy the demands of the question and its use of technical language means that it can cover a lot of content quite quickly. *Total: 19/20 marks*

3 'Trade unions can gain an increase in wage levels only at the expense of higher levels of unemployment.'

Assess the extent to which you agree with this statement. [20]

Example student response	Examiner comments
Trade unions are organisations that seek to represent labour in their place of work. They were set up and continue to exist because individuals (labour) have very little power to influence conditions of employment, including wages. Through collective bargaining, where trade union representatives get together with employers, trade unions generally aim to increase the wage rates of their members. The effect of a strong trade union can be illustrated in a labour market diagram – see below. 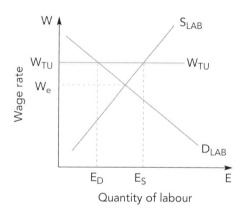 In this case, the trade union wage rate (W_{TU}) is fixed above the equilibrium wage rate (W_e). This means that workers are being paid more. Which, ultimately, was the aim of the trade union. However, economic theory suggest that will come at the expense of jobs. The higher wage rate leads to excess supply (E_s to E_D). Lots of people are willing and able to work at that wage rate but firms are less willing to hire them. This excess supply is 'unemployment', and this is why the quote suggests that trade unions may achieve higher wage rates but only at the expense of high level of unemployment. The extent to which this is the case is debateable. Firstly, it depends on just how large the increase in the wage rate is. If the trade union is only able to negotiate a small wage rise then the excess supply is relatively small. Secondly, it depends on the wage elasticity of demand and supply for this occupation. If they are both high (that is, the workers are highly skilled (inelastic supply) and are not easily replaced by machines (inelastic demand) then excess supply will be small. A good example of this might be footballers – highly skilled, not easily replaced. It should be noted, however, that they earn very high wages through the market system and do not need trade unions to bargain.	**AO1 Knowledge and understanding** The essay has a strong opening. The student demonstrates an excellent understanding of the key term ('trade unions') and already links to the question about wage rates. **AO2 Analysis** In the second paragraph, the diagram is drawn accurately and, again, the student demonstrates their understanding. By the end of this paragraph, the student has explained the general logic behind the quote in the stem of the question. This is important because the question asks the extent to which you agree. Showing that you understand the logic behind the quote is a great way to demonstrate that you have a strong appreciation of all of the key concepts. Later on, there is an excellent link to monopsony. Not many other students will have picked up on this point, and so the student has differentiated themselves with a very sophisticated piece of theory. *AO1 and AO2: 14/14* **AO3 Evaluation** There are two main lines of evaluation. Both are good points (very technical in nature). It would have been useful to have included diagrams to illustrate the points in diagrammatic terms (especially the penultimate paragraph on productivity).

Example student response	Examiner comments
Thirdly, it depends on the firm. If they are a monopsony employer then economic theory suggest that they are playing lower than equilibrium wages. In this case, a trade union can provide a counter-balance to the monopsony power of an employer. Far from leading to unemployment, the trade union is actually helping with job creation.	The conclusion answers the question, but it could have been longer.
Finally, it can be argued that higher wages might lead to an increase in productivity. In this case, the MRP of workers will rise. This is because each additional worker now brings in more revenue to the firm than before. This is beneficial for the firm. It will also lead to an increase in the demand curve for labour, since demand for labour is derived from MRP theory. Therefore, if demand increases then it may be the case that the 'trade union' wage actually represents a fair reward for the increased productivity of workers.	5/6
In conclusion, this quote is not justified. Whilst traditional economic theory might lead us to this conclusion, there are lots of exceptions to the rule. Therefore, I only agree with this statement to a small extent.	Total: 19/20 marks

4   Assess whether universal income or means-tested benefits would be better at improving equity and equality in a country.   [20]

Example student response	Examiner comments
The issue of improving equity and equality has been a subject of debate for many years. In recent times, the debate has intensified with the concept of universal basic income and means-tested benefits being proposed as potential solutions.	**AO1 Knowledge and understanding**
Universal basic income (UBI) is a system of providing a fixed income to all citizens of a country regardless of their job status. One of the main advantages of UBI is that it is universal, meaning that all citizens receive the same amount regardless of their income level. This ensures that the poorest members of society receive the necessary funds to cover their basic needs. Furthermore, UBI has the potential to increase social mobility by providing individuals with the resources they need to invest in education or start a business. This could lead to increased economic growth, as more people would have the ability to contribute to the economy.	The student demonstrates an excellent level of knowledge about the two policies: UBI and means-tested benefits. However, there is not a lot of understanding shown about the difference between equity and equality. Neither concept is defined, and although the understanding of equality is probably shown implicitly, there is little mention at all about equity.
However, one of the major criticisms of UBI is that it may discourage people from working. If individuals are given a fixed income without the need to work, they may choose not to participate in the labour force. This could lead to a decrease in economic productivity and potentially higher taxes to support the UBI system. Another issue with UBI is the cost. Providing a fixed income to all citizens of a country can be expensive, and it may not be sustainable in the long run.	

Example student response	Examiner comments

Means-tested benefits are a system of providing financial assistance to individuals based on their income level or other criteria. This system ensures that those who need assistance the most receive it. Means-tested benefits can be targeted to specific groups, such as the elderly or those with disabilities.

Means-tested benefits can also create a disincentive to work. If individuals receive assistance based on their income level, they may choose not to work as they may lose their benefits. This can create a cycle of poverty.

In conclusion, both universal basic income and means-tested benefits have their advantages and disadvantages. While UBI may provide a safety net for all citizens and encourage social mobility, it may not address the root causes of inequality and could be costly to implement. Means-tested benefits, on the other hand, are targeted to those who need assistance the most and can be more cost-effective, but they may create a stigma and disincentive to work. Ultimately, the choice between UBI and means-tested benefits will depend on the specific needs and circumstances of each country. A combination of both systems may provide the best solution to improve equity and equality in a country.

AO2 Analysis

The analytical paragraph about UBI is excellent. But, by contrast, the mean-tested benefits paragraph is rather short. For example, there was a missed opportunity to compare the relative costs of the two schemes. The student could have explained that means-tested benefits can be more cost-effective than UBI as they are targeted to those who need them the most.

AO1 and AO2: 10/14

AO3 Evaluation

As with the analysis, the evaluation of UBI is done very well, but the evaluation of means-tested benefits is less strong. The student should develop the comment which reads 'this can create a cycle of poverty' to say why it can create a cycle of poverty and why this is important.

4/6

Total: 14/20 marks

5   Assess the effectiveness of tradeable pollution permits in reducing global carbon emissions.   [20]

Example student response	Examiner comments
Tradeable pollution permits are a market-based solution to reducing negative production externalities associated with carbon emissions. The idea behind this policy is to set a cap on the socially optimal level of carbon emissions and make available permits up to that level, requiring polluting firms to buy permits. If they need more, then they will need to buy them from other firms, raising demand for permits and thus the price of polluting. This incentivises firms to cut pollution.	**AO1 Knowledge and understanding** The student demonstrates an excellent level of knowledge about the tradeable pollution permits. It may have been a good idea, however, to have at least one section of the answer focused on the market failure of carbon emissions, i.e., negative externalities.

Example student response	Examiner comments
One good thing about pollution permits is that they use the price mechanism to internalise the external cost of pollution. This means that companies that pollute pay the cost of the pollution, and the cost is reflected in the price of permits. This encourages firms to invest in clean technology as permits become more expensive, which can reduce carbon emissions over time. Additionally, pollution permits can be reduced over time, ensuring that carbon emissions fall over time. This is shown in the diagram below, where S shifts to S_1. This will reduce carbon emission from Q to Q_1 and thus help global emissions to fall. 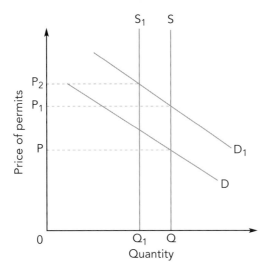 National governments can also raise funds from the initial sale of the permits, and the revenue can be used to clean up the environment. Firms are also encouraged to invest in green technology in developing countries, reducing global carbon emissions through carbon offset in other parts of the world. However, there are also bad things associated with tradeable pollution permits. One concern is that too many carbon permits may be issued by the government leading to little or no change in emissions. This could be due to information failure, leading to the price of carbon being too low, which does nothing to disincentivise the production of carbon. Additionally, too few permits could be issued, so production costs become too great, reducing profits and leading to job losses or firm closures. The burden may fall on smaller firms, and major polluting firms can buy up excess permits from elsewhere, which can strengthen the market power of large firms. Furthermore, carbon emissions are a global problem, and it may be difficult to manage a scheme such as this internationally, as there is no international regulator. This may lead to countries free-riding on others' efforts to reduce carbon emissions or other countries not participating at all.	**AO2 Analysis** The analysis starts off well and there is strong section on internalising the cost of pollution as well as a well-drawn diagram showing that permits can be reduced over time. However, the fourth paragraph simply makes assertions about raising funds and green tech investment without elaborating on them at all. *AO1 and AO2: 9/14* **AO3 Evaluation** The evaluative sections are good. In particular, there are good links to other market failures such as information failures and the free-rider problem. The conclusion is lengthy and comes to a well-articulated judgement. *6/6* *Total: 15/20 marks*

Example student response	Examiner comments
In conclusion, tradeable pollution permits have both good and bad aspects. They are effective in reducing carbon emissions by using the price mechanism to internalise the external cost of pollution and incentivising firms to invest in clean technology. However, given the fact that the cost of the permits is often passed on to consumers and that there is great difficulty in the management of such a scheme internationally, it is fair to say that policymakers may wish to consider other strategies like indirect taxes or green tech subsidies to reduce carbon emissions. Pollution permits are often too expensive and do not guarantee results.	

Here are two more practice questions which you should attempt. Use the guidance in the commentaries in this section to help you as you answer the questions.

6 Assess whether governments would have more to gain from increasing the size of the labour force or the increasing the labour participation rate. [20]

7 Using examples, assess whether behavioural insights and 'nudge theory' really can solve market failures. [20]

41 The circular flow of income

'Evaluate' means to judge or calculate the quality, importance, amount or value of something. For example, you may need to recognise any assumptions or limitations of any economic information provided or the strengths and weaknesses of arguments and then come to a conclusion. Judgement is particularly important. You need to analyse a question and then come to a conclusion based on the discussion you have provided.

A good answer requires precision. This is important in answering all questions and not just definition questions. Some students provide information that is not required or wander off the point of the question. You need to keep the question in mind and ensure that you write in clear, relevant sentences.

41.1 The multiplier

1 If national income rises by $20 billion as a result of a rise in investment by $5 billion, what is the size of the multiplier?

2 When will a closed economy without a government sector be in equilibrium?

3 If, in a closed economy with a government sector, mps is 0.1 and mrt is 0.1, what is the multiplier?

4 Why is the size of the multiplier likely to be smaller in an open economy with a government sector than in a closed economy with a government sector?

5 Copy and complete Table 41.1 by calculating apc, mpc, savings, aps and mps.

Income ($)	Consumer expenditure ($)	apc	mpc	Savings ($)	aps	mps
5000	5200	1.4	–	–200	–0.4	–
6000	6000	1.0	0.8	0	0	0.2
7000	6600					
8000	7000					
9000	7200					

Table 41.1: Income, consumer expenditure and savings

6 What is the difference between aggregate demand and aggregate expenditure?

In answering all the questions, remember the importance of precision. For example, in answering Question 7(b), you need to use the precise term for the piece of information.

7

India's multiplier

India is an open economy with a government sector. In recent years, the country's economy has grown rapidly. The country is a large exporter of technical and business services.

It has been estimated that the country has a marginal propensity to import of 0.2 and a marginal propensity to save of 0.3. To increase the effectiveness of fiscal policy, the Indian and other governments would welcome a large multiplier. However, a large multiplier would result in large fluctuations in economic activity. A rise in injections would cause a large increase in national income.

a Explain what is meant by an open economy. [2]

b Identify an additional piece of information which would be needed to calculate India's multiplier. [1]

c Explain why a large multiplier may increase the effectiveness of fiscal policy. [3]

d Analyse how an increase in India's export of technical and business services could benefit the Indian economy. [5]

UNDERSTAND THESE TERMS

- average propensity to consume (apc)

- average propensity to import (apm)

REFLECTION

In answering Question 7(d), did you remember the key areas to examine? In considering how an economy could benefit, you need to cover the key government macroeconomic aims. If you cannot remember all of them, check Chapter 21 in the coursebook.

≪ RECALL AND CONNECT 1 ≪

a   According to the circular flow of income, what is total income equal to?

b   What is the opportunity cost of households saving their income?

41.2 Components of aggregate demand and their determinants

1   Why would a more even distribution of income be likely to increase consumer expenditure?

2   a   An economy's consumption function is C = $10 billion + 0.8Y. What is consumer expenditure at a GDP of $380 billion?

    b   What is the difference between autonomous and induced consumer expenditure?

3   If the consumption function is $50 billion + 0.9Y, what is the savings function?

4   Copy Table 41.2. Match the questions with the terms in the word box on the components of aggregate demand. Note: the terms may fit more than one question, but you must end up with three of each component.

consumer expenditure	government spending
investment	net exports

Question	Answer
Which is an influence on investment?	
Which is a domestic component of aggregate demand?	
Which is an external component of aggregate demand?	
Which is influenced by advances in technology?	
Which is larger in a planned than in a market economy?	
Which is the most volatile component of aggregate demand?	
Which may decrease as a result of a rise in the interest rate?	
Which may increase as a result of a fall in the exchange rate?	
Which may increase during a recession?	
Which is influenced by changes in income?	
Which is usually the largest component?	
Which can be negative?	

Table 41.2: Components of aggregate demand

In answering the following essay-style question, remember that the command word 'evaluate' requires you to make a judgement. You need to explore both why investment may and why it may not increase and decide on the key influences and the most likely outcome.

5   Evaluate whether an increase in the apc and the mpc will increase investment.   [20]

> ## « RECALL AND CONNECT 2 «
>
> **a**   Why may a recession increase government spending?
>
> **b**   Why might net exports increase when a country experiences an unfavourable movement in its terms of trade?

> ### UNDERSTAND THESE TERMS
>
> • consumption function
> • savings function
> • accelerator theory
> • capital–output ratio

41.3 Full employment level of national income and equilibrium level of national income

> ### UNDERSTAND THESE TERMS
>
> • inflationary gap
> • deflationary gap

1   Why may a government choose to operate a budget surplus when there is an inflationary gap?

2   Why would a government seek to avoid a deflationary gap?

Question 3(c) asks you to explain three reasons and has six marks. This should indicate to you that you need to identify three reasons and then to make clear why these reasons mean that firms may not buy more capital goods when demand for consumer goods and services rise. Note that as the question asks for three reasons you will not gain any extra marks by explaining four reasons. Such a strategy would just reduce the time you have available to explain the three reasons you should explain.

3

The links between consumer expenditure, investment and national income

Consumer expenditure increased significantly in Bangladesh in 2022. This encouraged a rise in investment. Firms not only replaced worn-out capital goods, they also bought capital goods to expand production. Higher investment can have a multiplier effect. The resulting higher national income causes investment to increase by a greater percentage. The interaction of the multiplier and the accelerator can cause a significant change in national income. Figure 41.1 shows that the higher investment results in GDP increasing from Y to Y_1.

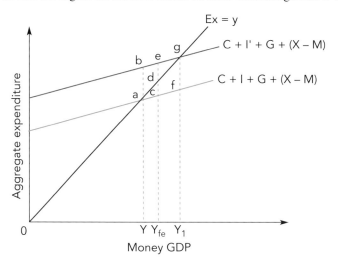

Figure 41.1: The effect of higher investment on national income

a   Identify, using Figure 41.1:

  i   the size of the multiplier   [1]

  ii   the inflationary gap.   [1]

b   Referring to investment, explain the difference between the multiplier and the accelerator.   [2]

c   Explain **three** reasons why an increase in demand for goods and services may **not** result in a proportionally larger increase in demand for capital goods.   [6]

REFLECTION

How confident did you feel in interpreting Figure 41.1? Could you produce a booklet of key diagrams? This can help you not only interpret the diagrams but also provides you with practice in drawing them and a reminder of the important ones.

≪ RECALL AND CONNECT 3 ≪

Why does full employment not mean zero unemployment?

SELF-ASSESSMENT CHECKLIST

Let's revisit the Knowledge focus and Exam skills focus for this chapter.
Decide how confident you are with each statement.

Now I can	Show it	Needs more work	Almost there	Confident to move on
explain the meaning of 'the multiplier'	Produce a flow chart, showing how much is passed on in spending from an injection of $100 if mpc is 0.5.			
calculate the multiplier using formulae in a closed economy without a government sector, a closed economy with a government sector and an open economy with a government sector	Calculate the multiplier if mps is 0.1, mrt is 0.07 and mps is 0.23.			
calculate the average and marginal propensities to save, consume and import	Calculate aps and mps if people save $3000 out of an income of $15 000 and would save $300 out of an extra income of $1000.			
calculate the average and marginal rates of tax	Calculate art and mrt if people pay $2200 in tax out of an income of $20 000 and would pay $400 out of an extra income of $1000.			

CONTINUED

analyse how national income is determined, using aggregate demand and income approach	Draw an AD/AS diagram and a Keynesian 45° diagram to show the effect of an increase in net exports.			
calculate the effect of changing aggregate demand on national income using the multiplier	Calculate the rise in national income if AD increases by $20 billion and the multiplier is 2.5.			
describe the determinants of aggregate demand	Identify the components of AD.			
explain the consumption function: autonomous and induced consumer expenditure	Give the consumption function if mpc is 0.7, income is $30 billion and $2 billion would be spent when income is zero.			
explain the savings function: autonomous and induced savings	Produce a multiple-choice question on the savings function.			
explain the determinants of investment	Produce a table on the key influences on investment.			
explain the difference between autonomous and induced investment	Identify the difference between autonomous and induced investment.			
explain the meaning of the accelerator	Explain the accelerator to a fellow student.			
analyse the determinants of government spending	Identify **three** key influences on government spending.			
describe the determinants of net exports	Identify **three** influences on net exports.			
explain the relationship between the full employment level of national income and the equilibrium level of national income	Draw an AD/AS diagram showing the full employment level of national income and a different level of national income.			

CONTINUED

analyse inflationary and deflationary gaps	Produce a table contrasting inflationary and deflationary gaps.			
understand the command word 'evaluate' and answer an evaluate question	Produce a plan for an answer to the question: Evaluate whether a deflationary gap is more harmful than an inflationary gap.			
understand the importance of precision in a good answer.	Define 'autonomous investment'.			

42 Economic growth and stability

KNOWLEDGE FOCUS

You will answer questions on:

42.1 Actual and potential economic growth

42.2 Positive and negative output gaps

42.3 The business cycle

42.4 Policies to promote economic growth

42.5 Inclusive economic growth

42.6 Sustainable economic growth

EXAM SKILLS FOCUS

In this chapter you will:

- show that you understand the command word 'analyse', used with the request for a diagram, and answer an analyse question requiring a diagram

- show that you can manage test anxiety by using a reward approach.

The command word 'analyse' requires you to explore a question in detail. Some questions may require you to do this with the use of a diagram. You will need to select an appropriate diagram: never make one up. Some students draw diagrams from their imagination: these never work. You will then have to draw it accurately to show the change that you will explain in writing.

It can be useful to follow a reward approach. After you have successfully completed a revision activity, why not reward yourself? This can be with a break, for example, with a cup of coffee.

42.1 Actual and potential economic growth

UNDERSTAND THESE TERMS

- actual economic growth
- potential economic growth

1   Copy the following text and fill in the missing words.

Actual economic growth can result from greater utilisation of existing _____ It may occur as an economy moves towards _____ employment. The result of actual economic growth is an increase in _____. When economists measure the _____ growth rate, they are measuring changes in _____ economic growth.

Potential economic growth occurs when there is an increase in _____ capacity. It may be the result of an increase in the quantity or _____ of resources. For example, net investment will increase the _____ stock and may incorporate advances in _____.

Potential economic growth will not result in _____ economic growth if there is not enough aggregate _____ to ensure that the rise in _____ capacity is used. What is most beneficial for economies is for actual economic growth to _____ potential economic growth.

≪ RECALL AND CONNECT 1 ≪

a   What are the **two** main causes of an increase in long-run aggregate supply?

b   Identify **two** possible causes of an increase in actual and potential economic growth.

42.2 Positive and negative output gaps

1   What are **two** indicators of a negative output gap?

2   What is the relationship between actual and potential output when there is a positive output gap?

3   Why is a positive output gap not sustainable?

UNDERSTAND THESE TERMS

- output gap
- negative output gap
- positive output gap

42.3 The business cycle

1   What economic problems may be encountered at the peak of the business cycle?

2   Why may a large expansion in bank lending cause an economic downturn?

3   What is meant by automatic stabilisers acting countercyclically?

The first two parts of Question 4 are relatively straightforward. As each has two marks, you should first state the evidence in Question 4(a) and the phase in Question 4(b). You should then make clear why you have given the answers for the second mark in each case.

In answering Question 4(c), consider how the economic growth rate has changed over the period shown.

In providing your answer to Question 4(d), you should bring out the meaning of negative economic growth and a government budget deficit; you should then examine the effects of a negative economic growth rate on both sides of a government's budget deficit.

Diagrams enable you to analyse. In your answer to Question 4(e), make sure your diagram is clear and accurately labelled. In your written analysis, make sure that you do not just describe what it shows, for instance, that a certain curve has shifted in a particular direction. What you need to do, in this case, is to interpret a negative output gap and to explain why the negative output gap may change.

UNDERSTAND THESE TERMS
• business cycle
• depression

4

Changes in the Hungarian economy

Hungary's output has fluctuated in recent years as shown by Figure 42.1.

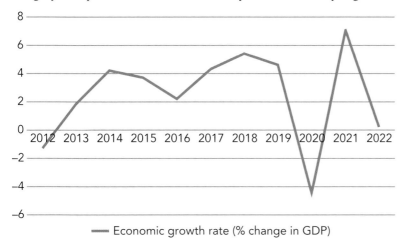

Figure 42.1: Hungary's economic growth rate 2012–2022

Hungary's economic performance in other respects also varied over the period 2012 and 2022. Its unemployment rate, for instance, was 11% at the start of the period. By 2019, this had fallen to 3.4%, the lowest rate in 50 years. By 2022, it had risen but only to 4.2%.

Throughout the period, Hungary had a budget deficit. Government spending fluctuated, as did consumer expenditure. At the end of the period, it was forecast that consumer expenditure would rise.

a   What evidence is there that Hungary experienced a low negative
    output gap in 2019?   [2]

b   Which phase of the economic cycle was Hungary in between 2014
    and 2016?   [2]

c   Explain how the pattern of Hungary's economic growth rate may have
    affected the country's investment over the period.   [4]

d   Explain the effect that the negative economic growth rate in 2020 was
    likely to have had on Hungary's government budget deficit.   [6]

e   Analyse, using a diagram, how an increase in consumer expenditure
    could reduce a negative output gap.   [6]

REFLECTION

Are you finding that you are now clear on the distinction between a government
budget deficit and a current account deficit? Students often confuse the two
but the more you apply your knowledge of them in answering questions, the
less likely this is to occur. You may also wish to produce revision cards on
a government budget balance and a current account balance.

« RECALL AND CONNECT 2 «

Over how long does real GDP have to fall for economists to declare a recession?

42.4 Policies to promote economic growth

1   What type of policy would a government use to promote economic growth?

2   What type of policy is a government likely to use to promote economic growth
    when there is a negative output gap?

« RECALL AND CONNECT 3 «

What other government macroeconomic objectives may be harmed by
government policies designed to promote actual economic growth?

42.5 Inclusive economic growth

1   Why may economic growth not be inclusive?

2   How may fiscal policy promote inclusive economic growth?

« RECALL AND CONNECT 4 «

Economic growth can be accompanied by a rise in structural unemployment.
Why are unskilled workers more likely to experience structural unemployment
than skilled workers?

UNDERSTAND THIS TERM

- gig economy

42.6 Sustainable economic growth

1 Why do governments try to ensure that tourism is spread throughout the country rather than concentrated in one area?

2 Copy and complete Table 42.1.

Change	Decrease or increase economic growth	Decrease or increase sustainability
Reduction in litter and the need to employ people to clean it up		
Cutting down rainforests to use their timber in a range of industries including furniture production		
Building wind farms		
Increase in the skills of workers		
Increase in air travel		
Increase in fishing which damages coral reefs		

Table 42.1: Effects on economic growth and sustainability

Question 3 involves a topic you may not be aware of. Data response questions can involve countries, products or topics you may not be familiar with. However, do not let this put you off. The data will give you all the information you need. They will form the basis for questions that allow you to apply your economic knowledge and skills.

In this case, you can answer Question 3(a) from the information in the data. In the case of Question 3(b) and Question 3(c) you need to apply relevant economic concepts to the topic described in the data.

3

> **The development of a circular economy**
>
> In manufacturing, raw materials are turned into finished goods. When the use of these goods is finished, many are sent to landfill sites or burnt. Now a number of industries are beginning to develop a circular economy. This involves not only recycling thrown away products but also extracting raw materials from them and then reusing them. For example, some car manufacturing factories are now recovering raw materials such as lithium, cobalt and nickel from old batteries and putting them into new batteries. This circular production not only reduces the harmful effects that may arise from disposing of goods but also can also help reduce the use of resources.

a Describe what is meant by a 'circular economy'. [2]

b Explain **two** government policy tools that could be used to encourage firms to adopt circular production. [6]

c Analyse how circular production can make economic growth more sustainable. [5]

REFLECTION

Did you make sure you explained two policy tools in your answer to Question 4(b)? Also did you devote approximately equal time to the two policy tools? If you did not, the next time you answer a similar question, why not underline the number of, for example, policy tools, examples, reasons or ways you are asked for?

SELF-ASSESSMENT CHECKLIST

Let's revisit the Knowledge focus and Exam skills focus for this chapter.
Decide how confident you are with each statement.

Now I can	Show it	Needs more work	Almost there	Confident to move on
explain the difference between actual growth and potential growth in national output	Draw **two** PPC diagrams to show the differences between actual and potential economic growth.			
explain the causes and consequences of positive and negative output gaps	Produce a table comparing the causes and consequences of positive and negative output gaps.			
describe the phases of the business (trade) cycle	List the phases of the business cycle.			
analyse the causes of the business cycle	Produce a table on the causes of the business cycle.			
explain the role of automatic stabilisers	Identify **two** automatic stabilisers.			
evaluate the effectiveness of policies to promote economic growth	Draw a mind map on the advantages and disadvantages of different policies to promote economic growth.			
explain the meaning of 'inclusive economic growth'	Define 'inclusive economic growth'.			
analyse the impact of economic growth on equity and equality	Identify a reason why economic growth may increase equality and one reason why it may reduce equality.			
analyse policies to promote inclusive economic growth	Produce a flow chart showing how government spending on education could promote economic growth and equality.			

CONTINUED

explain the meaning of 'sustainable economic growth'	Describe what is meant by 'sustainable economic growth'.			
explain the difference between using and conserving resources	Give an example of using and an example of conserving resources.			
analyse the impact of economic growth on the environment and climate change	Provide an example of an activity that could increase output an improve the environment and one which would increase output but harm the environment.			
evaluate policies to mitigate the impact of economic growth on the environment and climate change	Produce a table comparing the advantages and disadvantages of **two** government policies to reduce the impact of economic growth on the environment and climate change.			
understand the command word 'analyse', used with the request for a diagram, and answer an 'analyse' question requiring a diagram	Answer a past paper question with both written and diagrammatic analysis, such as Question 7(a) Paper 9708/42 Feb/March 2022.			
manage test anxiety by using a reward approach.	Think of a suitable reward you could give yourself when you have completed a revision activity.			

43 Employment and unemployment

EXAM SKILLS FOCUS

In this chapter you will:

- show that you understand the command word 'compare', used with the request to compare trends in economic data

- show that you can write high-quality essay answers.

The command word 'compare' requires you to identify and comment on similarities and/or differences. This command word is likely to appear in the data response question. You may be asked to compare, for example, trends in economic data. You will examine usually two items, explaining what they have in common and the ways in which they differ.

A high-quality essay answer is one which answers the question directly. To do this, you may have to adapt your knowledge and understanding. You need to be flexible. Prelearnt answers to essay questions are very unlikely to match the requirements of the actual questions set. Some students answer the question they would like to answer rather than the specific question set. It is useful to refer directly to the words of the question at the start of your answer. This can help focus your mind and structure your answer.

43.1 Full employment

Answering the following Knowledge recall question should help you in defining full employment. The definition of full employment in the context of the labour market is one which students sometimes struggle with.

1   Why is it impossible to get a 0% unemployment rate?

« RECALL AND CONNECT 1 «

Why may a fall in the number of people unemployed not increase the number of people employed?

UNDERSTAND
THIS TERM

• full employment

43.2 Equilibrium and disequilibrium unemployment

This section starts with a question requiring you to complete a table which should remind you of the key differences between equilibrium and disequilibrium unemployment. There is a short Knowledge recall question designed to make you think about a key feature of equilibrium unemployment and about a point you need to take into account when drawing diagrams showing equilibrium unemployment. You then have to define three key terms and finish with a Recall and connect question about the nature of the labour force.

UNDERSTAND
THESE TERMS

• equilibrium
  unemployment

• voluntary
  unemployment

• disequilibrium
  unemployment

1   Copy and complete Table 43.1, comparing equilibrium and disequilibrium unemployment.

	Equilibrium unemployment	Disequilibrium unemployment
Type(s) of unemployment included		cyclical
Effect of an increase in labour mobility	reduce	
Effect of an increase in labour market information		leave unchanged
Effect of a decrease in unemployment benefit	reduce	

Table 43.1: Effects on equilibrium and disequilibrium unemployment

2   Why does the gap between the aggregate labour force and the aggregate supply of labour widen as the wage rate falls?

« RECALL AND CONNECT 2 «

Identify **two** reasons for an increase in the proportion of people of working age in the labour force.

43.3 Voluntary and involuntary unemployment

The first knowledge-recall question here on involuntary employment should help you with the second one. Question 2 focuses on the nature of voluntary unemployment by asking you to consider how certain changes may affect voluntary unemployment.

1 When are people involuntarily unemployed?

2 Decide, in each case, whether the following will be likely to increase or decrease voluntary unemployment:

   a a decrease in the national minimum wage

   b a decrease in fringe benefits

   c a decrease in income tax

   d an increase in unemployment benefit

   e an increase in working hours.

> ### UNDERSTAND THIS TERM
>
> - natural rate of unemployment

REFLECTION

If you are still unsure about any of the answers to Question 2, even after you have thought about them, why not ask another student or teacher if they can clarify the point? You may be doing a fellow student a favour as explaining points to another person is one of the best ways of getting the points clear in your own mind. You can always return the favour on another question.

43.4 The natural rate of unemployment

1 According to the concept of the natural rate of unemployment, what effect would an increase in aggregate demand have on unemployment?

2 Copy and complete the following mind map. Each line represents a missing word.

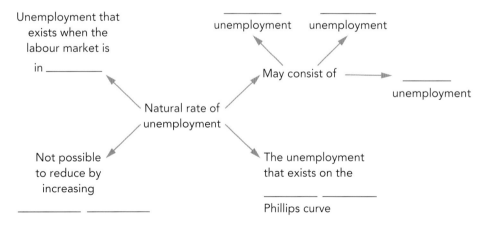

Figure 43.1: The natural rate of unemployment

Were you able to fill in most of the gaps? If you could not fill in all of them, think how you could strengthen your memory of these points. You could draw a second mind map showing government policy measures to reduce the natural rate of unemployment. This could help you in answering the following essay style question.

In answering Question 3, remember the advice given at the start of the chapter. You may be tempted to write about whether government policy can reduce unemployment in general rather than specifically the natural rate of unemployment. Many of the points you might mention in an essay question on whether government policy can reduce unemployment will be relevant here, but they must be directed towards reducing 'the natural rate of' unemployment.

3   Assess whether government policy can reduce the natural rate
    of unemployment.   [20]

Do you think you have answered the actual question? You could ask another student to read your answer and ask them what question they think you were answering.

43.5 Patterns and trends in unemployment

The questions here may help you consider how different groups can be affected by unemployment.

1   Decide which of the following groups are likely to experience higher or lower than average unemployment.

   a   occupationally mobile workers

   b   old workers

   c   university graduates

   d   workers with IT skills

   e   young workers

« RECALL AND CONNECT 3 «

Why may the children of parents who have experienced long periods of unemployment be more likely to be unemployed than the average worker?

43.6 Patterns and trends in employment

1 Matching the questions to the correct answers here will enable you to apply your knowledge and understanding of the patterns and trends in unemployment. You may find at first that more than one answer can match a question. This may mean that you need to change a couple to ensure that there is an appropriate answer for each question.

Question	Answer
Why may more women enter the labour force?	Declines as the pattern of employment changes
What usually happens to the proportion of workers employed in the public sector as a country moves towards a market economic system?	Rise in pay and more job opportunities
Why may part-time employment rise?	Rise in the national minimum wage
What usually happens to the proportion of the labour force employed in the primary sector as a country develops?	Need to look after family members and inability to find the type of job with the hours wanted
Why may there be a fall in the number of people working in the informal economy?	Declines as a result of privatisation

Table 43.2: Causes of changes in the pattern of employment

UNDERSTAND THIS TERM

• self-employed

≪ RECALL AND CONNECT 4 ≪

What are **three** possible reasons why people may prefer to work in the public sector rather than the private sector?

43.7 The forms of labour mobility

1   Table 43.3 shows some of the key influences on labour mobility.
    Copy the table and match the causes with relevant examples.

UNDERSTAND
THESE TERMS

•   occupational
    mobility

•   geographical
    mobility

Causes of labour immobility	Example
A long term contract and lack of qualifications	A plumber not moving to a higher paid job in a different area
Immigration controls and inability to speak the language	A disabled worker staying in a low-paid job
Difference in house prices and family ties	A Malian farmer not moving to the USA for higher wages
Attachment to employer and reluctance to work unsocial hours	A footballer not becoming an accountant
Discrimination and lack of information about job opportunities	A gardener not becoming a night porter in a hotel

Table 43.3: Causes of labour immobility

43.8 Policies to reduce unemployment

1   Why may a cut in income tax reduce unemployment more in other countries than
    in the home country?

2   Why may a cut in income tax be considered to be both a fiscal policy tool and
    a supply-side policy tool?

Question 3 gives you the opportunity to explore your skills across not only government
policies but also the pattern of unemployment and labour mobility. It involves both
a line diagram and written text. Look over the information first, getting a general view
of the topic. Then read the questions. Go back to the data. Check what the diagram
is showing and pick out key comparisons for your answer to Question 3(a). Do not
just state what is happening in each year. It is important that you interpret the data.
As mentioned at the start of the chapter, think about how the rates and trends differ
and how they are similar. In answering Question 3(b), you should find that you could
explain a number of reasons, but note that you only have to cover two. There are also
only four marks for this question, so you do not have to go into much depth. However,
try to make sure that you include economic terms and concepts in your answer. In your
answer to Question 3(c), you need to consider what 'assess' is asking you to do and to
draw on both the data and your knowledge of economics.

3

Unemployment in Argentina

Between 2018 and 2022, Argentina was in recession. The country's unemployment rate and youth unemployment rate fluctuated over this period and over the longer period of 2010 to 2021 as shown in Figure 43.2.

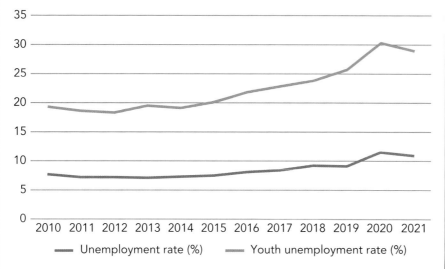

Figure 43.2: Argentina's unemployment rate and youth unemployment rate 2010–2021

In recent years, Argentina has experienced unemployment in a number of industries including construction. Workers do not always find it easy to move from working in one industry to working in another industry. Few workers who lose their jobs in construction are likely to become air pilots, for example.

To reduce youth unemployment, some economists have suggested that the government should increase its spending on education. Argentinian employers are looking for more IT skills and more soft skills, including communication and ability to participate in teamwork. In 2022, Argentina experienced a surplus of medical and law graduates, not all of whom found jobs.

a Compare Argentina's unemployment rate and youth unemployment rate over the period shown. [4]

b Explain **two** reasons why unemployed construction workers may not become air pilots. [4]

c Assess whether an increase in government spending on education in Argentina would reduce youth unemployment. [8]

REFLECTION

Are you now enjoying interpreting diagrams? Do you think your answers were clear? Why not try explaining the data and your answers to a non-economist? If you can make them understand, it should mean that you have a good grasp of the topic.

SELF-ASSESSMENT CHECKLIST

Let's revisit the Knowledge focus and Exam skills focus for this chapter.
Decide how confident you are with each statement.

Now I can	Show it	Needs more work	Almost there	Confident to move on
define the meaning of full employment	Describe the meaning of 'full employment'.			
explain the difference between equilibrium and disequilibrium unemployment	Identify **two** differences between equilibrium and disequilibrium unemployment.			
explain the difference between voluntary and involuntary unemployment	Define voluntary and involuntary unemployment.			
define the meaning of the natural rate of unemployment	Describe the meaning of the natural rate of unemployment.			
explain the determinants of the natural rate of unemployment	Identify **five** determinants of the natural rate of unemployment.			
analyse the policy implications of the natural rate of unemployment	Produce a flow chart showing the links between improvements in infrastructure and a decrease in the natural rate of unemployment.			
describe patterns and trends in (un)employment	Draw a line graph to show the unemployment rate of your country over the last 10 years.			
explain the forms of labour mobility: geographical and occupational	Explain geographical and occupational mobility of labour and give an example of each.			
analyse the factors affecting labour mobility	List **three** factors affecting geographical and **three** factors affecting occupational mobility of labour.			

CONTINUED

evaluate the effectiveness of the policies to reduce unemployment	Produce a table comparing the advantages and disadvantages of **two** different policy tools used to reduce unemployment.			
understand the command word 'compare', used with the request to compare trends in economic data	Compare trends in your country's unemployment rate for the last 10 years with that of another country.			
write high-quality essay answers.	Produce a plan for the following past paper question: Question 7 Paper 9708/41 June 2022.			

44 Money and banking

EXAM SKILLS FOCUS

In this chapter you will:

* further practise answering questions with the command word 'calculate'
* further practise answering questions with the command word 'outline'.

The command word 'calculate' involves working out from given facts, figures or information. You will need to use an economic concept or formula in your calculation. The more you practise these calculations, the more confident you will become. Remember you are allowed to use a calculator in the exams. Make sure your calculator matches Cambridge Assessment International Education requirements.

The command word 'outline' means to set out main points. This command word indicates that you do not have to go into depth in your answer. However, you do need to write about the key points. This means that you have to show the skill of selecting the main points and writing about them in a clear and coherent way.

44.1 Introduction to money

UNDERSTAND THESE TERMS

- money
- double coincidence of wants

1   Over time all the following items have been used to buy and sell goods and services. Which of the following are now used for this purpose:

   a   bank deposits

   b   bank notes

   c   buttons

   d   coins

   e   cryptocurrencies

   f   sea shells.

2   After a period of hyperinflation, a government introduces a new currency. Decide which of the following characteristics of the new currency would encourage or discourage firms and households to use it as money:

   a   easy to counterfeit

   b   homogeneous

   c   perishable

   d   portable

   e   recognisble

   f   unlimited in supply.

《 RECALL AND CONNECT 1 《

Hyperinflation can mean that money does not carry out its functions. Which function would have to be lost for people to resort to barter?

44.2 The money supply

UNDERSTAND THIS TERM

- money supply

1   What is the difference between narrow and broad money?

2   What is narrow money also known as?

44.3 The quantity theory of money

1   Copy the paragraph below on the quantity theory of money and fill in the missing words.

The quantity theory of money is based on the _____ equation. Both sides of the equation can be considered to represent total _____. As the right hand side equals price multiplied by _____, it can also be regarded as total _____. The _____ equation is turned into the quantity theory of money by assuming that the _____ and _____ are constant in the short run. Such assumptions suggest that the cause of inflation is increases in the _____. A group of economists known as _____, however, argue that the equation cannot be used to make predictions as any of the four variables can change.

2   Carry out the following calculations that are linked to the quantity theory of money.

a   If GDP is $90 billion and the money supply is $12 billion, what is the velocity of circulation?

b   If the money supply is $75 billion, the price level, as measured by average price, is $60 and the velocity of circulation is 8, what is output?

c   Initially output is 320 billion, the money supply is $48 billion, the price level is $30 and the velocity of circulation is 24. If the money supply rises by 12%, according to the quantity theory of money, what will be:

i   the initial price level

ii   the % rise in the price level?

REFLECTION

How well did you do on these calculations? If you did not get them right, was it because of a numerical error? Did you rush your answers? If you did not get them right because you were unsure about the quantity theory, look over Section 44.3 in the coursebook. You could then try writing your own questions, checking with your teacher if they are right.

44.4 Functions of commercial banks

UNDERSTAND THESE TERMS

- government securities
- equities
- reserve ratio
- capital ratio
- liquidity

1 Decide whether the following statements are true or false:

a Commercial banks' most profitable activity is lending.

b Commercial banks' main objectives are profitability, liquidity and security.

c A bank loan allows someone to borrow up to a set amount, with interest only charged on the amount borrowed. The interest charged is usually higher than that charged on the other main form of borrowing.

44.5 Causes of changes in the money supply

UNDERSTAND THESE TERMS

- bank credit multiplier
- quantitative easing
- total currency flow

1 Why is confidence important in banking?

2 Identify a reason why a commercial bank that has the ability to lend an extra $50 million only lends $35 million more.

3 Copy and complete the following flow chart to show the monetary transmissions mechanism:

Increase in the money supply

↓

———

↓

———

↓

Increase in output and/or the price level

In answering Question 4(a), think about what formulae you need to use.
The calculations in Question 4(a) and Question 4(b) are relatively straightforward, but you may find it helpful to use a calculator in answering them.

4   Complete the following calculations:

a   If a commercial bank creates $90 million in new loans as a result of a change in its liquid assets of $15 million, what is its bank credit multiplier?

b   A commercial bank, which has a bank credit multiplier of 9, attracts $20 million in new deposits. What is the maximum amount its:

i   total deposits can increase by

ii   lending can increase by?

REFLECTION

Did you show your workings in your answers to Question 4(a) and Question 4(b)? Why do you think it is a good idea to show your workings? It is possible that you may gain a mark or marks for an answer that is partially correct. It is also good practice as it should ensure that you follow the right approach.

44.6 The effectiveness of policies to reduce inflation

1   A government overestimates the risk of future demand-pull inflation and uses policy tools to avoid it. What effect may this have on economic growth?

2   Why is it difficult for central banks to control the money supply?

The next question builds up the assessment objectives, in a similar way to Question 1 on Paper 2: AS Level Data Response and Essays and Paper 4: A Level Data Response and Essays. It starts with the lowest order objective (known as AO1 Knowledge and understanding) and finishes with the highest order (AO3 Evaluation). You should be prepared for this increase in the skills required as you progress through the questions. It is also usually best to answer the questions in order. This is because answering relatively straightforward questions can build up your confidence and because there will be a logical structure to the questions.

Note the word 'not' in Question 3(b). It is in bold to reduce the chance of you missing it. Question 3(b) also has the command word 'outline'. After writing a sentence on a reason in each case, you can then write another sentence making the reason clear.

Remember in your answer to Question 3(c) to base your answer on both Figure 44.1 and your knowledge and understanding of economics. In your answer to Question 3(d), note that the focus needs to be on households and not firms or the economy as a whole.

3

Causes and consequences of interest rate changes

The Monetary Policy Committee of the Central Bank of Kenya raised its interest rate from 8.25% to 8.75% in November 2022. It was concerned about the growth in bank loans given by the country's commercial banks, all aiming to make a profit. The number of commercial banks in the country was increasing. Most of these kept similar reserve ratios. Kenyan households were demanding more bank loans for a variety of reasons including to pay school fees and to purchase homes.

Some economists expressed concerns that while a high rate of interest might reduce inflation, it could bring disadvantages to households and could cause unemployment. Figure 44.1 shows the relationship between the interest rate and unemployment rate in six selected countries.

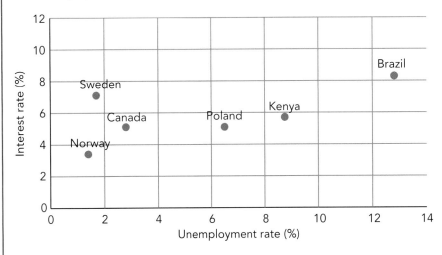

Figure 44.1: Interest rate and unemployment rate in selected countries 2022

a Identify what type of inflation the action of the Central Bank of Kenya would have been designed to reduce. [1]

b Outline **two** reasons why a commercial bank may decide **not** to lend to a household. [4]

c Analyse, using Figure 44.1, the relationship between the rate of interest and the unemployment rate. [6]

d Assess whether Kenyan households would have benefited from the rise in the interest rate in November 2022. [8]

≪ RECALL AND CONNECT 2 ≪

a   What are the **two** main causes of deflation?

b   What are **two** possible costs of inflation?

44.7 The liquidity preference theory

1   The left-hand side of Table 44.1 has the motives for holding money. The right-hand side has influences on these motives. Copy the table and rearrange the right-hand side so that each influence matches an appropriate motive.

Motive	Influence
transactions	concerns about the future
transactions	cost of insurance
transactions	expectations of future bond prices
precautionary	frequency of pay
precautionary	income
speculative	interest rate changes
speculative	prices of goods and services

Table 44.1: Influences on the motives for holding money

UNDERSTAND THESE TERMS

- liquidity preference
- active balances
- idle balances

44.8 Interest rate determination

1   According to Keynesians, what determines the rate of interest?

2   In what circumstance would the existence of the liquidity trap reduce the effectiveness of monetary policy?

3   According to the loanable funds theory, what effect would an increase in borrowing have on the rate of interest?

≪ RECALL AND CONNECT 3 ≪

a   Apart from the rate of interest, identify **two** influences on saving.

b   What is the formula for the savings ratio?

c   What are **two** reasons why people can spend more than their income?

SELF-ASSESSMENT CHECKLIST

Let's revisit the Knowledge focus and Exam skills focus for this chapter.
Decide how confident you are with each statement.

Now I can	Show it	Needs more work	Almost there	Confident to move on
define the meaning of money	Identify the main forms of money used today.			
explain the functions and characteristics of money	List the **four** functions of money and **five** characteristics an item has to possess to act as money.			
define the meaning of the money supply	Distinguish between narrow money and broad money.			
analyse the quantity theory of money	Calculate the price level if the money supply is $50 billion, output is 60 billion and velocity of circulation is six.			
explain the functions of commercial banks, including providing deposit accounts; lending money; holding or providing cash, securities, loans, deposits, equity; reserve ratio and capital ratio; and the objectives of commercial banks	List **four** functions of commercial banks.			
analyse the causes of changes in the money supply in an open economy including credit creation, government deficit financing, quantitative easing and change in the balance of payments	Identify **three** causes of a change in the money supply.			
explain the role of the bank credit multiplier	Produce a flow chart to show the link between a rise in bank deposits of $100 billion, when the credit multiplier is 20, and the money supply.			

CONTINUED

explain the role of the central bank	List **four** functions carried out by a central bank.			
evaluate the effectiveness of policies to reduce inflation	Produce a table showing the advantages and disadvantages of using fiscal, monetary and supply-side policies to reduce inflation.			
explain demand for money (liquidity preference theory)	Identify the **three** motives for holding wealth in the form of money.			
evaluate interest rate determination according to both the loanable funds theory and the Keynesian theory	Draw a diagram to show how the rate of interest is determined according to the loanable funds theory and the Keynesian theory.			
further practise answering questions with the command word 'calculate'	Calculate the money supply if GDP is $200 billion and the velocity of circulation is four.			
further practise answering questions with the command word 'outline'.	Outline **two** reasons why the number of commercial banks in your area may have changed.			

Exam practice 9

This section contains practice questions. These questions draw together your knowledge on a range of topics that you have covered up to this point and will help you prepare for your assessment.

The following question has an example student response and commentary provided. Work through the question first, then compare your answer to the example student response and commentary.

1   Evaluate how the relative size of injections into and leakages from the circular flow of income can affect the ability of a government to achieve its macroeconomic aims.   [20]

Example student response	Examiner comments
Injections are additions to the circular flow of income. They are extra spending which do not arise in the usual flow of spending between households and domestic firms. They are government spending, investment and exports.	**AO1 Knowledge and understanding** Good knowledge and understanding of injections and leakages is shown. It might have been useful to have identified government macroeconomic aims at the start of the answer.
In contrast, leakages are withdrawals from the circular flow. They are saving, taxation and imports. Leakages remove spending from the circular flow.	**AO2 Analysis**
If injections exceed leakages, there will be a net injection. This will cause aggregate demand (AD) to increase. The more injections exceed leakages, the greater will be the rise in AD and possibly in GDP. Whereas if leakages exceed injections, AD will fall and the greater the difference, the more AD will rise.	In examining how a change in injections and leakages would affect a government's macroeconomic aims, it would have been useful to have included reference to the multiplier effect.
An increase in AD will reduce cyclical unemployment and will help a government to achieve its macroeconomic aim of low unemployment.	The analysis could also have been strengthened by the inclusion of an AD/AS diagram. The meaning of cyclical unemployment could have been brought out. The difference between actual and potential economic growth might also have been examined.
If an economy initially has spare capacity, an increase in AD will result in actual economic growth. One of the main aims of any government is likely to be economic growth.	*AO1 and AO2: 10/14*
Higher AD, however, may cause inflation if it occurs when the economy is operating close to full capacity. The excess demand may cause demand-pull inflation. Although if net injection is the result of higher investment or government spending on, for example, infrastructure, both aggregate demand and aggregate supply may increase.	

Example student response	Examiner comments
If a rise in net injections is the result of higher net exports, a current account deficit is reduced. If there is a net injection into the circular flow, GDP will rise until again injections equal leakages. Higher GDP is likely to result in higher spending on imports, incomes moving into higher tax brackets and a higher proportion of income being saved.	**AO3 Evaluation** There is some evaluation in the second half of the answer. This is linked to whether there is spare capacity in the economy and how differences in injections and leakages will be eliminated in the long run. However, a strong concluding paragraph that sums up these points and that recaps the significance of injections and leakages would have been useful. 4/6 Total: 14/20 marks

Here is another practice question which you should attempt. Use the guidance in the commentaries in this section to help you as you answer the question.

2   Assess whether a decrease in the average and marginal propensities to save will benefit an economy.   [20]

The following question has an example student response and commentary provided. Work through the question first, then compare your answer to the example student response and commentary.

3   Equilibrium national income is a key concept in the study of economics. Assess the relative merits of policies a government might use to cause the equilibrium level of national income to change in an open economy.   [20]

Example student response	Examiner comments
Equilibrium national income is the level of a country's income where injections equal leakages. In an open economy, the three injections are investment (I), government spending (G) and exports (X). The three leakages are saving (S), taxation (T) and imports (M). So national income is in equilibrium where $I + G + X = S + T + M$. The diagram shows the economy is in equilibrium at an income of Y. 	**AO1 Knowledge and understanding** There is good knowledge and understanding shown of equilibrium national income in terms of injections equaling leakages and the nature of fiscal and monetary policy. However, equilibrium national income could also have been defined in terms of aggregate expenditure equaling output (income) and in terms of aggregate demand equaling aggregate supply. This would have strengthened the analysis and would have provided the basis for more analysis and evaluation in terms of supply-side policy.

Example student response	Examiner comments
To change the equilibrium national income, a government could use fiscal or monetary policy. A cut in corporation tax could increase investment. This is because firms will have more funds to invest and will have a greater incentive to invest, knowing that a smaller proportion of profits will be taken in tax. A cut in the rate of interest would also increase investment. The cost of borrowing will fall and firms will expect to sell more as the lower cost of borrowing and lower reward from saving are also likely to increase consumer expenditure. Higher investment will increase injections into the circular flow of income. It will set in place a multiplier effect on national income. The larger the size of the multiplier, the greater the effect of any change in an injection. For example, if mps + mrt + mpm equals 0.5, the multiplier will be 1/0.5 = 2. An injection of extra investment of $10bn will cause equilibrium national income to rise by $20bn. If, however, mps + mrt + mpm equals 0.1, the multiplier will be 1/0.1 = 10 and the same injection will cause equilibrium national income to increase by $100bn.	**AO2 Analysis** Again, there is some good analysis particularly in terms of the multiplier effect. The two diagrams are clear, accurate and useful. However, a clearer link to the diagrams would have been established if there had been reference to aggregate expenditure equaling output. Alternatively, diagrams showing injections equaling leakages could have been used. Supply-side policy designed to increase aggregate supply might also have been analysed. *AO1 and AO2: 11/14*
A rise in government spending on goods and services also acts as an injection. If the government raised its spending by $50bn and the multiplier is 3, equilibrium national income will rise by $150bn. A government could encourage a rise in exports in a variety of ways. It might instruct or encourage its central bank to sell its currency to lower the exchange rate. An increase in exports will again cause a multiple rise in national income.	
When there is an injection into the circular flow, national income will rise until injections again equal leakages. So, if injections total $50bn, national income will keep increasing until $50bn leaks out of the circular flow in the form of saving, taxation and leakages.	
The effect of some government policy tools on equilibrium national income are uncertain. This is because it can be difficult to predict how firms and households respond to changes in tax rates and interest rates. If firms and households are pessimistic about the future, they may save a high proportion of any rise in disposable income and may continue to save even if the rate of interest is reduced. In such a situation, an increase in government spending may be a more reliable government policy tool to get extra spending into the circular flow.	
In practice, it can be difficult to estimate the size of the multiplier effect. If a government underestimates it, expansionary demand-side policies may result in demand-pull inflation. The diagram shows that increasing government spending from G to G_1 results in an economy moving from a deflationary gap of ab to an inflationary gap of ca.	

Example student response	Examiner comments
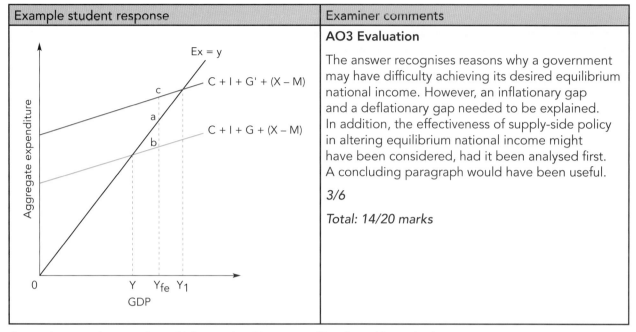	**AO3 Evaluation** The answer recognises reasons why a government may have difficulty achieving its desired equilibrium national income. However, an inflationary gap and a deflationary gap needed to be explained. In addition, the effectiveness of supply-side policy in altering equilibrium national income might have been considered, had it been analysed first. A concluding paragraph would have been useful. *3/6* *Total: 14/20 marks*

Here is another practice question which you should attempt. Use the guidance in the commentaries in this section to help you as you answer the question.

4 Assess how a change in the equilibrium level of income resulting from the multiplier process might lead to unemployment or inflation in a mixed economy with foreign trade. [20]

The following question has an example student response and commentary provided. Work through the question first, then compare your answer to the example student response and commentary.

5 'The use of quantitative easing (QE) has the same effect on the economy as the use of Keynesian fiscal demand management policy. Both policies create employment in the short run at the expense of inflation in the long run.'

How far would you support this view? [20]

Example student response	Examiner comments
Quantitative easing (QE) involves the central bank buying government bonds and other long-term securities. The intention is to raise the price of these financial assets and so lower the long-term rate of interest. For example, if a government bond that is initially sold for $100 pays $6 interest, the interest rate will be 6%. Increased demand for government bonds could raise the price to $120, reducing the interest rate to 5%. A lower interest rate paid on government securities tends to reduce interest rates throughout the economy, including mortgage interest rates.	**AO1 Knowledge and understanding** There is good knowledge of quantitative easing (QE) and fiscal demand management policy shown. **AO2 Analysis** There is good and detailed analysis of QE, but there should have been more examination of fiscal demand management. The links between higher government spending, for example, and higher output and employment could have been established. *AO1 and AO2: 9/14*

Example student response	Examiner comments
Lower interest rates can increase consumer expenditure and investment. Higher investment may also occur because the lower return on government bonds may encourage financial institutions and individuals to buy shares. Financial institutions would also have more money available from the sale of government bonds. Higher share prices will provide more funds for investment. The money used by the central bank in conducting QE is created digitally. It adds to the money supply. The increase in the money supply and resulting higher aggregate demand may result in demand-pull inflation. To try to get round this, central banks have reversed QE when there is evidence of inflationary building up. Selling government securities to push up long term interest rates is referred to as quantitative tightening (QT). Keynesian fiscal demand management policy involves the government changing government spending and/or taxation to influence aggregate demand. To stimulate economic activity, a government will use expansionary fiscal policy. It may increase government spending and/or lower tax rates or tax coverage. Keynesian and new classical economists agree that higher aggregate demand, resulting from expansionary fiscal policy, may increase output and employment in the short run. New classical economists, however, argue that higher AD can only increase output and employment in the short run. In the long run, they think that output will return to the long run equilibrium but at a higher price level. The diagram shows that initially the higher aggregate demand, AD_1, causes national output to rise to Y_1. In the long run, however, the higher AD pushes up wage rates and other costs of production. This causes short run aggregate supply to decrease from SRAS to $SRAS_1$. Real GDP returns to Y level of national output but at a higher price level.	

Example student response	Examiner comments
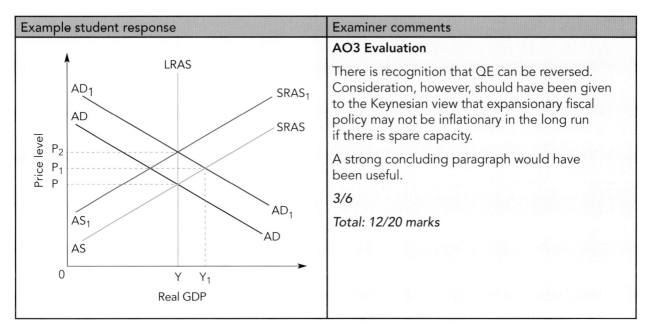	**AO3 Evaluation** There is recognition that QE can be reversed. Consideration, however, should have been given to the Keynesian view that expansionary fiscal policy may not be inflationary in the long run if there is spare capacity. A strong concluding paragraph would have been useful. *3/6* *Total: 12/20 marks*

Here is another practice question which you should attempt. Use the guidance in the commentaries in this section to help you as you answer the question.

6 Some Japanese economists have argued that higher interest rates would, unusually, improve Japan's economic growth.

Evaluate the view that the link between higher interest rates and economic growth is unusual and that economic growth is always good for an economy. [20]

The following question has an example student response and commentary provided. Work through the question first, then compare your answer to the example student response and commentary.

7 Firms say that high interest rates are not desirable because they prevent investment. Government ministers say that high interest rates are sometimes necessary because they encourage saving and control inflation.

Evaluate these two opinions and decide whether they are always true. [20]

Example student response	Examiner comments
Interest is the reward for saving and lending and the cost of borrowing. High interest rates may prevent investment for three reasons. One is that it increases the cost of borrowing to undertake investment projects such as building a new office block or buying new machinery. The higher cost may be greater than the expected return from the investment. Firms may expect that their sales may decline as households may spend less as borrowing would be discouraged while the reward for saving would be increased. Lower demand would reduce firms' profits and would be likely to reduce output and so the need and incentive to invest. High interest rates may also encourage firms to place their funds in financial institutions rather than buying capital goods.	**AO1 Knowledge and understanding** There is clear understanding of the possible influence of a higher interest rate on investment and the relationship between higher interest rates and demand-pull inflation.

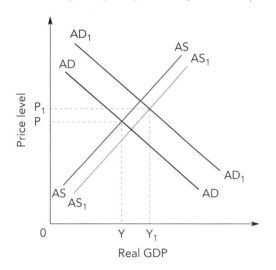

Example student response	Examiner comments
However, a government may want its central bank to raise interest rates to reduce demand-pull inflation. Consumer expenditure may be rising rapidly. This may result in aggregate demand increasing at a faster rate than aggregate supply. The diagram below shows that the larger shift in the AD curve to the right than the shift in the AS curve, pulls up the price level from P to P_1. 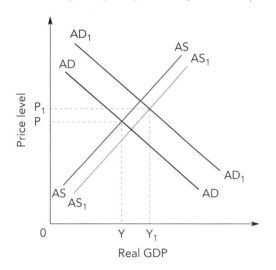 In this case, higher interest rates could reduce consumer expenditure, or the growth in consumer expenditure. Consumers may be discouraged from borrowing and may be encouraged to save more, given the higher return. Investment may also be reduced. So, two of the components of AD may decline or, at least, the growth may be slowed. Whether higher interest rates are desirable or not will depend on the level of economic activity. If there is a low level of economic activity, lower interest rates may be more appropriate as aggregate demand will be low. In this situation, a government may need to stimulate consumer expenditure and investment.	**AO2 Analysis** The analysis provided is clear and relevant. The diagram is clear and integrated into the answer. However, there needs to be more depth and width of analysis. For example, the relationship between greater saving and more funds being available for banks to lend to firms and the effect of higher interest rates on costs of production and cost-push inflation might be examined. *AO1 and AO2: 9/14* **AO3 Evaluation** There is a clear and relevant conclusion. With greater width and depth of analysis, the evaluation could have been stronger. For example, if the role of expectations on investment had been analysed, it might have been concluded that a small rise in interest rates might not reduce investment and AD if firms and households are optimistic about the future. In this case, higher interest rates may not control inflation. *3/6* *Total: 12/20 marks*

Here is another practice question which you should attempt. Use the guidance in the commentaries in this section to help you as you answer the question.

8 Assess the effects of lower interest rates in reducing a country's unemployment rate. [20]

The following question has an example student response and commentary provided. Work through the question first, then compare your answer to the example student response and commentary.

9 Assess the effectiveness of the policies a government might use to reduce an inflationary gap. [20]

Example student response	Examiner comments
An inflationary gap occurs when total spending is greater than the maximum output an economy can produce with all of its resources employed. The diagram shows that at the full employment level of GDP, Yfe, C + I + G + (X – M) is greater than potential output. 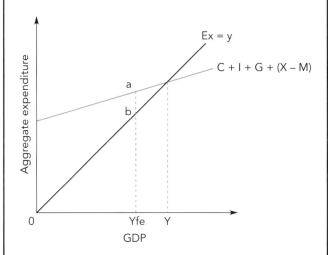 There is an inflationary gap of ab. To eliminate this gap, a government could use contractionary demand-side policies or supply-side policy. Contractionary fiscal policy would involve a cut in government spending and/or a rise in taxation. Lower government spending on goods and services directly reduces aggregate demand. Increases in income tax would reduce taxpayers' disposable income. This will reduce their purchasing power and is likely to reduce consumer expenditure, another component of aggregate demand. Higher corporation tax may reduce a third component of aggregate demand, investment. This is because firms will have less funds to invest and less incentive to invest. Contractionary monetary policy involves decreases in the money supply and increases in the rate of interest. A government may reduce the money supply by selling government bonds to the banking sector. This would reduce the funds they have available to lend to firms and households. A higher rate of interest would also tend to reduce consumer expenditure and investment. This is because it will increase the cost of borrowing and the reward for saving. A higher interest rate may also increase the exchange rate as it could attract hot money flows and so demand for the currency. A higher exchange rate may reduce exports and increase imports, lowering the net exports component of aggregate demand.	**AO1 Knowledge and understanding** There is a good understanding of an inflationary gap and the policies a government might use to reduce an inflationary gap. **AO2 Analysis** The analysis, which includes an accurate diagram, is good and relevant. The answer could have been improved by having more depth of analysis of supply-side policy. The answer could also have been rather better organised. If supply-side policy had been analysed earlier, then the conclusion could have referred back to it. *AO1 and AO2: 12/14* **AO3 Evaluation** There is some good evaluation, recognising some possible limitations of demand-side policies and concluding that supply-side policy might be a better option. This conclusion could, however, be built on stronger analysis of supply-side policy tools. *5/6* *Total: 17/20 marks*

Example student response	Examiner comments
Contractionary fiscal and monetary policy, however, may reduce output and employment in the long run. This is because they are likely to reduce investment which, in turn, can reduce productive capacity. Some contractionary demand-side policy measures may also reduce the living standard of certain groups. For example, cuts in spending on state education may affect the poor more than the rich. There is also the possibility that a government may underestimate the size of the multiplier and may turn an inflationary gap into a deflationary gap. A better way to reduce an inflationary gap may be to raise productive capacity rather than reduce aggregate expenditure. This might be achieved by using supply-side policy. For example, an increase in spending on education and training may raise labour productivity. Higher spending on infrastructure projects may reduce transport costs and encourage firms to increase their output.	

Here is another practice question which you should attempt. Use the guidance in the commentaries in this section to help you as you answer the question.

10   Assess whether an inflationary gap or a deflationary gap is likely to be more harmful for an economy. [20]

The following question has an example student response and commentary provided. Work through the question first, then compare your answer to the example student response and commentary.

11   Assess, using the liquidity preference theory, why people demand money and the possible consequences of an increase in the supply of money. [20]

Example student response	Examiner comments
Liquidity preference is the desire to hold wealth in a money form. There are three main reasons why people demand money. One is the transaction motive. This is the desire to hold money to buy goods and services. The second motive is the precautionary motive. This is money held to meet unexpected expenses and spending opportunities. The money held for these two motives is sometimes known as active balances. This is because they are likely to be spent on goods and services. These motives tend to be interest inelastic. This means that a fall in the rate of interest is likely to cause a smaller percentage extension in demand for money. The third motive for holding money is the speculative motive. People, mainly those working in financial institutions, may hold money to take advantage of changes in the price of financial assets, including government bonds, and the rate of interest.	**AO1 Knowledge and understanding** Very good awareness is shown of the meaning of liquidity preference and the three motives for holding money. There is also an understanding of the relationship between an increase in the money supply and the rate of interest. **AO2 Analysis** The analysis that is included is relevant. There might have been some explanation of why demand for money in the case of the speculative motive tends to be interest-elastic and a diagram showing the liquidity trap would have been useful. *AO1 and AO2: 12/14*

Example student response	Examiner comments
The price of government bonds and the rate of interest move in opposite directions. For example, if the price of a $200 government bond paying $24 interest (12%) rises to $300, the $24 interest will fall to 8%. People are likely to buy bonds when the price of bonds is low and expected to rise. This is because the rate of interest is likely to be high and there is the possibility that a profit will be made if the price of the bonds does rise in value. Money held for a speculative motive is sometimes called idle balances. Such money is likely to be interest elastic.	**AO3 Evaluation** The evaluation could have been improved by including a judgement about which motive is likely to account for the greatest value of money held. The student could also have made a link between the liquidity trap and the use of quantitative easing. *3/6* *Total: 15/20 marks*
An increase in the money supply will be likely to result in people having higher money balances than they want to hold. As a result, they are likely to use some of the extra money to purchase government bonds. The higher demand for government bonds will raise their price and lower the rate of interest. The diagram shows that the increase in the supply of money from M to M_1 results in the rate of interest falling from R to R_1. The quantity of money held rises from Q to Q_1. 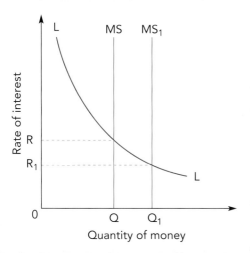 The effect of an increase in the supply of money, however, is not always certain. When the price of bonds is very high and the rate of interest is very low, an increase in the money supply may have no effect on the rate of interest. This is because people will hold all of the extra money that has come into circulation. The inability to drive down the rate of interest by increasing the money supply is known as the liquidity trap.	

Here is another practice question which you should attempt. Use the guidance in the commentaries in this section to help you as you answer the question.

12 Assess whether the liquidity preference theory or the loanable funds theory provides a better explanation of how the rate of interest is determined. [20]

45 Government macroeconomic policy objectives

EXAM SKILLS FOCUS

In this chapter you will:

* show that you can identify a mark scheme's expectations.

It is useful to become familiar with mark schemes issued by the exam board. Having looked at several past papers, you could try writing an essay question and an accompanying mark scheme. You could then try it out on another student.

45.1 Inflation

1 Use an aggregate demand and aggregate supply diagram to explain the possible effect on a country's inflation rate of an increase in the inflation rate of a country's main trading partner.

2 Why do central banks often discuss with each other their plans for interest rate changes?

3 Decide whether the following would increase or decrease the chances of an inflation rate target being successful:

   a It is set at a rate eight percentage points below the country's annual average inflation rate over the last ten years.

   b Trade unions are confident that the inflation rate target would be achieved.

   c Consumers think that the inflation rate will be above the target rate.

   d The global price of energy doubles.

   e There is a global spread of technological developments in food processing.

   f Other countries' governments impose inflation targets.

≪ RECALL AND CONNECT 1 ≪

a If a country has an inflation rate target, which institution sets it?

b If a country is at the natural rate of unemployment, what is happening to its inflation rate?

45.2 Balance of payments stability

1 Copy and complete the following paragraphs by filling in the missing words.

Governments aim for a stable balance of payments in the long run. If the _____ items on the current account balance equal the debit items, the government will not have to use _____, monetary and _____ policy to achieve its objective.

The avoidance of a long run current account _____ would mean that the government does not have to, for example, increase income tax which could reduce _____. There would not be a current account _____, which would put upwards pressure on the exchange rate.

If there is balance of payments stability, the country will not be getting into international _____ and will not be forgoing the opportunity to _____ goods and services.

≪ RECALL AND CONNECT 2 ≪

Why may a trade in goods and services deficit not be a cause for concern?

45.3 Unemployment

1 Identify **two** aims a government is likely to have for unemployment.

2 Decide which of the following a government may be seeking to achieve by lowering unemployment:

   a a decrease in the inflation rate

   b a decrease in welfare payments

   c an increase in the country's economic growth rate

   d an increase in living standards

   e an increase in productive potential

   f an increase in tax revenue.

« RECALL AND CONNECT 3 «

What is the difference between someone being unemployed and someone being economically inactive?

45.4 Economic growth

1 What are **two** reasons why economic growth may not be accompanied by a fall in unemployment?

2 Decide, in each case, which of the following would increase or decrease a government's aim for its economic growth rate:

   a a global recession

   b net immigration

   c discovery of natural resources

   d rise in educational standards

   e rise in health of population

   f rise in unemployment.

« RECALL AND CONNECT 4 «

What type of policies are used to increase actual economic growth and potential economic growth?

45.5 Economic development

1   From the details on the five fictional countries in Table 45.1, rank them from the likely most developed to the least developed.

Country	Income per head ($)	Life expectancy (years at birth)	Migration	Unemployment rate (%)	Proportion of output accounted for by the primary sector (%)
A	31 000	71	−3 million	9%	25
B	30 000	86	0.5 million	3%	20
C	30 000	88	1 million	4%	5
D	28 000	74	−2 million	6%	10
E	25 000	75	−5 million	8%	25

Table 45.1: Levels of development

45.6 Sustainability

1   What are **two** ways a government could increase sustainability?

2   How may CO_2 emissions reduce sustainability?

UNDERSTAND THIS TERM
• sustainable development

45.7 Redistribution of income and wealth

1   Is an extra $50 worth the same to everyone?

2   What effect would a rise in the rate of interest be likely to have on the distribution of income?

In answering Question 3, take careful note of the marks awarded. These indicate the time you spend on the question parts and the depth of your answers.

3

> ### Slow down in economic growth in high-income countries
>
> In recent years, the economic growth rate of high-income countries has slowed. There are a number of reasons for this. One is that the growth in the countries' labour force has declined. These countries' populations are having fewer children, a higher proportion of people over retirement age and a slowdown in the growth of the female labour participation rate. Some high-income countries have actually experienced a fall in population.
>
> Gains in productivity have also declined. The growth in the proportion of students going to university declined in some countries, which affected the growth in their aggregate supply and their current account balances. In addition, there were fewer reductions in trade restrictions. Indeed, some countries increased their trade restrictions. The imposition of import quotas, for example, may result in a decline in global output.
>
> In some high-income countries, residents have become more concerned with how green output is rather than the quantity of output. There are a number of factors which influence whether higher output is sustainable. It is also debatable as to whether economic growth will benefit everyone in a country.

a Using the information, identify **two** causes of a decrease in the size of a country's labour force. [2]

b Explain **two** government macroeconomic objectives that low productivity growth may harm. [4]

c Analyse how the imposition of import quotas may reduce global output. [5]

d Explain **two** reasons why economic growth may not be sustainable. [6]

e Assess whether economic growth benefits everyone in a country. [8]

REFLECTION

Both Question 1(b) and Question 1(c) have the command word 'explain'. However, Question 1(d) has two more marks. Did you provide more links in your answer to Question 1(d)? If not, see if you can provide more depth to your answer.

SELF-ASSESSMENT CHECKLIST

Let's revisit the Knowledge focus and Exam skills focus for this chapter.
Decide how confident you are with each statement.

Now I can	Show it	Needs more work	Almost there	Confident to move on
analyse macroeconomic policy objectives in terms of inflation, balance of payments, unemployment, growth, development, sustainability and redistribution of income and wealth	Identify **two** reasons, in each case, why a government seeks to achieve price stability, balance of payments stability, low unemployment, economic growth, development, sustainability and redistribution of income.			
identify a mark scheme's expectations.	Recognise how questions with the same command word but with different marks will require different depth of answers.			

46 Links between macroeconomic problems and their interrelatedness

EXAM SKILLS FOCUS

In this chapter you will:

* show that you understand the benefits of planning your response before writing it

* show that you can interpret diagrams.

You should think about all your answers before you start writing them. Think about what the command word is asking you and the information you will need to draw on. In the case of assess and evaluate questions, you may find it beneficial to write down the key points you want to include. You can provide a logical structure, ordering the points into two sides and an overview and conclusion.

There is a wide variety of diagrams that you may be asked to interpret. These include not only economic diagrams, such as Laffer curve and Phillips curve diagrams, but also standard diagrams such as line diagrams, bar charts, scatter diagrams and pie charts that can illustrate economic data. Make yourself familiar with these diagrams.

46.1 The relationship between the internal and external value of money

When presented with a table or a diagram, first check what the data are showing, then read the questions and then go back to the data in the table or diagram.

1

Year	Inflation rate (%)	Exchange rate (US$s per Japanese yen)
2012	−0.04	0.013
2013	0.34	0.011
2014	2.76	0.010
2015	0.80	0.008
2016	−0.13	0.010
2017	0.48	0.009
2018	0.99	0.009
2019	0.47	0.009
2020	−0.02	0.009
2021	−0.23	0.008
2022	2.50	0.007

Table 46.1: Japan's inflation rate and exchange rate 2012–2022

Identify a year when:

a   the internal and external value of the Japanese yen rose and explain the evidence for your choice

b   the internal and external value of the Japanese yen fell and explain your choice

c   the internal value of the Japanese yen rose and the external value of the Japanese yen fell and explain your choice.

≪ RECALL AND CONNECT 1 ≪

Why might a person's purchasing power rise despite a fall in the value of money?

46.2 The relationship between the balance of payments and inflation

1   Copy and complete the following paragraphs by filling in the missing words.

A current account surplus may increase the inflation rate as it will increase _____ demand and may result in _____ inflation. However, it can cause a rise in the _____ rate. This will reduce the price of _____ raw materials and _____ goods and so may lower _____ inflation.

Inflation can also affect the current account balance. If a country's inflation rate is _____ than rival countries, demand for _____ is likely to fall while demand for _____ is likely to rise, which may increase a current account deficit. Export revenue, however, may not fall if demand for exports is price _____.

It is also possible that if other countries' inflation rates rise and the demand for imports is price _____, there may be _____ inflation.

REFLECTION

How many of the missing words could you fill in? If there were any words you could not fill in, how would you find the relevant information on the topics of the current account of the balance of payments and inflation?

« RECALL AND CONNECT 2 «

How might a country's firms increase their international competitiveness despite a rise in the price of their products?

46.3 The relationship between growth and inflation

1   Copy and complete Table 46.2. Decide, in each case, whether the following changes will be likely to decrease or increase economic growth and inflation.

Change	Economic growth	Inflation
Increase in consumer expenditure		
Increase in investment		
Increase in labour productivity		
Increase in the price of imported raw materials		
Increase in unemployment		

Table 46.2: Effects of changes in economic variables on economic growth and inflation

2 Copy and complete the following two flow charts:

Increase in _____   Increase in _____

↓   ↓

May cause _____ economic growth   May cause _____ economic growth

↓   ↓

May cause _____ inflation   May cause reduced inflation

↓   ↓

If there is no _____ in the economy   If aggregate _____ increases by
                                       more than aggregate _____

≪ RECALL AND CONNECT 3 ≪

Why may inflation reduce investment?

46.4 The relationship between growth and the balance of payments

Data response questions usually, but not always, follow the order of the data provided. In this case, the information for Question 1(a), for example, is not at the start and actually appears in two places.

You may find that Question 1(e) is harder than the other questions. This may be because you are unlikely to have answered such a question before, but do not let that put you off. You should be able to apply your knowledge and skills to answering this question with help from the data.

1

Challenges facing Malawi

Malawi, in recent years, has experienced rising consumer expenditure and a fall in the internal and external value of its currency. Its economic performance has been affected by negative supply-side shocks. As well as the COVID-19 pandemic, it has suffered from floods and rises in the price of imported fuel.

Most of Malawi's 7 million labour force is employed in the primary sector. Figure 46.1 shows the percentage of the country's labour forced employed in the three sectors of production.

CONTINUED

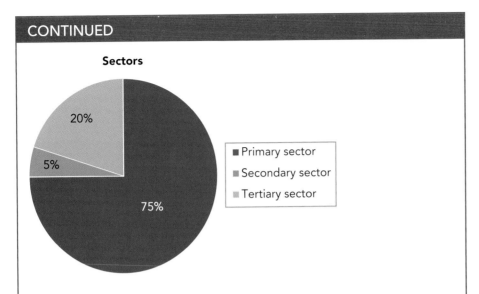

Figure 46.1: The share of Malawi's labour force employed in the three sectors of production in 2021

Malawi's economic growth rate picked up from 0.8% in 2020 to 2.8% in 2021. This rise in the increase in the country's output is thought, however, to have contributed to the rise in the country's current account deficit from $1.4 billion in 2020 to $1.6 billion in 2021.

There have been occasions when the Malawian government has banned the exports of food. The intention behind such a ban has been to reduce inflationary pressure and help the poor. However, some economists argue that banning the export of food can harm the country's macroeconomic performance.

a   Calculate the number of Malawian workers employed in the tertiary sector in 2021.   [2]

b   Explain how an increase in consumer expenditure may reduce both the internal and external value of a country's currency.   [4]

c   Explain how an increase in a country's economic growth rate can result in an increase in its current account deficit.   [5]

d   Analyse, using an aggregate demand and supply diagram, the effect of a negative supply-side shock on an economy.   [6]

e   Assess whether a government should ban the export of food.   [8]

REFLECTION

How did you find Question 1? Did you remember to devote approximately two minutes per mark? This means you should have spent 48 minutes on this question, including reading and thinking time.

46.5 The relationship between inflation and unemployment

1   What is the implication of the expectations-augmented Phillips curve for macroeconomic policy?

2   Use the information in Table 46.3 to plot a Phillips curve diagram. Comment on whether the diagram supports the relationship suggested by the traditional Phillips curve.

Year	Inflation rate (%)	Unemployment rate (%)
2015	4.4	6.5
2016	3.8	6.7
2017	2.8	7.0
2018	2.1	7.2
2019	1.9	7.3
2020	1.5	11.2
2021	4.5	9.1

Table 46.3: Chile's inflation rate and unemployment rate 2015–2021

Before writing your answer to Question 3, produce a brief plan. This can be in point form. It should indicate the points you want to make on each side, the name of the diagram(s) you will include and the evaluative points you could make.

3   Assess, using an appropriate diagram or diagrams, whether a decrease in unemployment will increase the inflation rate.   [20]

UNDERSTAND THESE TERMS

- Phillips curve
- expectations-augmented Phillips curve

SELF-ASSESSMENT CHECKLIST

Let's revisit the Knowledge focus and Exam skills focus for this chapter.
Decide how confident you are with each statement.

Now I can	Show it	Needs more work	Almost there	Confident to move on
describe the relationship between the internal value of money and external value of money	Produce a flow chart to show the possible links between a fall in the internal value of money and a decrease in the external value of money.			
explain the relationship between the balance of payments and inflation	Produce a table comparing the effects of a current account deficit and a current account surplus on inflation.			
explain the relationship between growth and inflation	Draw an AD/AS diagram to show the possible different effects of actual and potential economic growth on inflation.			
explain the relationship between growth and the balance of payments	Produce a table comparing how economic growth may increase a current deficit and how it may reduce it.			
explain the relationship between inflation and unemployment	Produce a flow chart to show how inflation may cause a rise in unemployment.			
analyse the traditional Phillips curve	Produce a revision card explaining the traditional Phillips curve.			
analyse the expectations-augmented Phillips curve (short- and long-run Phillips curve)	Draw the expectations-augmented Phillips curve.			
understand the benefits of planning my response before answering it	Plan an answer to the question: Assess whether a government can achieve both high economic growth and a deficit on the country account of its balance of payments.			
interpret diagrams.	Interpret a pie diagram, (e.g., Figure 36.6 in the coursebook) and plot and interpret a Phillips curve diagram, using data on your own country's inflation rate and unemployment rate over the last ten years.			

47 Effectiveness of policy options to meet all macroeconomic objectives

KNOWLEDGE FOCUS

You will answer questions on:

47.1 The effectiveness of fiscal policy in relation to different macroeconomic objectives

47.2 The effectiveness of monetary policy in relation to different macroeconomic objectives

47.3 The effectiveness of supply-side policy in relation to different macroeconomic objectives

47.4 The effectiveness of exchange rate policy in relation to different macroeconomic objectives

47.5 The effectiveness of international trade policy in relation to different macroeconomic objectives

47.6 The problems arising from conflicts between policy objectives

47.7 Government failure in macroeconomic policies

EXAM SKILLS FOCUS

In this chapter you will:

- show that you can practise and improve your answers
- show you can revise more effectively by taking movement breaks.

The best form of revision is active revision. This involves you using your knowledge and skills, rather than just reading your notes. The more you can use your knowledge and skills, the stronger they will become. Think about sportspeople and professional economists. Sportspeople not only practise by training. They analyse their previous performance and look at ways to improve their performance. The job of professional economists involves them using their knowledge and skills to interpret economic data and world affairs, explaining them and advising governments and firms. They seek to improve their performance by, for example, attending conferences and carrying out research.

Movement breaks are likely to increase the efficiency of your revision. Standing up, moving around, taking walks, cycling and other physical activities can keep your mind fresh, and allow you to improve your performance.

47.1 The effectiveness of fiscal policy in relation to different macroeconomic objectives

1 Which group of economists think that crowding out can be a significant problem?

2 Do all economists agree that the Laffer curve proves that a rise in the rate of income tax will always reduce tax revenue?

3 Copy Table 47.1. Rearrange the combination of fiscal policy tools in the table to match the appropriate macroeconomic objectives.

Macroeconomic policy objective	Policy tool 1	Policy tool 2
Balance on the current account	Decrease government spending on public sector pay.	Increase the standard rate of income tax.
Low unemployment	Increase government spending on research and development.	Increase customs duties.
Price stability	Increase government spending on solar energy.	Increase taxes on the production of plastic bottles.
Redistribution of income from the rich to the poor	Increase government spending on training.	Reduce the lowest rate of income tax.
Sustainable economic growth	Increase progressive income tax.	Increase welfare payments.

Table 47.1: Fiscal policy tools to achieve macroeconomic objectives

« RECALL AND CONNECT 1 «

What are the main objectives of expansionary fiscal policy?

47.2 The effectiveness of monetary policy in relation to different macroeconomic objectives

1 Why might quantitative easing not result in a rise in lending by commercial banks?

2 What effect would a recession in the USA and China be likely to have on the effectiveness of an expansionary monetary policy introduced by India's central bank?

3   Copy and complete the following flow chart by filling in the missing words and phrases:

Pakistan experiences a decrease in aggregate demand

↓

The Pakistan central bank uses _____ monetary policy

↓

It increases the _____

↓

The _____ theory of money suggests

↓

This will increase the _____

↓

As the theory assumes that the _____ and _____ are constant in the short run

≪ RECALL AND CONNECT 2 ≪

Which type of government policy would conflict with an expansionary monetary policy?

47.3 The effectiveness of supply-side policy in relation to different macroeconomic objectives

1   For each case in Table 47.2, decide whether the following would be appropriate supply-side policy tools to achieve the government macroeconomic objective.

Supply-side policy tool	Macroeconomic objective	Appropriate or inappropriate
A cut in the top rate of income tax	Redistribute income from the rich to the poor	
Deregulation	Reduce pollution	
Increase government spending on infrastructure projects	Increase economic growth	
Increase government spending on education	Reduce current account deficit	
Privatisation of an inefficient industry	Reduce inflation	

Table 47.2: The appropriateness of supply-side policy tools

REFLECTION

Would you be able to explain the choices you have made? If you think you would struggle to provide an explanation, think of specific actions that you should take to ensure that you could justify your decision.

≪ RECALL AND CONNECT 3 ≪

Why are supply-side policy tools not used to stop deflation?

47.4 The effectiveness of exchange rate policy in relation to different macroeconomic objectives

1   Why may a rise in the value of the exchange rate reduce inflation?

2   What are **two** reasons why a central bank's attempts to raise the value of its exchange rate by purchasing its own currency might not succeed?

≪ RECALL AND CONNECT 4 ≪

a   What are **three** reasons why foreign currency is purchased?

b   When would a fall in export prices increase export revenue?

47.5 The effectiveness of international trade policy in relation to different macroeconomic objectives

1   Decide whether the following circumstances would decrease or increase the chances of a policy of free trade being successful.

   a   Firms from other countries are dumping goods in the home country.

   b   Other countries' firms have monopsony power.

   c   Other governments are not subsidising their domestic industries.

   d   The country's government currently has low tariffs on imports.

   e   The country has flexible factors of production.

   f   The country has similar health and safety standards as other countries.

   g   The country has the same opportunity costs in its production as its trading partners.

≪ RECALL AND CONNECT 5 ≪

What are **three** types of industries that a government may seek to protect?

47.6 The problems arising from conflicts between policy objectives

1   If a government introduces a contractionary fiscal policy, which **two** policy objectives is it unlikely to be trying to achieve?

2   Why may an increase in competition from foreign firms make it easier for a country to achieve a rise in economic growth and a fall in unemployment without causing inflation?

Question 3 draws on a number of areas of this chapter. There are two key points to note about the parts of Question 3. One is that the mark for Question 3(a)(ii) is higher than that for Question 3(a)(i). This indicates that there are more stages involved in answering Question 3(a)(ii). The other point to note is that Question 3(c) has the command word 'describe' rather than 'explain'. This means that you should pick out the key features of the trends, but you do not have to give reasons for these trends.

3
> ### Changes in Sierra Leone's macroeconomy
>
> Sierra Leone is a West African country with one of the lowest incomes per capita in the world. In 2021, the country's GDP was $4.2 billion, and its population was 8.5 million. Consumer expenditure made up 95%, investment 18% and government spending 12% of the country's GDP. Imports were 55% of GDP.
>
> In recent years, Sierra Leone's inflation rate and economic growth rate have fluctuated quite considerably as shown in Figure 47.1.

CONTINUED

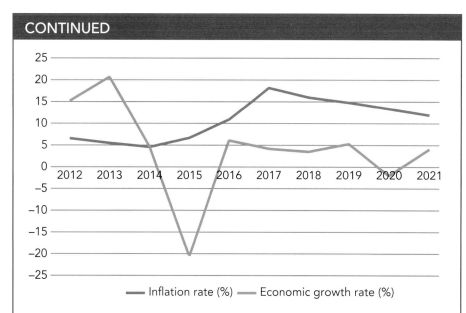

Figure 47.1: Sierra Leone's inflation and economic growth rates 2012–2021

Sierra Leone's unemployment rate was more stable than its inflation rate and economic growth rate over this period, varying only between 4.4% and 5.6%. The country's youth unemployment has fallen in recent years. One reason for this might be rising educational standards in the country.

The Sierra Leone government doubled its spending on education between 2018 and 2022. In 2021, 20% of its spending went to education. This represented 9.1% of the country's GDP compared to a global average of 4.3%. For example, the USA spends 6.1% of its GDP on education.

The Sierra Leone government has abolished tuition fees and now provides some free textbooks. The higher government spending has encouraged more children to attend school. It is likely that this will result in more children wanting to progress on to university.

The Sierra Leone government has a budget deficit, but it is thought that higher government spending on education could reduce the deficit in the long run.

a Calculate

   i Sierra Leone's GDP per capita in 2021 [1]

   ii the value of Sierra Leone's exports in 2021. [3]

b Explain whether Sierra Leone or the USA would have spent more on education in 2021. [2]

c Describe, using Figure 47.1, the trends in Sierra Leone's inflation rate and economic growth rate over the period shown. [4]

d Assess whether an increase in government spending on education will reduce a budget deficit. [8]

47.7 Government failure in macroeconomic policies

UNDERSTAND THESE TERMS

- government macroeconomic failure
- counter-cyclically

1. A government decides to reduce aggregate demand by using contractionary monetary policy. What may happen between it making its decision and the policy having an impact, for the policy to make macroeconomic performance worse?

2. What effect does corruption have on the allocation of resources?

REFLECTION

How well did you do on this topic? You will find that in economics you will apply concepts to a range of different topics and situations. The more you apply your knowledge and use your skills, the stronger your knowledge and skills will become. At this stage, where do you think your strengths are? Which areas could you improve on?

SELF-ASSESSMENT CHECKLIST

Let's revisit the Knowledge focus and Exam skills focus for this chapter.
Decide how confident you are with each statement.

Now I can	Show it	Needs more work	Almost there	Confident to move on
evaluate the effectiveness of fiscal policy including Laffer curve analysis in relation to different macroeconomic objectives	Produce a table covering the advantages and disadvantages of fiscal policy and in achieving macroeconomic objectives and draw a Laffer curve.			
evaluate the effectiveness of monetary policy in relation to different macroeconomic objectives	Write a multiple-choice question on the effectiveness of monetary policy to reduce inflation with an explanation of why the distractors are wrong and the key is right.			

CONTINUED

evaluate the effectiveness of supply-side policy in relation to different macroeconomic objectives	Identify **two** reasons why a supply-side policy may be effective in promoting economic growth and **two** reasons why it may not.			
evaluate the effectiveness of exchange rate policy in relation to different macroeconomic objectives	Produce a revision card on the advantages and disadvantages of using exchange rate policy to reduce unemployment.			
evaluate the effectiveness of international trade policy in relationship to different macroeconomic objectives	Identify a reason why the imposition of import tariffs may increase economic growth and a reason why it may reduce economic growth.			
analyse problems and conflicts arising from the outcome of the different policies	Produce a table showing how different macroeconomic objectives may conflict.			
explain the existence of government failure in macroeconomic policies	Identify **three** causes of government failure.			
practise and improve my answers	Review your overall performance on the questions in this chapter and consider which areas could be improved.			
revise more effectively by taking movement breaks.	Compare how you performed on answering a question after a movement break with how you performed on a question when you had been sitting still for more than an hour.			

Exam practice 10

This section contains practice questions. These questions draw together your knowledge on a range of topics that you have covered up to this point and will help you prepare for your assessment.

The following question has an example student response and commentary provided. Work through the question first, then compare your answer to the example student response and commentary.

1   'Keynesian policies to solve the problem of unemployment will not work because they will conflict with the attainment of other key macroeconomic aims.'

Assess the accuracy of this statement.   [20]

Example student response	Examiner comments
The types of policies Keynesian would recommend to solve the pattern of unemployment depend on the type of unemployment.	**AO1 Knowledge and understanding**
Low unemployment is one of a government's key macroeconomic aims. The other aims include price stability, economic growth and balance of payments stability.	There is good knowledge of structural and cyclical unemployment and an awareness of government macroeconomic aims.
To reduce structural unemployment, Keynesian and other economists would also support policies to increase labour skills and mobility. The key policy tool would be education and training. A more skilled labour force would raise productivity and labour market flexibility. This could help a government achieve all of its key macroeconomic aims. A more flexible labour force would be more able to move from declining to expanding industries and be more able to adapt to new technology. A more productive labour force is also likely to be in higher demand.	**AO2 Analysis**
	There is good analysis which includes two relevant and accurate diagrams. What is missing both in terms of knowledge and understanding and analysis is consideration of frictional unemployment. This could be covered relatively briefly by reference to the provision of information and how such a policy is unlikely to conflict with any other macroeconomic aim.
As well as reducing structural unemployment, a more productive labour force will increase potential economic growth. It could also reduce inflation and a current account deficit, if productivity rises by more than wages. In this case, costs of production will fall.	*AO1 and AO2: 12/14*
The Keynesian policies to reduce cyclical unemployment are expansionary fiscal and monetary policies. Cutting taxes, increasing government spending and reducing interest rates are likely to increase aggregate demand. For example, lower interest rates would be likely to reduce saving and increase borrowing, consumer expenditure and investment. The higher aggregate demand may encourage firms to employ more workers. Higher employment may also make income more evenly distributed and may increase economic growth.	

Example student response	Examiner comments
It is possible that a government may underestimate the extent to which unemployment is the result of a lack of demand or the size of the multiplier. In this case, the government will have increased AD by too much. The diagram shows that the higher AD has resulted in economic growth but also a rise in the price level. 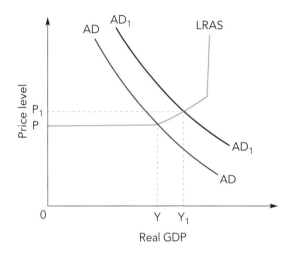 New classical economists argue that demand-side policies designed to reduce unemployment may work in the short run. However, they think that such policies will only be successful in the short run. They think that in the long run, unemployment will return to the natural rate of unemployment but at a higher price level. The diagram shows output initially rising to Y_1 but then returning to Y as a result of higher costs of production. 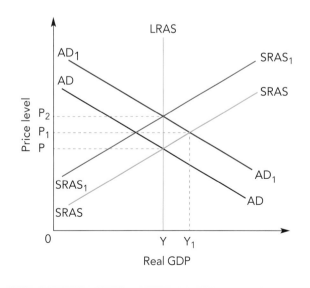	**AO3 Evaluation** There is some good evaluation linked to the extent to which Keynesian policies to reduce unemployment may conflict with the aims of price stability and a current account deficit. However, a new concept, crowding out, is introduced in the concluding paragraph. This should have been explained beforehand. *5/6* *Total: 17/20 marks*

Example student response	Examiner comments
If the higher AD does result in a higher inflation rate, the country's products will become less price competitive. This is likely to increase imports and reduce exports. If demand for exports and imports is price elastic, the value of net exports will fall and a current account deficit would increase. Expansionary demand-side policies may help reduce income inequality and may promote economic growth. It is possible that they may reduce cyclical unemployment without causing inflation not only if there is spare capacity but also if the policies result in a rise in productivity and investment. However, if the rise in AD takes output beyond full capacity, inflation and a large current account deficit may be the unintended consequences. It Is also possible that expansionary fiscal policy, financed by borrowing, may crowd out private sector investment and just shift demand from the private to the public sector.	

Here is another practice question which you should attempt. Use the guidance in the commentaries in this section to help you as you answer the question.

2 'When a government wishes to lower unemployment, its only method of reducing it is by the use of fiscal policy tools.'

   Evaluate this opinion.   [20]

The following question has an example student response and commentary provided. Work through the question first, then compare your answer to the example student response and commentary.

3 Cyclical and structural unemployment are the most common types of unemployment.

   Explain the causes of these types of unemployment and assess the effectiveness of government policies to reduce them.   [20]

Example student response	Examiner comments
Cyclical unemployment is caused by a lack of aggregate demand. It gets its name from its connection with the economic cycle. When an economy experiences a downturn or a recession, demand for products produced by most industries would be likely to decrease, causing workers throughout the economy to lose their jobs. In contrast to cyclical unemployment, structural unemployment is restricted to particular industries. It arises because of changes in the structure of the economy. Demand for some products may decline and/or new methods of production and technology may be introduced. These changes can result in a mismatch between the skills and location of workers and the jobs available. Some industries decline while other industries expand. Some workers may lack the geographical or occupational mobility to move from the declining to expanding industries.	**AO1 Knowledge and understanding** There is good awareness shown of the nature of structural and cyclical unemployment and the policies which can be used to reduce them. **AO2 Analysis** Greater width of analysis would have been useful. For example, another supply-side policy tool might have been examined. *AO1 and AO2: 10/14*

Example student response	Examiner comments
In practice, frictional unemployment is likely to occur more often than cyclical unemployment. If an economy is expanding there may be little or no cyclical unemployment. There will, however, always be some frictional unemployment. This type of unemployment occurs when workers are in between jobs.	**AO3 Evaluation**
Governments try to reduce frictional unemployment by increasing the information available about job vacancies. They may also provide more incentive to move to a new job by cutting unemployment benefits and or the lower rate of income tax.	There is thoughtful consideration shown of whether structural and cyclical unemployment are the most common types of unemployment. Evaluation of government policies to reduce unemployment would have been stronger if more tools had been assessed. For example, the effectiveness of privatisation as a way of reducing unemployment may have been considered.
To reduce structural unemployment, governments use supply-side policy tools. A government, for example, may provide training for unemployed workers in the skills required by expanding industries.	*3/6*
In contrast, governments use demand-side policy tools to reduce cyclical unemployment. For example, a government may cut personal income tax to increase aggregate demand. Lower personal income tax rates will increase disposable income. Some of this higher disposable income will be spent. Higher consumer expenditure will encourage firms to produce a higher output. To produce more, firms may take on extra workers.	*Total: 13/20 marks*
To be successful, a government has to identify the cause of unemployment. If a government thinks that the unemployment is structural whereas it is actually cyclical, providing training is unlikely to be successful. Workers may gain new skills but if there is a shortage of job vacancies, they will not gain employment.	

Here is another practice question which you should attempt. Use the guidance in the commentaries in this section to help you as you answer the question.

4   Assess whether a decrease in structural unemployment is likely to be more beneficial than a decrease in cyclical unemployment.   [20]

The following question has an example student response and commentary provided. Work through the question first, then compare your answer to the example student response and commentary.

5   Assess whether achieving a fall in unemployment should be the main macroeconomic objective of a government.   [20]

Example student response	Examiner comments
A fall in unemployment from a high rate should be an important objective of a government. This is because a high level of unemployment can impose a number of significant costs. One is a loss of potential output. When there are unemployed workers, an economy will be producing less than it is capable of. It will be producing inside its production possibility curve. The diagram shows that the economy is producing at point X. This is an inefficient use of resources. In contrast, point Y would be an efficient point. Moving to point Y would not involve an opportunity cost. Higher output could increase both a country's economic growth rate and living standards.	**AO1 Knowledge and understanding**
	There is knowledge and understanding of unemployment and macroeconomic objectives shown throughout the answer. However, it would have been useful to have stated the main macroeconomic objectives at the start.

Example student response	Examiner comments

Example student response

Lower unemployment would raise tax revenue and reduce government spending on transfer payments. With more people gaining jobs, income tax revenue is likely to increase. Indirect tax revenue and corporation tax revenue would also increase as a result of consumer expenditure rising. Government spending on unemployment benefits and other welfare benefits is also likely to fall. This may enable the government to spend more on, e.g., infrastructure projects.

However, if the unemployment rate is close to the full employment rate or is expected to reach it soon, lowering unemployment should not be the government's main macroeconomic objective. In deciding whether it should take action to reduce unemployment, a government will consider not only the rate of unemployment, but also the cause and duration. Frictional unemployment is likely to be regarded as a less serious problem than structural and cyclical unemployment.

The government may be faced with other more serious macroeconomic problems. These may also have an impact on unemployment. There may be a growing current account deficit. If the government does not adopt measures to stop the rising deficit, unemployment could increase. A rising inflation rate, may have a number of significant costs. These include menu costs, shoe leather costs, inflationary noise and a random redistribution of income. If it is cost-push inflation, it is also likely to be accompanied by falling output and rising unemployment.

There may be occasions when a government has to decide between different macroeconomic policy objectives. For example, if a government uses deflationary demand-side policies to reduce demand-pull inflation, it may increase cyclical unemployment. However, macroeconomic objectives tend to be interlinked. For example, on many occasions, promoting economic growth and reducing a current account deficit may reduce unemployment. Some supply-side policy tools, such as education, introduced to reduce inflation, may also reduce unemployment.

Examiner comments

AO2 Analysis

There is some good analysis with good use of a PPC diagram. The analysis covers not only why a government should keep unemployment low but also some problems that may arise from other macroeconomic objectives not being achieved.

AO1 and AO2: 13/14

AO3 Evaluation

There is clear evaluation in terms of what should determine whether unemployment should be the main focus of government policy and why other objectives may need to take priority. A final sentence or couple of sentences coming to an overall conclusion would have been useful. For example, the student might have concluded that, in the long run, a government should aim to achieve all its macroeconomic objectives. While, in the short run, if unemployment is high and increasing, it may need to be its main aim.

5/6

Total: 18/20 marks

Here is another practice question which you should attempt. Use the guidance in the commentaries in this section to help you as you answer the question.

6 Assess whether achieving a fall in inflation should be the main macroeconomic objective of a government. [20]

The following question has an example student response and commentary provided. Work through the question first, then compare your answer to the example student response and commentary.

7 Assess why some macroeconomic policies may conflict with each other and which macroeconomic policy should be given priority. [20]

Example student response	Examiner comments
Contractionary monetary policy will conflict with expansionary fiscal policy. A central bank may raise the rate of interest to reduce demand-pull inflation. The intention would be to reduce consumer expenditure. A higher interest rate would make borrowing more expensive while increasing the reward for saving. A reduction in consumer expenditure may reduce aggregate demand. This could stop the upward pressure on the price level. If, however, at the same time, the government is pursuing an expansionary fiscal policy, there may still be upward pressure on the price level. A government may reduce taxes or increase government spending to promote economic growth, reduce unemployment or reduce a current account surplus. Lower direct taxes and indirect taxes could increase aggregate demand by raising consumer expenditure and investment. Higher government spending on goods and services will directly increase aggregate demand.	**AO1 Knowledge and understanding** The student clearly understands government policies. However, it would have been useful to have defined the different types of policies at the start. **AO2 Analysis** The analysis is accurate and relevant. At the end of the first, rather long paragraph, it would have been useful to have linked back to demand-pull inflation. *AO1 and AO2: 11/14* **AO3 Evaluation** There is clear and supported evaluation based on the analysis. The student might have considered how the extent to which policies might conflict may be influenced by the level of economic activity. *5/6* *Total: 16/20 marks*
It is possible that fiscal policy measures may conflict with each other. For example, a government may raise taxation or reduce demand-pull inflation. If, however, it is raising spending on education because of an increase in the number of schoolchildren, it may actually be injecting extra demand into the economy.	
Supply-side policy, if successful, is unlikely to conflict with its other policies. This is because it aims to improve all the macroeconomic objectives by increasing aggregate supply. For example, government spending on training may increase labour productivity. This may increase employment and economic growth and reduce demand-pull inflation and a current account deficit.	
If supply-side policy tools are not successful, they may harm government macroeconomic objectives. For example, if government spending on training does not raise labour productivity, it may just be inflationary.	
Without careful co-ordination, it is possible that government policies may conflict in terms of their effect on aggregate demand. Supply-side policy aims to increase aggregate supply but it is not always successful and so may offset the effect of demand-side policies. Which policy should be given priority would depend on which macroeconomic problems the country is facing.	

Here is another practice question which you should attempt. Use the guidance in the commentaries in this section to help you as you answer the question.

8   Explain why an increase in consumer expenditure and investment might increase economic growth and assess whether this will conflict with other government macroeconomic policy objectives. [20]

The following question has an example student response and commentary provided. Work through the question first, then compare your answer to the example student response and commentary.

9   'Monetarists insist that control of the money supply is the key to solving the problem of inflation; Keynesians argue that inflation can only be controlled by controlling expenditure.'

To what extent do you agree that both these approaches are only partially correct? [20]

Example student response	Examiner comments
Monetarists do argue that control of the money supply is the key to solving the problem of inflation. This is because they think that the cause of inflation is the money supply growing faster than output: 'too much money chasing too few goods'. They use the quantity theory of money in support of this view. The quantity theory is based on the Fisher equation, $MV = PT$. Monetarists think that V and T are constant in the short run. As a result, they think that an increase in M will cause a proportional increase in P.	**AO1 Knowledge and understanding** The knowledge and understanding was good, although the role of commercial banks could have been identified, as this could have been built on in terms of analysis and evaluation.
To control the growth of the money supply, monetarists argue that the government should avoid adding to the money supply by financing government spending by borrowing from the banking sector.	**AO2 Analysis** There is some good analysis. There is relevant examination of the quantity theory and the use of AD/AS analysis. However, the diagrams needed to be explained in the text.
However, the quantity theory can be questioned as V and T may not be constant. Increases in the money supply may also be the result rather than the cause of inflation. Firms experiencing higher costs of production because of inflation, may borrow from commercial banks. Higher bank loans will add to the money supply.	*AO1 and AO2: 10/14*
Keynesians do argue that inflation can be controlled by 'controlling expenditure' if the inflation is of a demand-pull nature. If aggregate demand (AD) has increased by more than aggregate supply (AS), the price level will rise. Higher AD becomes particularly inflationary when it occurs when the economy is operating at full capacity. At this level of economic activity, higher expenditure will cause inflation but will leave national output unchanged.	

Example student response	Examiner comments
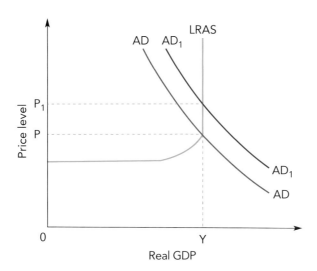	**AO3 Evaluation** There is some relevant evaluation in terms of whether an increase in the money supply will cause inflation, whether it is cause or a consequence of inflation and why higher expenditure is not the only possible cause of inflation. If the role of commercial banks had been covered, the difficulty of controlling their lending might have been covered. 4/6 *Total: 14/20 marks*
However, Keynesians do not think controlling expenditure will reduce inflation if the inflation is cost-push inflation. In this case, it will be the rise in the costs of production which will be pushing up prices. In this case, a government is likely to aim to reduce increases in costs of production in the short run and to increase aggregate supply in the long run. For example, a government may restrict wage rises for public sector workers. It may introduce supply-side policy tools to reduce inflationary pressures in the long run. For example, infrastructure projects may reduce transport costs and increase long-run aggregate supply.	
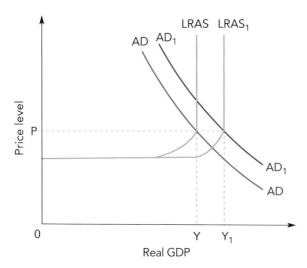	
Monetarists, but not all economists, would argue that control of the money supply is the way to control inflation. Keynesians, however, think that control of expenditure should be the approach only if inflation is of a demand-pull nature.	

Here is another practice question which you should attempt. Use the guidance in the commentaries in this section to help you as you answer the question.

10 Evaluate the opinion that the most effective way to reduce inflation is for the government to achieve a budget surplus. [20]

The following question has an example student response and commentary provided. Work through the question first, then compare your answer to the example student response and commentary.

11 Assess whether it is better for a government to raise the economy's rate of productivity growth or to control the rate of inflation. [20]

Example student response	Examiner comments
There is a range of policy tools that a government could use to control the rate of interest. One is for its central bank to increase the rate of interest. This could cause households to reduce their spending and increase their saving. Households will find that it is more expensive to borrow to finance some of their expenditure. They will also find that they could earn more interest on any saving they undertake. Lower consumer expenditure could reduce demand-pull inflation.	**AO1 Knowledge and understanding** There is good knowledge and understanding shown. However, in the first sentence the student writes 'interest' rather than 'inflation'. The student's mind was probably thinking ahead to the next sentence. As it is relatively easy to make such a mistake, it is useful to read over an answer when completed.
A government could also use contractionary fiscal policy to control the rate of inflation. It could raise taxes or lower government spending to reduce aggregate demand. There may also be occasions when a government may want to raise the price level, if the economy is experiencing deflation or is at risk of experiencing deflation. In this case, it may use expansionary fiscal policy or its central bank may lower the rate of interest.	**AO2 Analysis** The analysis is clear. However, the structure of the answer could have been stronger. For example, the third paragraph could have come first and might have referred directly to the question. The inclusion of a diagram might also have been useful, and the student might have explained that supply-side policy could also reduce demand-pull inflation.
Controlling the rate of inflation can be very important in the short run, if it is at a high rate. High inflation can cause a number of significant problems. It can reduce the country's international price competitiveness of the country's products, lowering exports and increasing imports. If the inflation was unexpected, people can lose out. Savers may experience negative real interest. Those on fixed incomes may struggle to buy basic necessities and taxpayers may find that that their incomes are dragged into higher tax brackets.	*AO1 and AO2: 10/14*
Cost-push inflation can be particularly serious as it is associated with lower output. This can be accompanied by a rise in unemployment.	
To raise the economy's rate of productivity growth, a government would use supply-side policy tools. For example, a government may increase its spending on education. This may raise workers' skills, enabling them to produce more per hour. A rise in the rate of productivity growth will help all the government's macroeconomic objectives. It is likely to increase economic growth as productive capacity will increase. Higher productivity may reduce costs of production. This may increase exports as the country's products may become more internationally competitive. If more exports are sold, output may rise and employment may increase. A higher rate of productivity growth can also enable the increase in aggregate supply to rise along with an increase in aggregate demand, avoiding inflation.	

Example student response	Examiner comments
Higher productivity can improve all the macroeconomic policy objectives including controlling inflation. It should be a constant government objective. In the short run, however, if inflation gets out of control, a government may have to concentrate on reducing a high and accelerating inflation rate.	**AO3 Evaluation** A little more might have been made of the difference between objectives in the short run and long run, perhaps supported with a diagram or diagrams, but overall there is good evaluation. *5/6* *Total: 15/20 marks*

Here is another practice question which you should attempt. Use the guidance in the commentaries in this section to help you as you answer the question.

12 Assess whether it is better for a government to raise the country's economic growth rate or to reduce its deficit on the current account of the balance of payments. [20]

48 Policies to correct disequilibrium in the balance of payments

KNOWLEDGE FOCUS

You will answer questions on:

48.1 The components of the balance of payments

48.2 Effect of fiscal, monetary, supply-side, protectionist and exchange rate policies on the balance of payments

48.3 Expenditure-switching and expenditure-reducing policies

EXAM SKILLS FOCUS

In this chapter you will:

- show that you can structure long-form responses

- learn how to test your understanding of topics that you find challenging.

When you are writing answers to the higher mark questions in Section A and the essay questions in Sections B and C of Paper 4: A Level Data Response and Essays, it is advisable to write in paragraphs. Devote a paragraph to each major point. Make sure that there is a logical structure to your answer, with a point following on from the previous point. Planning will help with this and should avoid you jumping back and forward.

The more you test your knowledge, the stronger it is likely to become. In the case of topics that you find more challenging, you should test your understanding several times. Follow the motto 'test and test again': TATA.

48.1 The components of the balance of payments

It can be difficult to remember the components of the balance of payments. Try answering a number of questions, including multiple-choice questions on this topic. This can enable you to test your understanding of the components several times: TATA.

1   Match the questions with the right answers.

Questions		Answers	
a	What would a net debit position on portfolio investment in the balance of payments mean?	**i**	The value of shares and government securities purchased by the country's residents must be greater than the value of financial assets purchased by foreigners from the country.
b	What is the connection between the financial account and the primary income balance of the current account?	**ii**	The items in the financial account generate the receipt and payment of profit, interest and dividends. These forms of investment income appear in the primary income balance.
c	What must be the position on a country's combined financial and capital account if there is a deficit on its current account?	**iii**	A surplus on its combined financial and capital account. This is because the total value of debit items must be matched by credit items.
d	What does it mean if there is a positive net errors and omissions figure in a country's balance of payments account?	**iv**	More money must have come into the country than has been recorded. This may be the result of mistakes or delays in the recording of some of the transactions and payments made and received.

2 Calculate the missing figures in the balance of payments account in Table 48.1.

	$ billion
Exports of goods	620
Imports of goods	
Trade in goods	−230
Exports of services	240
Imports of services	180
Trade in services	
Primary income balance	45
Secondary income balance	8
Current account balance	−117
Capital account balance	5
Direct investment	84
Portfolio investment	
Other investments	−6
Net reserves	8
Financial account	121
Net errors and omissions	

Table 48.1: Calculating balance of payments figures

≪ RECALL AND CONNECT 1 ≪

a Why might an increase in firms' spending on research and development reduce a trade in goods and services deficit?

b Why might a firm borrow from a foreign bank rather than a domestic bank?

48.2 Effect of fiscal, monetary, supply-side, protectionist and exchange rate policies on the balance of payments

1 Why might privatisation result in both a trade goods and services surplus and a positive balance on direct investment?

2 Why may protectionist policy actually increase a current account deficit?

3 What unintended consequence might an increase in government spending on welfare benefits have on the balance of payments?

4 Why is the effect that a rise in the interest rate may have on a current account deficit uncertain?

≪ RECALL AND CONNECT 2 ≪

a Which supply-side policy tool conflicts with the protectionist measure of red tape?

b What effect would a fall in the exchange rate have on the value of workers' remittances?

48.3 Expenditure-switching and expenditure-reducing policies

1 Decide, in each case, whether the following are expenditure-switching or expenditure-reducing policy tools.

    a cut in government spending on healthcare

    b cut in the money supply

    c quota on imports

    d rise in income tax

    e rise in the rate of interest

    f subsidies to producers

    g tariffs.

2

Rise in US protectionism

The USA has had a current account deficit since 1980. In 2021, the USA had a GDP of $22 996 billion. Table 48.2 shows the US current account deficit and unemployment rate between 2016 and 2021.

Year	Current account deficit as % of GDP	Unemployment rate (%)
2016	−2.4	4.3
2017	−2.3	3.8
2018	−2.4	3.5
2019	−2.2	3.3
2020	−2.9	7.3
2021	−3.6	4.7

Table 48.2: US current account deficit as % of GDP and unemployment rate 2016 and 2022

During this period the USA became more protectionist. It increased trade restrictions against the European Union and a number of countries including Brazil, Canada, China and Mexico. Among the products the US government increased its tariffs on were aluminium, solar panels, steel and washing machines.

CONTINUED

Increased protectionism by one country can lead to a trade war. It is thought that the US government was prepared to take the risk as it would be less affected by a trade war than many countries. Figure 48.1 shows the extent to which countries engaged in international trade in 2021.

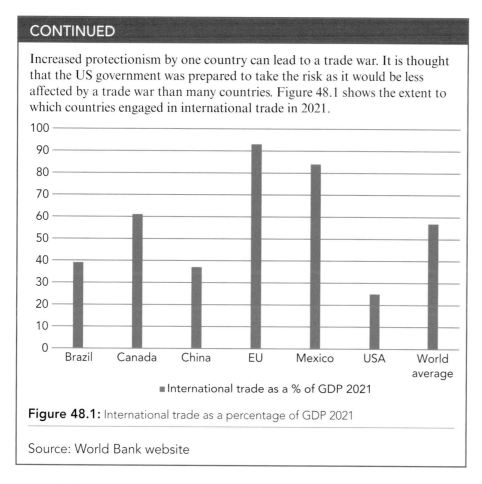

Figure 48.1: International trade as a percentage of GDP 2021

Source: World Bank website

a   Calculate the US current account deficit in US dollars in 2021.   [1]

b   Explain what happened to the US combined capital and financial
    accounts between 2019 and 2020.   [3]

c   From the evidence, consider the relationship between the US current
    account deficit and unemployment rate.   [5]

d   Assess whether the US economy is likely to be harmed by engaging
    in a trade war.   [8]

In answering Question 3, remember to write in paragraphs and ensure that each paragraph follows on logically from the previous paragraph.

3   'Expenditure-reducing policy is likely to be more effective than expenditure-
    switching policy in reducing a deficit on the current account of the balance
    of payments.' Evaluate this statement.   [20]

REFLECTION

Are you getting more confident in analysing economic data? Analysing macroeconomic data on your own country and relationships between the data would be useful practice and can provide information that you may be able to draw on in some answers. Did you know what to include in your answer to Question 2(d)? If you were not sure what to include, look over both Chapter 26 and Chapter 48 in the coursebook.

SELF-ASSESSMENT CHECKLIST

Let's revisit the Knowledge focus and Exam skills focus for this chapter.
Decide how confident you are with each statement.

Now I can	Show it	Needs more work	Almost there	Confident to move on
explain the components of the balance of payments: current account, financial account and capital account	Identify the items that appear in the different accounts of the balance of payments.			
evaluate the effects of fiscal, monetary, supply-side, protectionist and exchange rate policies on the balance of payments	Produce a table with **one** advantage and **one** disadvantage each of using fiscal, monetarist, supply-side, protectionist and exchange rate policies to improve the country's balance of payments.			
explain the difference between expenditure-switching and expenditure-reducing policies	Distinguish, with examples, between expenditure-switching and expenditure-reducing policies.			
structure long-form answers	Structure an answer to the question: Assess whether monetary policy is an effective way to reduce a current account surplus.			
test my understanding of topics that I find challenging.	Identify **three** different ways you could test your knowledge on expenditure-reducing policy and expenditure-switching policy.			

49 Exchange rates

EXAM SKILLS FOCUS

In this chapter you will:

* improve your ability to make connections between concepts by using key concept cards.

* discover techniques that will help you learn definitions more effectively.

You may have to analyse or evaluate connections between concepts you have not linked together before. However, you will have the skills and knowledge to do this. You just need to adapt that knowledge and those skills to new connections. There is an activity you could try to improve your ability to make connections. This involves you making 30 or more cards. Have one side of each card blank. On the other side, write 30 or more key concepts such as aggregate demand, cost-push inflation, depreciation, disequilibrium unemployment, inflation, money supply, Phillips curve, recession, tariffs and wealth. When you have made the cards, shuffle them face down and select two cards. See if you can explain connections between the two concepts you have selected.

As well as possibly answering a question with the command word 'define', you may also find it useful to define terms in some essay answers. To learn definitions, there are a number of techniques you could try. One is to read the definition aloud several times. Another is to explain the definition to another student. A third technique is to write this and other terms and their definitions on separate cards and, after a gap in time, match them up.

49.1 Measurement of exchange rates

1 Why does the real exchange rate provide a more accurate view of a country's international competitiveness than the nominal exchange rate?

2 What determines the weights in a trade weighted exchange rate?

REFLECTION

How comfortable are you with the definitions in the 'understand these terms' box in this section? These are quite difficult terms to define. You may find it useful to follow one of the pieces of advice given at the start of the chapter.

« RECALL AND CONNECT 1 «

What are **two** benefits of a higher exchange rate?

UNDERSTAND THESE TERMS

- real exchange rate
- trade-weighted exchange rate

49.2 Determination of exchange rates

1 What are the **two** main ways a central bank maintains a fixed exchange rate?

2 In what sense is a managed exchange rate system a mixture of a floating exchange rate system and a fixed exchange rate system?

3 Decide whether the following statements relate to a fixed exchange rate or a floating exchange rate:

a It can be set at a level to achieve a government's macroeconomic objectives.

b It can encourage trade by creating certainty.

c It is determined by market forces.

d It may be difficult to maintain its value.

e It may restrict the use of interest rate changes to achieve price stability.

f It may require the use of foreign currency reserves.

g It means the exchange rate is no longer a policy objective.

UNDERSTAND THESE TERMS

- fixed exchange rate
- devaluation
- revaluation
- managed system

« RECALL AND CONNECT 2 «

How may a floating exchange rate automatically eliminate a current account deficit without the need for a change in government policy?

49.3 Revaluation and devaluation of a fixed exchange rate

1   Copy the text below and fill in the missing words and phrases.

A fixed exchange rate has been set at the _____ level. As a result, there are no market forces putting pressure on the exchange rate to change. However, the government decides to devalue the exchange to gain a _____. A lower exchange rate will _____ export prices and _____ import prices. This may increase net exports and so raise _____ demand. As a result, economic growth may increase and _____ may fall. There is risk that other governments may consider that this is _____ competition and may take action including placing _____ on imports from the country. A devaluation can also cause a rise in the country's _____, which can offset the effect of the reduction in the exchange rate on the relative price of the country's products.

2   For each of the following groups, decide whether they are likely to gain or lose from a revaluation of the currency, and provide a brief explanation.

a   domestic consumers

b   domestic firms that export a high proportion of their output

c   domestic firms that import a high proportion of their raw materials

d   foreign citizens who hold the country's government bonds

e   foreign governments that have borrowed from the country's government

f   foreign workers who work in the country but have families abroad

49.4 Changes in the exchange rate under different exchange rate systems

1   Why may speculation force a government to devalue its currency?

2   Why may central bank action to stop upward pressure on the exchange rate cause inflation?

> **≪ RECALL AND CONNECT 3 ≪**
>
> What effect may a fall in the exchange rate have on tourism?

49.5 The effects of changing exchange rates on the external economy

1 Why may demand for exports and imports be price inelastic in the short run?

Note that Question 2(e) is asking about the relationship between changes in the budget deficit and the exchange rate. Students often confuse the budget deficit and the current account deficit. You might have been expecting to see the current account deficit. That would have been a more straightforward question. You might find the actual question more challenging and more interesting. It will enable you to show the links between a change in an internal deficit and an external deficit.

2

Changes in the value of the South Korean won

In 2022 South Korea's GDP rose to $1 800 billion. However, the value of the South Korean won fell by 18%. This was for a number of reasons. One was the increase in the country's inflation rate from 2.6% to 5.5%. Higher inflation can reduce the exchange rate and a lower exchange rate can increase the inflation rate.

To try to stop the fall in the value of the won, South Korea's central bank raised its interest rate and used some of its foreign currency reserves to purchase the won.

Some South Korean economists argued that the country's central bank should allow the exchange rate to fall as this could increase the country's current account surplus if the Marshall–Lerner condition was met. Other economists argued that fluctuations in the value of the won could become destabilising. Figure 49.1 shows how the value of the won has changed over the last 15 years.

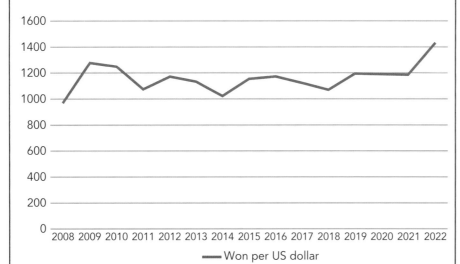

Figure 49.1: South Korean won per US dollar 2008—2022

It has been suggested that a change in the country's budget balance could affect the current account balance and so the value of the won. In the period 2020–2022, South Korea had a budget deficit. In 2022, the budget deficit was 2.7% of GDP with government revenue being $479.4 billion.

a   Calculate South Korea's government spending in 2022.
    Show your workings.   [3]
b   Explain how:
    i   inflation can reduce the exchange rate   [3]
    ii   a lower exchange rate can increase the inflation rate.   [5]
c   Explain the relevance of the Marshall–Lerner condition and J-curve
    effect in determining whether a fall in the exchange rate will
    move the current account balance from a deficit into a surplus.   [4]
d   Explain what:
    i   happened to the value of the won in 2009   [2]
    ii   is likely to have happened to export prices in 2018.   [2]
e   Assess whether a reduction in a government's budget deficit will
    reduce a current account deficit.   [8]

Question 3 is a relatively straightforward essay question. Remember to structure your answer and note that the instruction to include diagram(s) may help you recognise a concept you could include. You may also find it useful to give a numerical example of the effects of a revaluation to strengthen your analysis.

3   Assess, using a diagram(s), whether a revaluation of the exchange rate
    will reduce a current account surplus.   [20]

REFLECTION

How well do you think you did on these questions? Did you look carefully at Figure 49.1 to determine what was happening to the exchange rate? Were you able to work out the connection between the budget deficit and the current account deficit? Do you need to look over these topics?

SELF-ASSESSMENT CHECKLIST

Let's revisit the Knowledge focus and Exam skills focus for this chapter.
Decide how confident you are with each statement.

Now I can	Show it	Needs more work	Almost there	Confident to move on
identify the three main ways exchange rates are measured: nominal, real and trade-weighted exchange rates	Name the **three** main ways exchange rates are measured.			
explain the difference between nominal and real exchange rates	Define nominal and real exchange rates.			

CONTINUED

explain trade-weighted exchange rates	Decide what weight would be given to the currency of a foreign country that accounts for 40% of a country's international trade.			
analyse how exchange rates are determined under fixed and managed systems	Draw diagrams to show how exchange rates are determined under fixed and managed systems.			
explain the difference between revaluation and devaluation of a fixed exchange rate	Define revaluation and devaluation and consider how a devaluation affects export and import prices.			
analyse the causes of changes in the exchange rate under different exchange rate systems	Produce a table comparing a fixed and a floating exchange rate system.			
evaluate the effects of changing exchange rates on the external rates on the external economy using the Marshall–Lerner condition and J-curve analysis	Define the Marshall–Lerner condition and the J-curve effect.			
improve my ability to make connections between concepts by using key concept cards	Examine the connection between the budget surplus and a current account surplus.			
discover techniques that will help me learn definitions more effectively.	Define a fixed exchange rate.			

50 Economic development

363 >

Read questions very carefully. Students sometimes confuse terms not only in their answers but also in the questions themselves. They also do not always notice whether a question is asking about, for example, a decrease or an increase. In addition, they do not notice if a diagram has been requested. Do not rush answering the question. When you have answered the question, you may want to read it again to check that your answer has focused on the specific question.

Working with other students can increase your understanding and performance. You might be able to form a study group with one or more of your fellow students. For example, you could each produce a table that summarises a topic and then you could compare them, or each member of the study group could produce a revision card on a topic and these could be shared. Working with other students can give you new ideas, enable you to see if you can explain your knowledge and understanding in a clear way and provide you with useful revision material. You may also find it makes revision more stimulating and enjoyable.

50.1 How economies are classified in terms of development and national income

1   The World Bank classified countries into four income groups. What are these?

2   Why may low income per head result in low productivity?

3   Complete the virtuous circle in a copy of Figure 50.1.

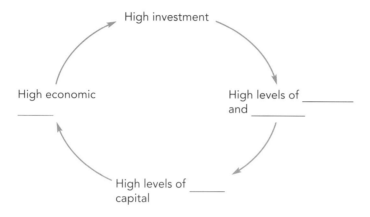

Figure 50.1: Virtuous circle

UNDERSTAND THESE TERMS

- poverty cycle
- development traps

« RECALL AND CONNECT 1 «

What is the difference between GDP per head and GNI per capita?

50.2 Other indicators of living standards and economic development

UNDERSTAND THESE TERMS

- purchasing power parity (PPP)
- Multidimensional Poverty Index (MPI)

1 What are the **three** components of the HDI?

2 When is a family poor according to the Multidimensional Poverty Index?

3 What does the Kuznets curve suggest?

4 Match the following influences with the explanations as to whether they will increase or decrease living standards or whether their effects will be uncertain.

Influence	Effect on living standards and development
High CO_2 emissions per head	Increase as likely to raise the health of the population
High number of car accidents per head	Increase as likely to be less destruction of buildings and loss of life
High number of cars per head	Decrease as will reduce the health of those affected
High number of hospital beds per head	Increase as will allow more people to participate fully in society
High percentage of population with internet connection	Decrease as can result in a range of illnesses
Long paid holiday time	Uncertain as may indicate better or more inefficient healthcare
Low number of days of extreme weather	Uncertain as may give people greater freedom of movement but may also cause pollution

Table 50.1: Influences on living standards

« RECALL AND CONNECT 2 «

Which curve suggests that a cut in income tax may increase income tax revenue?

50.3 Comparison of economic growth rates and living standards

Remember to read Question 1 carefully. For example, note that Question 1(d) is asking about economic development and not economic growth. Economic development is wider than economic growth.

1

Changes in Bangladesh's economic growth and economic development

Bangladesh's population has experienced a rise in income, a fall in poverty and a rise in life expectancy in recent years. Since 2000, the economy has grown at an average annual rate of 5%. Between 2021 and 2022, the country's GDP grew by 6.5% and reached $461 billion in 2022. Life expectancy increased by six years between 2000 and 2020. By 2020, Bangladesh's life expectancy equalled global life expectancy as shown in Table 50.2.

Country	GDP per head ($)	Life expectancy at birth (years)	Male life expectancy at birth (years)	Female life expectancy at birth (years)
Bangladesh	2 233	72	70	74
Canada	43 258	82	80	84
Indonesia	3 894	69	67	71
Lesotho	990	55	52	58
Russia	10 168	71	66	76
South Korea	31 721	83	81	87
UAE	37 620	79	78	81
Global average	10 882	72	70	75

Table 50.2: GDP per head and life expectancy in selected countries 2020

Source: The World Bank

The growth in Bangladesh's economy has attracted more foreign firms to set up in the country. Firms in a range of industries including energy, food processing, telecommunications and textiles have set up in Bangladesh. These firms export some of their output and sell some on the home market. For example, foreign textile firms sell clothes in Bangladesh.

While more firms are coming into Bangladesh, some Bangladeshi workers are still leaving the country to work abroad. In 2022, remittances sent home by Bangladeshi workers, employed mainly in Saudi Arabia and the UAE, accounted for 7% of GDP.

a   Calculate Bangladesh's GDP in 2021.   [2]

b   Explain how Bangladesh's balance of payments is affected by:
  i   foreign firms setting up in Bangladesh   [2]
  ii   Bangladeshi workers sending money home from the UAE.   [2]

c   Using Table 50.2:
  i   comment on the difference between male and female life expectancy   [3]
  ii   analyse the relationship between GDP per capita and life expectancy.   [5]

d   Assess whether the presence of foreign textile firms in a country will promote economic development.   [8]

REFLECTION

Did you remember the different components of the balance of payments?
If not, look over this topic. Did you focus on textile firms in the last question?
You do not need detailed information on such firms. You just need to apply
economic concepts in the context of textile firms.

SELF-ASSESSMENT CHECKLIST

Let's revisit the Knowledge focus and Exam skills focus for this chapter.
Decide how confident you are with each statement.

Now I can	Show it	Needs more work	Almost there	Confident to move on
describe how economies are classified in terms of their level of development and level of national income	Outline how the World Bank classifies countries according to their income levels and consider other influences on living standards and economic development.			
evaluate indicators of living standards and economic development including real per capita national income statistics, purchasing power parity, non-monetary indicators and composite indicators	Produce a table comparing the advantages and disadvantages of different indicators of living standards and economic development.			
explain the Kuznets curve	Draw the Kuznets curve.			
compare economic growth rates and living standards over time and between countries	Using the CIA World Factbook, compare the economic growth rate and **three** indicators of living standards of your country and one other country.			
show that I know what a question is asking	Identify the key words in **three** exam style questions.			
improve my understanding by working with other students.	Identify **three** benefits of working with other students.			

51 Characteristics of countries at different levels of development

KNOWLEDGE FOCUS

You will answer questions on:

51.1 Population growth and structure

51.2 Income distribution

51.3 Economic structure

EXAM SKILLS FOCUS

In this chapter you will:

- show that you can recognise signs of test anxiety

- show that you can evaluate your progress.

Are you losing sleep worrying about your exams? Anxiety can cause loss of sleep and loss of sleep can cause anxiety, creating a negative cycle. Anxiety can be reduced by preparing well, thinking positively and practising exam questions. The quality of sleep can be improved in a number of ways. Try to go to bed at a regular time and avoid looking at electronic devices at least an hour before.

Evaluating your own progress can help you improve your performance. If you set goals for what you want to achieve, for example answering at least eight out of ten multiple-choice questions correctly or gaining 15 marks or more for an essay answer, you can assess whether you have achieved your aims. If you have achieved your goals, you may wish to consider if you can increase your aims. If you have not reached them, you can reflect on why this may have been the case and what strategies you can use to increase your performance.

51.1 Population growth and structure

1   What causes a natural increase in population?

2   Why may the population of a high-income country:

   a   decline

   b   increase

   c   move from rural to urban areas?

3   What effect may the discovery of natural resources such as gold have on the size of a country's optimum population?

4

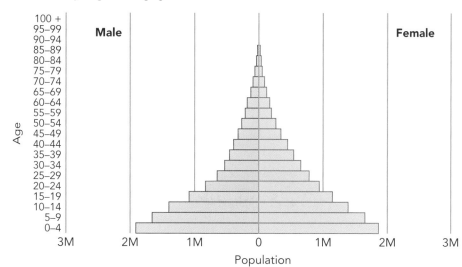

Figure 51.1: Mali's population pyramid

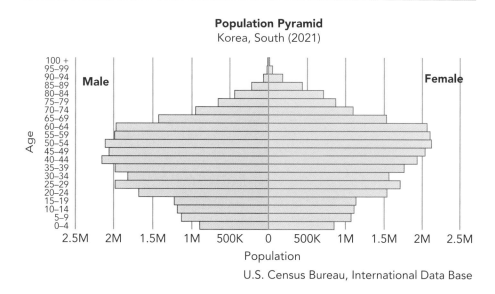

Figure 51.2: South Korea's population pyramid

UNDERSTAND THESE TERMS

- demographers
- birth rate
- death rate
- infant mortality rate
- dependency ratio

Source: CIA World Factbook

Which country:

a   is likely to experience the highest growth in population?

b   is likely to have the highest birth rate?

c   has the highest proportion of population aged over 64?

d   is likely to decline in population in the future?

51.2 Income distribution

1   What would a Gini coefficient of 0.7 indicate?

2   What does the 45° diagonal line on a Lorenz curve indicate?

3   Which of the following diagrams shows the highest degree of income inequality?

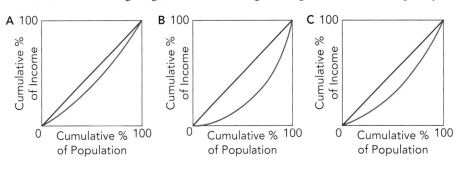

Figure 51.3: Lorenz curves

≪ RECALL AND CONNECT 1 ≪

What are **four** policy measures governments use to make income more evenly distributed?

51.3 Economic structure

1   As economies develop, what usually happens to the proportion of workers employed in the tertiary sector?

2   What are **two** disadvantages of exporting primary products?

3   Are there any high-income countries that export mainly primary products?

4

Changes in Mexico's and Japan's population sizes and population structures

Mexico's economy and population structure are changing. The proportion of the country's labour force employed in the primary and secondary sectors has declined in recent years. In 2022, the proportion was 37%. The country is ageing fast. In 1960, life expectancy at birth was 57. In 2022, this had increased to 75. In that year, 12% of the population was aged over 60 and by 2050, it will be 25%. A relatively high proportion, 38%, of the elderly population are poor, and many do not enjoy good health.

In 2022, the country's birth rate was 13.7, its death rate 7.7 and its net migration rate was −1.45. Table 51.1 shows the net migration rate and GDP per capita of a number of countries.

Country	Net migration (per 1 000)	GDP per capita ($)PPP
Australia	7.41	56 281
Benin	0.25	3 649
Japan	0.75	42 940
Lesotho	−4.59	2 521.5
Luxembourg	12.01	134 545
Mauritius	0	23 035
Mexico	−0.76	20 277
UK	3.59	49 675

Table 51.1: The net migration rate and GDP per capita of selected countries 2021

Japan's population is ageing even more rapidly than Mexico's. In 2022, the average age of Japan's population of 126 million was 48.5, whereas Mexico's 128 million population had an average age of 29.3. Japan is adapting to an ageing population in a variety of ways. It has raised the retirement age and is making use of robots in care homes. There is also some pressure on the government to reduce its strict immigration laws.

a   Calculate the proportion of Mexico's labour force employed in the tertiary sector in 2022. [1]

b   Calculate Mexico's natural increase in population in 2022. [3]

c   Explain **two** effects on a government's budget of a rise in the retirement age. [4]

d   Explain why a country with a higher average age population may have a lower output than a country with a smaller sized population but a younger average age. [4]

e   Consider whether the evidence provided supports a positive relationship between GDP per capita and positive migration. [6]

f   Assess whether positive migration will benefit an economy. [8]

REFLECTION

Try marking your answers before you check the answers and marks in the Answers section. Assess how well you have performed and whether your performance has met your aims. What strategies do you think you could use to raise your performance?

« RECALL AND CONNECT 2 «

What are **two** influences on what products countries export?

SELF-ASSESSMENT CHECKLIST

Let's revisit the Knowledge focus and Exam skills focus for this chapter.
Decide how confident you are with each statement.

Now I can	Show it	Needs more work	Almost there	Confident to move on
explain how the birth rate, death rate, infant mortality and net migration are measured	Define the birth rate, death rate, infant mortality and net migration.			
analyse the causes of changes in birth rate, death rate, infant mortality and net migration	Identify **two** causes of changes in birth rate, death rate, infant mortality and net migration.			
explain the concept of the optimum population	Draw a diagram to show the optimum population.			
explain how the level of urbanisation changes as countries develop	Identify **three** reasons why people move from rural to urban as development increases.			
explain how income distribution can be measured	Plot a Lorenz curve using the information: poorest 20% of the population receive 3% of income, next 20% of population receive 6% of income, middle 20% receive 12% of income, next 20% receive 20% and the richest 59%.			
calculate and interpret the Gini coefficient	Tell another student what a fall in a country's Gini from 0.6 to 0.2 would mean.			

CONTINUED

analyse and draw Lorenz curves	Draw a Lorenz curve.			
explain employment composition in terms of primary, secondary and tertiary sectors	Give an example of a primary industry, a secondary industry and a tertiary industry.			
analyse the pattern of trade at different levels of development	Produce a flow chart showing how the pattern of trade changes as the level of development increases.			
show that I recognise signs of anxiety	List **four** things you could do to ensure you get good quality sleep.			
show that I can evaluate my progress.	Think of a strategy that you could use to increase your performance on one of the activities in this chapter.			

52 Relationship between countries at different levels of development

EXAM SKILLS FOCUS

In this chapter you will:

- show that you understand what knowledge you need to demonstrate

- show that you know the most suitable environment for you to revise in.

By now you will have covered a range of economic topics and concepts. You will have developed an economics toolkit that you can apply to a wide range of topics. You need to use the toolkit selectively. You need to know not only what to include in answers but also what not to include. The quality of what is written is more important than the quantity of what is written. Students are sometimes tempted to write all they know about a topic rather than focus on the aspects that are required.

Some students revise best in a room without any distractions. Others find it more relaxing to revise with music in the background. There is no one right environment in which to revise, and what is likely to be the most productive environment may depend on what type of revision activity you are undertaking. You have to find the environment that will suit you best.

52.1 International aid

1. What are **two** reasons why investment may be low in a low-income country?

2. What are **two** disadvantages of relying on international aid?

3. Match the forms of international aid in Table 52.1 with the motives.

Forms of international aid	Motive
Bilateral tied aid in the form of a low-interest loan	Reduce illegal immigration
Bilateral untied aid in the form of providing the services of experts at no cost	Promote international trade
Bilateral untied aid in the form of a gift of military equipment	Increase demand for the donor country's exports
Multilateral tied aid in the form of grants given to strengthen border controls	Gain political support
Multilateral untied aid given in the form of a loan to cover a current account deficit	Raise living standards in the recipient country

Table 52.1: Reasons for giving aid

> ## ≪ RECALL AND CONNECT 1 ≪
>
> Why is investment so important for economic growth?

52.2 Trade and investment

1. What are **two** reasons why a firm's average costs may fall when it starts to engage in international trade?

2. Why does food in high-income countries tend to have low income elasticity of demand?

3. What are **two** characteristics of emerging economies?

> ## ≪ RECALL AND CONNECT 2 ≪
>
> Identify **four** reasons why a government subsidy given to domestic farmers does not result in higher exports of agricultural products.

UNDERSTAND THESE TERMS

- International Monetary Fund (IMF)
- aid
- virtuous cycle

UNDERSTAND THIS TERM

- emerging economies

52.3 The role of multinational companies

UNDERSTAND THIS TERM

* foreign direct investment (FDI)

1   What are **two** disadvantages a country may experience due to the presence of foreign multinational companies?

2   Decide whether the following would encourage or discourage foreign direct investment:

    a   high education standards

    b   high government subsidies

    c   high level of government regulations

    d   high supply of natural resources

    e   low corporation tax

    f   low income tax

    g   low labour productivity.

《 RECALL AND CONNECT 3 《

Multinational companies may engage in price discrimination in their different markets. What are the **three** conditions needed for a firm to engage in price discrimination?

Remember to focus on the specific question. In Question 3 you do not have to write about the effects of FDI on the poor in the country or countries that the MNCs have come from (home country/countries).

3   Evaluate whether foreign direct investment (FDI) is likely to benefit the poor in low-income countries.   [20]

52.4 The causes and consequences of external debt

1   What are **three** reasons why a country may have a high level of external debt?

2   What effect will defaulting on past loans have on a government's ability to borrow in the future?

《 RECALL AND CONNECT 4 《

What are the **three** main objectives of commercial banks?

52.5 The role of the International Monetary Fund and the World Bank

1   Why does the IMF promote exchange rate stability?

2   What is the aim of the Washington consensus?

3   What are the **two** goals the World Bank has set for itself to achieve by 2030?

4

> **Challenges facing the Ghanaian economy**
>
> Ghana is a West African country rich in natural resources including gold, oil and gas. The country's GDP per head increased from $1259 in 2010 to $2363 in 2021. This rise was combined with a rise in urbanisation. In 2021, 58% of Ghana's population lived in urban areas.
>
> Ghana has had a current account deficit for a number of years. It has also had a government budget deficit. The government has been spending a large proportion of its tax revenue on paying interest on its national debt. By December 2022, Ghana's public sector debt had built up due to budget deficits and higher interest rates. In 2021, the government had spent more on education, healthcare and infrastructure projects. In previous years, the government had cut taxes and removed some import tariffs. By 2022, the government budget deficit had reached 12% of GDP. To cover the widening gap between government spending and revenue, the Ghanaian government increased its borrowing including by selling government bonds to foreign commercial banks.
>
> In 2022, Ghana's inflation rate rose to 50% and its interest rate increased to 27%. The value of the country's currency, the cedi, fell by 48% on the foreign exchange market. Lack of confidence in the country caused some financial investors to move their money out of the country, and the country's credit rating went down.
>
> In December 2022, Ghana defaulted on interest payments it owed to foreign governments and financial institutions. The Ghanaian government turned to the IMF, and it received a $3 billion loan. In return, it agreed to negotiate a restructure of its debt with its creditors and a cut in government spending. The announcement of the loan stopped the fall in the value of the cedi. Some economists predicted that if Ghana's debt reduced, foreign direct investment would increase.

a   Identify **three** reasons why Ghana's budget deficit increased.   [3]

b   Explain why foreign commercial banks may have bought Ghanaian government bonds.   [2]

c   Why may a reduction in government debt encourage FDI?   [3]

d   Analyse the relationship between GDP per head and urbanisation.   [4]

e   Assess whether international aid promotes economic development.   [8]

REFLECTION

How did you get on with the questions in this chapter? Were there any that you could not answer or which you think you could have done better on? If there were, think about specific ways you could improve your performance.

SELF-ASSESSMENT CHECKLIST

Let's revisit the Knowledge focus and Exam skills focus for this chapter.
Decide how confident you are with each statement.

Now I can	Show it	Needs more work	Almost there	Confident to move on
describe different forms of international aid	Identify the main forms of international aid.			
explain reasons for giving aid	Identify **three** reasons for giving aid.			
evaluate the effects and importance of aid	Produce a table comparing the advantages and disadvantages of receiving aid.			
analyse the role of trade and investment between countries	Identify **three** reasons why firms trade with and invest in other countries.			
define the meaning of multinational companies	Define a multinational company.			
evaluate the activities and consequences of multinational companies	Produce a mind map on the advantages and disadvantages that an MNC may have on its home country and on a host country.			
define the meaning of foreign direct investment	Describe what is meant by foreign direct investment.			
evaluate the consequences of foreign direct investment	Give **three** consequences of foreign direct investment.			
explain the role of the International Monetary Fund	Identify **three** functions of the IMF.			
explain the role of the World Bank	Identify the key aims of the World Bank.			
understand what knowledge I need to demonstrate	Give **three** economic concepts that you could apply in answering a question on the benefits of receiving aid.			
know the most suitable environment for me to revise in.	Find an environment in which you can do your best work.			

53 Globalisation

KNOWLEDGE FOCUS

You will answer questions on:

53.1 What is globalisation?

53.2 Trade blocs

53.3 Trade creation

53.4 Trade diversion

EXAM SKILLS FOCUS

In this chapter you will:

* further practise navigating synoptic questions

* show that you can manage distribution of your time.

Synoptic questions assess your understanding of links between different topics of the syllabus. Data response questions draw on a range of economic topics, as do some essay questions. Some questions may require you to draw on both macroeconomic concepts, such as the multiplier, and microeconomic concepts, such as market power. Think through which are the appropriate concepts to use, and ensure that you link them in a clear and logical way.

It would be a good idea to answer a whole past paper under exam conditions. This would be good practice and could help you identify both topics you need to go over and whether you can divide up your time appropriately.

53.1 What is globalisation?

> ### UNDERSTAND THIS TERM
>
> • globalisation

1 What are **two** ways internal trade differs from external trade?

2 Why have advances in technology helped to increase the number of multinational companies?

3 Why may globalisation:

   a reduce income inequality?

   b increase income inequality?

4 What effect does globalisation have on the ability of a government to charge higher taxes than governments of other countries?

> ### ≪ RECALL AND CONNECT 1 ≪
>
> **a** Globalisation can enable countries to exploit their comparative advantage to a greater extent. What is the significance of opportunity cost ratios in the theory of comparative advantage?
>
> **b** Globalisation can increase economic growth. What would be **two** possible advantages of higher world output?

53.2 Trade blocs

1 How does a customs union differ from a free trade area?

2 What are the key features of a monetary union?

3 Match the countries in Table 53.1 with the trade blocs they are members of.

Country	Trade bloc
Brazil	ASEAN
France	Caricom
Jamaica	EAC
Nigeria	ECOWAS
Qatar	EU
Rwanda	GCC
Thailand	Mercosur
USA	USMCA

Table 53.1: Members of trade blocs

> ### UNDERSTAND THESE TERMS
>
> • trade bloc
> • full economic union

53.3 Trade creation

1 What effect may trade creation have on the pattern of trade of a new member country to a trade bloc?

2 Students can find the diagrams showing trade diversion and trade creation relatively difficult. Figure 53.1 is intended to show trade creation. show this but it contains a number of mistakes. Identify these mistakes.

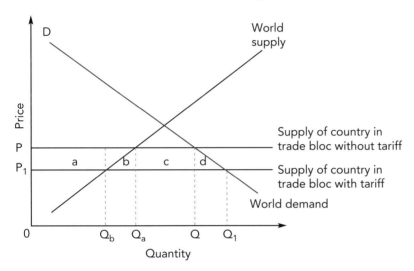

Figure 53.1: Trade creation

53.4 Trade diversion

1 Why does trade diversion result in a loss in efficiency?

In thinking about your answer to Question 2(c), think about a microeconomic concept you could use.

2

Sri Lanka's economic problems

In 2022, the Sri Lankan economy ran into difficulties. Inflation soared, reaching 74% in September when the rate of interest was 15%. Shortages of food lead to not only price rises but also long queues. It was expected that the unemployment rate was going to rise. Figure 53.2 shows the country's unemployment rate in the years just before 2022.

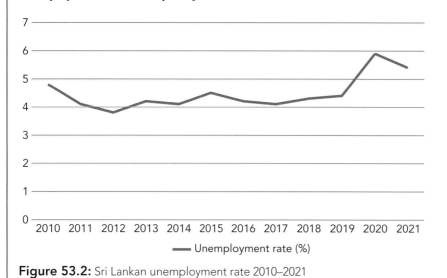

Figure 53.2: Sri Lankan unemployment rate 2010–2021

Tourism is a major industry in the country, contributing 12.6% of the country's GDP in 2019. The COVID-19 pandemic and resulting fall in global output caused a serious decline in the number of tourists visiting Sri Lanka. Tourism was also hit by the fall in the country's currency, the Sri Lankan rupee. The Sri Lankan government was not able to stop the depreciation in the exchange rate as it had almost run out of foreign exchange reserves. The reserves had been used up not only trying to support the currency but also servicing the country's external debt. The lack of foreign exchange reserves reduced the country's ability to import not only food but also raw materials. This reduced the country's output.

Sri Lanka has a number of foreign multinational companies (MNCs) operating in the country, including in banking and telecommunications. However, the economic problems facing Sri Lanka led some economists and politicians to express concern that some MNCs might move out of the country.

---

  a Calculate the real rate of interest in Sri Lanka in September 2022.   [1]

  b Describe the trend in Sri Lanka's unemployment rate shown in Figure 53.1.   [2]

  c Explain **two** reasons why tourism may increase in Sri Lanka in the future.   [4]

  d Analyse, using a diagram, how a depreciation in the exchange rate could initially cause a rise in a country's current account deficit.   [5]

  e Assess whether foreign MNCs moving out of the country would harm the economy of that country.   [8]

REFLECTION

Did you know what diagram to draw for the answer to Question 2(d)? It may be useful to draw the key diagrams you are likely to need on revision cards.

3 Complete the answers to the following crossword.

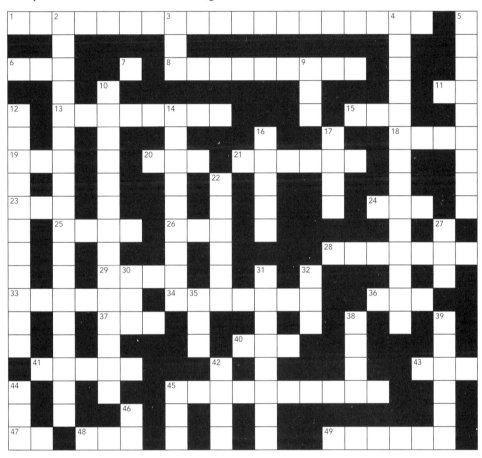

Across

1 The desire to hold wealth in a money form (9, 10).

6 The initials of an institution of the World Bank that provides grants to the world's poorest countries (3).

7 The name of the curve that shows how a devaluation of the exchange rate may initially increase a current account deficit (1).

8 The permission given by a bank to a customer to spend more than is in their account (9).

11 The answer to the question, 'Is government spending on education a market-based supply-side policy?' (2).

13 The name for a situation where governments retaliate to tariffs being placed on their products (5,3).

15 The initials of a measure of living standards produced by the UN (3).

18 The description of aid which is given with conditions (4).

19 The initials of an indirect tax (3).

20 The initials of the term for the proportion of income taken in tax (3).

21 The term for the type of government policy involved with government spending and taxation (6).

23 A term for permitting someone to do something (3).

24 The initials for a measure of living standards designed by William Nordhaus and James Tobin (3).

25 The type of money balances kept to speculate on interest rate changes (4).

26 The type of chart where numerical values are shown by the height or length of columns (3).

28 A union which is a type of trade bloc (7).

29 Money given by a bank to a customer which has to be repaid (4).

33 The unemployment rate if 5.5 million workers out of a labour force of 50 million are out of work (6).

34 A curve which shows the relationship between economic growth and income inequality (7).

36 The position on a curve which shows the optimum population (3).

37 A country, firm or individual who is in debt is said to be in this (3).

40 When an increase in government spending results in a fall in private sector spending, there is said to be crowding _____. (3).

41 An exchange rate which is set by a government (5)

43 The initials of an indirect tax (3).

45 The effect which occurs when national income changes by more than a change in an injection (10).

47 Crowding _____ is a term that describes a situation when an increase in government spending increases private sector spending (2).

48 The initials of a firm that operates in more than one country (3).

49 A curve that shows the relationship between tax revenue and tax rates (6).

Down

2 A central bank buying securities to increase the money supply and economic activity (12,6).

3 The number of countries in USMCA excluding the USA (3).

4 The making of money by commercial banks (6,8).

5 The sector which includes manufacturing and construction (9).

9 The initials for the term for the proportion of income saved (3).

10 The condition needed for a devaluation to be successful in reducing a current account deficit (8,6).

12 The improvement in the quality of life (11).

14 The international organisation which offers financial support to low- and middle-income countries (5,4).

16 The rate which records how many babies are born per 1 000 of the population (5).

17 A financial institution that lends money (4).

22 The curve which measures the distribution of income or wealth (6).

27 The initials of the international organisation which helps countries with balance of payments difficulties (3).

30 The real rate of interest if the nominal interest rate is 9% and the inflation rate is 8% (3).

31 Policy measures which are designed to reduce a current account deficit which are not expenditure switching are expenditure _____ (8).

32 What countries do with resources to produce goods and services (3).

35 The initials of the federation of the seven states of Abu Dhabi, Ajman, Dubai, Fujairah, Ras al Khaimah, Sharjah and Umm al Quwain (3).

38 The migration rate if 150 000 people enter a country with 30 million people (4).

39 The equation on which the quantity theory is based. (6).

42 A group of countries that have entered into a trade agreement is called a trade _____ (4).

44 The initials for the term that covers the setting up of production units or the purchase of existing production units in other countries (3).

45 The initials of the term for the proportion of income that is taxed (3).

46 The initials for the cost per unit of output (2).

SELF-ASSESSMENT CHECKLIST

Let's revisit the Knowledge focus and Exam skills focus for this chapter.
Decide how confident you are with each statement.

Now I can	Show it	Needs more work	Almost there	Confident to move on
define the meaning of globalisation	Describe what is meant by globalisation.			
analyse the causes and consequences of globalisation	Produce a mind map on the causes, advantages and disadvantages of globalisation.			
analyse the difference between a free trade area, a customs union, a monetary union and full economic union	Produce a table summarising the different features of trade blocs.			
explain the difference between trade creation and trade diversion	Produce a revision card on trade creation and trade diversion.			
further practise navigating synoptic questions	Try a data response question from a recent past paper.			
manage distribution of my time.	Sit a past paper under exam conditions.			

Exam practice 11

This section contains practice questions. These questions draw together your knowledge on a range of topics that you have covered up to this point and will help you prepare for your assessment.

The following question has an example student response and commentary provided. Work through the question first, then compare your answer to the example student response and commentary.

1 'Both developed and developing economies can experience high rates of unemployment, high rates of inflation and large current account deficits. Therefore there is now no real difference between these two types of economy.'

How far would you agree with the view that this statement is misleading?   [20]

Example student response	Examiner comments
Developed and developing economies can both experience high rates of unemployment, high rates of inflation and large current account deficits.	**AO1 Knowledge and understanding** Some key differences between developing and developed countries might have been mentioned at the start of the answer. However, this is a thoughtful and well-structured answer. It shows a clear awareness of some of the possible differences between developed and developing economies.
Some causes of unemployment may be the same in both types of economy. For example, a recession may cause high cyclical unemployment in both types of economy. However, unemployment is usually relatively low in developed economies. It may be higher for longer in developing economies if they are moving employment opportunities from the primary to the secondary and tertiary sectors. In this case, structural unemployment may arise. The governments of developing economies may have less government revenue to spend on education and training to reduce such unemployment.	
	AO2 Analysis The answer examines some of the key influences on unemployment, inflation and current account balance in the two types of economy and other potential differences. The answer brings out possible differences in the causes with a good use of a poverty cycle diagram. The information in this diagram could have been linked back to differences in inflation rates and current account balance in the two types of economies. *AO1 and AO2: 12/14*
Both types of economy may experience cost-push inflation as a result of negative supply-side shocks such as a sudden and significant rise in the price of oil. However, developing economies may be more likely to experience hyperinflation if their governments are tempted to print money to finance government spending because of a lack of tax revenue.	
It is also possible that the cause of a current account deficit may vary. A developing economy may be producing agricultural products that have low income elasticity of demand and the supply of which can be significantly reduced by bad weather and diseases. In contrast, current account deficits may occur in developed economies because high incomes may increase spending on imports.	

Example student response	Examiner comments
Income per head is a much more significant difference between developed and developing economies than the macroeconomic problems they face. Developed economies have a higher income per head than developing economies. This is, in part, because they have higher productivity. Developing economies may experience a poverty cycle, such as that shown in the diagram. 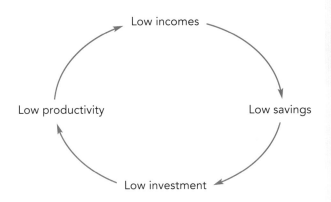 Some developing economies experience higher levels of absolute poverty than developed economies. A number also have lower life expectancy, lower number of years of schooling and higher rates of population growth. The statement is misleading as differences do remain among economies. These are largely linked to differences in income per head. This is one reason why more institutions, including the World Bank, now group countries according to levels of income per head rather than in terms of developed and developing economies.	**AO3 Evaluation** There is clear evaluation throughout with a supported conclusion. *5/6* *Total: 17/20 marks*

Here is another practice question which you should attempt. Use the guidance in the commentaries in this section to help you as you answer the question.

2 Assess whether higher government spending will increase a country's economic development.   [20]

The following question has an example student response and commentary provided. Work through the question first, then compare your answer to the example student response and commentary.

3 'Labour is a resource; the use of economic resources increases well-being. The main aim of the government of a developing country keen to increase well-being should, therefore, be to support an increase in the population of its country.'

Assess this argument and decide whether you agree with it. [20]

Example student response	Examiner comments
An increase in population may increase the well-being of people living in a developing country if it results in an increase in the size of its labour force. An increase in the immigration of skilled workers, for example, would increase the country's productive capacity. The extra workers may increase both the quantity and quality of output. For example, some of the immigrant workers may be doctors and teachers. This could increase the provision and quality of healthcare and education. With more skilled workers, GDP per head could rise and absolute poverty may be reduced. However, developing countries may experience net emigration rather than net immigration of skilled workers. Its skilled workers may move to other countries in search of higher wellbeing.	**AO1 Knowledge and understanding** There is good knowledge and understanding shown of the causes of an increase in population. It is good to refer to the concept of the optimum population and the dependency ratio, but their meaning might have been brought out more. Rather more understanding of well-being might also have been shown.
An increase in population may also be caused by an increase in the country's birth rate. A higher birth rate will increase the dependency ratio, at least in the short run. There will be more children to support and some parents may leave the labour force to look after their children. Output may decrease while the number of people requiring to consume the output will rise. More pressure may be put on the country's social infrastructure. This could reduce some the population's well-being. More resources may have to be devoted to meeting the needs of the children. This may involve an opportunity cost with less resources being available to, for example, improve the country's transport infrastructure. In the long run, a higher birth rate may increase the size of the labour force. However, a lower birth rate may enable parents to educate their children for longer. This may raise the quality of the labour force.	**AO2 Analysis** There is some good analysis linked to different possible causes of an increase in population. The analysis of the effect of a fall in the death rate might have been stronger. The student might have explained that this could increase both the number of workers and the number of retired people. The effect of a higher population on the environment might also have been analysed. *AO1 and AO2: 10/14*
Population may rise because of a fall in the death rate. A government would welcome people living longer due to better healthcare and living standards. However, the priority of the government may be to increase the number of years its population lives rather than to increase the size of the country's population.	
A developing country's population may already be above its optimum level. Having more people will put more pressure on its resources. The immigration of skilled workers would increase the country's labour resources but, even in this case, a developing country may lack the capital or natural resources to take full advantage of the extra workers.	

Example student response	Examiner comments
The governments of some countries that are experiencing ageing populations may welcome a rise in their birth rates as it would increase the size of their labour force in the long run. However, many developing countries have relatively young populations with already relatively high birth rates. The governments of these countries may try to raise the quality of the education their children receive in order to increase productivity. They may also try to increase investment so that their workers can work with more capital goods. They may be more likely to try to achieve these two aims to increase well-being rather than to aim for an increase in population.	**AO3 Evaluation** There is some good, relevant evaluation. It may have been strengthened by bringing out the difference between an increase in GDP and an increase in GDP per head. A country with a high population growth may experience a rise in GDP with higher AD and AS. However, if output rises at a slower rate than population, GDP per head will fall. This is likely to reduce well-being. *4/6* *Total: 14/20 marks*

Here is another practice question which you should attempt. Use the guidance in the commentaries in this section to help you as you answer the question.

4   'High-income countries face more serious population problems than low-income countries.' Evaluate this statement.   [20]

The following question has an example student response and commentary provided. Work through the question first, then compare your answer to the example student response and commentary.

5   Assess the extent to which the Human Development Index (HDI) and the Measure of Economic Welfare (MEW) provide better measures of living standards than gross national income (GNI).   [20]

Example student response	Examiner comments
The HDI and MEW have the potential to be better measures than GNI as they include more influences on living standards. GNI is the total income received by a country's population. It is calculating by measuring GDP and then adding net income (property income and compensation of employees). It is GNI per capita which is used in measures of living standards. The higher GNI per head is, the more goods and services people are likely to be able to consume. The HDI takes into account not only GNI per capita but also schooling (mean and expected) and life expectancy at birth. Education is an important influence on living standards. A more educated population has a greater chance of gaining good quality, well-paid jobs. A more educated population is also likely to enjoy better health and have more choices in life.	**AO1 Knowledge and understanding** There is good knowledge and understanding shown of the three measures of living standards.

Long life expectancy suggests a good quality of healthcare. However, it can be argued that a better measure would be good quality years of life. People may live a long time, but if a significant proportion of this is spent in poor quality health, they will not be enjoying a high standard of life.	**AO2 Analysis** The answer is structured well. It starts with the narrowest measure and ends with the widest measure. The analysis would have been strengthened by consideration of the possible difficulties of measuring GNI in different economies where there may be differences in, for instance, the size of undeclared economic activity. There could also have been an explanation of the difficulties of measuring environmental damage. This could have brought out the difference between private and external costs.
MEW again has GDP as its starting point. It then adds an assessment of the value of leisure time and deducts a value for environmental damage.	
There are other measures of living standards. That take into account even more influences on living standards. For example, the Index of Sustainable Economic Welfare (ISEW) develops MEW by, for example, deducting defence spending and car accidents.	
	AO1 and AO2: 10/14
The HDI and MEW can give a more complete picture of living standards than GNI per capita. However, it can be difficult to estimate expected years of schooling in the case of HDI and even more difficult to measure environmental damage in the case of MEW. The HDI and MEW also do not take into account all the factors that influence living standards such as crime rates and working conditions.	**AO3 Evaluation** If the problems of measurement had been analysed, there could have been a stronger conclusion. The answer, however, started well with an evaluative statement, which is then supported by some clear evaluation in the rest of the answer. *4/6* *Total: 14/20 marks*

Here is another practice question which you should attempt. Use the guidance in the commentaries in this section to help you as you answer the question.

6   Assess whether an increase in a country's HDI ranking means that everyone in the country's population is enjoying a higher standard of living.   [20]

The following question has an example student response and commentary provided. Work through the question first, then compare your answer to the example student response and commentary.

7   Assess whether a rise in its exchange rate or a fall in its exchange rate is more beneficial for an economy.   [20]

Example student response	Examiner comments
A rise in a country's foreign exchange rate may benefit a country in a number of ways. It will increase export prices in terms of foreign currency and lower import prices in terms of the domestic currency.	**AO1 Knowledge and understanding** There is good and widespread knowledge and understanding shown. While some terms including the exchange rate and terms of trade are not defined, their meaning is brought out in the comments made.
This will improve a country's terms of trade. It will enable a given value of exports to purchase more imports. It may enable a country's producers to buy good quality imported raw materials and capital goods.	

A higher exchange rate may also reduce inflation. This is because it will lower the price of imported raw materials and capital goods. Cheaper raw materials and capital goods will lower firms' costs of production which can reduce cost-push inflation.

A higher exchange rate may also reduce a current account deficit if demand for exports and imports is price inelastic. In this case, export revenue will rise and import expenditure will fall.

If demand for exports and imports is elastic, export revenue will fall and import expenditure will rise. This might be beneficial if a country has a current account surplus. In this case a country's households may be able to consume more goods and services. Lower net exports may also reduce demand-pull inflation.

However, if there is elastic demand for exports and imports and the country starts with a current account deficit, the effect may not be beneficial. After a period of adjustment to the new prices, a current account deficit will increase. A reverse J-curve effect will be experienced as shown in the diagram.

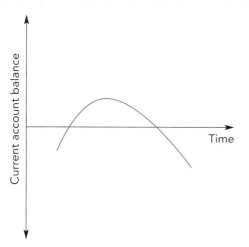

Lower net exports could reduce output. This may result in a rise in unemployment. This unemployment may be experienced in both those industries which export some of their output and also those industries which compete with imports.

A rise in an exchange rate may also not be beneficial if the exchange rate is driven above its equilibrium level by speculation. In this case, the exchange rate will not be sustainable and it could result in a large current account deficit.

A fall in the exchange rate to the equilibrium level, where demand for and supply of the currency is equal, is likely to be beneficial. A lower exchange rate may reduce a current account deficit if the Marshall–Lerner condition is met with the price elasticity of demand for exports and imports being greater than 1. If net exports increase, the country may experience a higher economic growth rate with a fall in unemployment. However, if the economy is currently operating at full capacity, it will be difficult to increase output.

AO2 Analysis

In analysing the effects of a higher exchange rate, it would have been useful to have examined the possible greater pressure on domestic firms to be efficient in order to compete with cheaper imports.

There is, nevertheless, some good analysis including use of the reverse J-curve and the Marshall–Lerner effect.

AO1 and AO2: 12/14

Example student response	Examiner comments
Whether a rise or a fall in the exchange rate will be more beneficial will depend on a number of factors. A rise in the exchange rate is likely to be more beneficial if the exchange rate is currently below the equilibrium level, if there is inelastic demand for exports and imports and if the currently has an inflationary gap.	**AO3 Evaluation** There is some good evaluation throughout and a good concluding paragraph. However, while the answer has examined the possible effect of a higher exchange rate on inflation, in the concluding paragraph 'an inflationary gap' is mentioned. It would have been useful to have explained this earlier in the answer. 5/6 *Total: 17/20 marks*

Here is another practice question which you should attempt. Use the guidance in the commentaries in this section to help you as you answer the question.

8 Assess whether a government should be more concerned by an unstable foreign exchange rate or by an unstable domestic price level. [20]

The following question has an example student response and commentary provided. Work through the question first, then compare your answer to the example student response and commentary.

9 'Developing countries have a low standard of living, yet many have much wealth in natural resources which multinational companies would like to exploit.'

Assess which is the better way of increasing the standard of living: to allow multinational companies to exploit all of the country's natural resources or for the government to increase expenditure on education and health. [20]

Example student response	Examiner comments
Some developing countries may experience a low standard of living. They may have a low income per capita and some of the population may be living in poverty, perhaps even in absolute poverty. Children in the country may not receive many years of schooling and the schooling may not be of a high quality. It is also possible that many of the population may not receive good quality healthcare and life expectancy may be low. There is a possibility that allowing multinational companies (MNCs) to exploit all of its resources may increase its people's standard of living, in the short run, because MNCs may employ local workers and may pay them more than the wages operating in the developing country.	**AO1 Knowledge and understanding** The answer shows a good awareness of some of the key characteristics of developing countries and the key factors that MNCs and higher government expenditure and health may affect.

Example student response	Examiner comments
The MNCs will contribute to the country's output and exports, bringing in scarce foreign currencies. Although the MNCs may send some of their profits home, it is possible that they may pay some corporation tax to the developing country's government. If MNCs do not replace local firms, they may also increase employment which may reduce poverty and raise tax revenue. Some of the additional tax revenue could be spent increasing people's living standard.	**AO2 Analysis** There is some strong analysis, especially in terms of the short-run and long-run effects. However, at the start of the fifth paragraph, the answer loses objectivity. The first two sentences are unsupported opinions. It would have been better to have written that the MNCs *may* create pollution and that they *may be less concerned* about the harmful environmental effects they *may* cause.
If MNCs do deplete the developing country's natural resources, it will mean the country will not be able to gain revenue from them in the future. There is the possibility that the price of natural resources may increase in the future and the country may lose out on future higher profits. Making more gradual use of natural resources may also mean that other industries can be developed before the natural resources wear out.	*AO1 and AO2: 13/14*
MNCs create pollution when they exploit natural resources. They will not care about the harmful environmental effects they cause in a country they will not stay in. Pollution may damage the health of the population and cause the destruction of, for example, wildlife habitats and clean beaches and can reduce the ability to earn income from tourism for generations to come.	**AO3 Evaluation** There is clear and thoughtful evaluation. The answer comes to a clear conclusion based not only the possible effects of the two options but also on the possible restrictions on the choice in a developing country.
However, there is the possibility that MNCs may leave some lasting benefits. They may train workers in skills that the workers can use in other industries. They may also develop infrastructure, including roads and ports that could be used for many years.	*6/6*
But increasing spending on education and healthcare is likely to be a more effective way of increasing the standard of living of a developing country's population in the long run.	*Total: 19/20 marks*
A more educated and healthier population is likely to be better informed and to live a longer and healthier life. It is also likely to be more productive. Higher productivity can increase employment and incomes. A virtuous circle may be created, with healthy and educated parents providing more education and better healthcare to their children and raising their expectations. A more educated population might also be able to make good use of the country's natural resources.	
Of course, a developing country may lack the tax revenue or aid to spend more on education and tax revenue. In this case, it may need to rely on attracting MNCs to raise employment, income and tax revenue. If this is the case, it should try to ensure that the MNCs do provide good quality training, pay most of their taxes in the country, avoid creating pollution and do not use up the natural resources too quickly. Of course, given the financial power of many MNCs, this may not be easy.	
Increasing government spending on education and health is likely to be a better option in the long run, but the ability to do this may not be available to all developing countries.	

Here is another practice question which you should attempt. Use the guidance in the commentaries in this section to help you as you answer the question.

10 Explain, using a diagram, how income distribution can be measured and assess whether international aid reduces income inequality.   [20]

The following question has an example student response and commentary provided. Work through the question first, then compare your answer to the example student response and commentary.

11 The International Monetary Fund (IMF) lends money to developing countries but requires that these countries reduce existing restrictions on imports, focus on the export of primary goods and accept a devaluation of their currencies.

Based upon the preceding information, assess whether developing countries should continue to borrow money from the IMF.   [20]

Example student response	Examiner comments
If developing countries get into financial difficulties due to large external debt arising from current account deficits, they may seek to borrow from the IMF. A loan from the IMF may restore confidence in the recipient countries' economies. This can enable the countries to attract foreign direct investment and may give them time to reduce current account deficits.	**AO1 Knowledge and understanding** The knowledge and understanding shown on, for example, the role of the IMF in this context, import restrictions, primary products and devaluation was accurate and relevant.
However, IMF loans come with conditions. If the IMF requires recipient countries to reduce their existing restrictions on imports, this may improve their macroeconomic performance and reduce their current account deficits. This could occur if the domestic firms respond to the increased competitive pressure by becoming more efficient. The removal of import restrictions may also reduce domestic firms' costs of production if imported raw materials fall in price.	**AO2 Analysis** The analysis was good, but there could have been more depth on infant industries. For example, the effect on the ability of infant industries to experience economies of scale might have been considered.
However, the removal of import restrictions may reduce the recipient countries' output and employment and may increase their current account deficits. This may occur if it reduces protection of infant industries and if other countries are engaging in dumping. Declining industry may go out of business very quickly before other industries have had time to expand. The removal of import tariffs will also reduce government revenue.	*AO1 and AO2: 12/14* **AO3 Evaluation** There is thoughtful evaluation which comes to a judgement supported by analysis. *5/6* *Total: 17/20 marks*
Requiring recipient countries to focus on primary products may be an advantage if the recipient countries have a comparative advantage in these products and if the demand for the products is increasing. However, the demand for some primary products, particularly agricultural products, tend to be income-inelastic. Over time, the terms of trade tend to move against agricultural products and in favour of manufactured goods and services. More agricultural products have to be exchanged to gain a given value of manufactured goods and services. Wages and working conditions may also be lower than in secondary and tertiary industries.	

Example student response	Examiner comments
The supply of agricultural products can be unstable as they are affected by changes in weather and the outbreak of diseases. Developing countries may also be keen to diversify their output so as not to be at risk from sudden falls in demand for a few products. Devaluation may benefit recipient countries as it will reduce export prices and raise import prices. This could raise output. Lower unemployment and reduce a current account deficit. However, demand for many agricultural products is price inelastic. This will mean that while demand for imports may rise, it will rise by a smaller percentage than the fall in price. As a result, export revenue will fall. Demand for imports may be price inelastic, if they do not have close domestic substitutes. While a devaluation can initially increase a current account deficit before it reduces it, there is the possibility that demand does not become elastic over time, if the Marshall-Lerner condition is not met. A devaluation will increase the size of the current account deficit. A devaluation can also increase inflation in the recipient countries. It will increase the cost of imported raw materials, raising domestic firms' costs of production. It may also reduce pressure on domestic firms to keep their price rises low as imports will become more expensive. Borrowing from the IMF will also impose a commitment to repay the loan and to pay interest. There is a risk that the conditions imposed for loans may reduce the macroeconomic performance of recipient countries. However, developing countries with large current deficits may have no choice but to borrow from the IMF. This is because no other international organisation, government or financial institution may be willing to lend to them.	

Here is another practice question which you should attempt. Use the guidance in the commentaries in this section to help you as you answer the question.

12 Assess whether attracting more foreign direct investment or obtaining a loan from the World Bank is more likely to increase employment in a low-income country. [20]